KU-504-862

Information networks
Planning and design

David Etheridge and *Errol Simon*

University of Central England in Birmingham

New York   London   Toronto   Sydney   Tokyo   Singapore

First published 1992 by
Prentice Hall International (UK) Ltd
Campus 400, Maylands Avenue
Hemel Hempstead
Hertfordshire, HP2 7EZ
A division of
Simon & Schuster International Group

© Prentice Hall International (UK) Ltd, 1992

All rights reserved. No part of this publication may be
reproduced, stored in a retrieval system, or transmitted,
in any form, or by any means, electronic, mechanical,
photocopying, recording or otherwise, without prior
permission, in writing, from the publisher.
For permission within the United States of America
contact Prentice Hall Inc., Englewood Cliffs, NJ 07632

Typeset in 10/12pt Baskerville
by Mathematical Composition Setters Ltd, Salisbury, Wiltshire

Printed and bound in Great Britain by
Dotesios Limited, Trowbridge, Wiltshire

Library of Congress Cataloging-in-Publication data

Etheridge, David
    Information networks : planning and design / David Etheridge and
Errol Simon.
        p.   cm.
    Includes bibliographical references and index.
    ISBN 0-13-465402-1 (pbk)
    1. System design.   2. Computer networks.   I. Simon, Errol.
II. Title.
QA76.9.S88E74   1992
004.6'068—dc20   92-7244
                                                        CIP

British Library Cataloguing in Publication Data

A catalogue record for this book is available from
the British Library

ISBN 0-13-465402-1

1   2   3   4   5   96   95   94   93   92

UNIVERSITY OF
CENTRAL ENGLAND
Book no. 07280270
Subject no. 004. 6 Eth
INFORMATION SERVICES

To Annette.

Dave Etheridge

To Herline, Stuart and Sasha-Louise.

Errol Simon

Contents

Contents

ix

Contents

Preface

Rationale

There are several textbooks which deal with the technical aspects of voice and data communications. Most of these books also examine the protocols and standards used in communication systems. Furthermore, some texts present a mathematical treatment of the design of communication networks. There are very few books, however, that take the process of analysis and design of networks as their principal theme or contain a significant section devoted to this. This book, unlike others, approaches the task of developing information networks by adopting a systems-oriented view. Aspects of the analysis of communication requirements, in particular, are dealt with in this way. Planning is approached from a strategic level and is viewed as integral to the process of strategic planning for information systems. Design is dealt with as a modelling exercise, with the emphasis on the input requirements for network modelling and the interpretation of the output from such an exercise.

Aims and objectives

The primary aim of this book is to present a methodology for the process of developing information networks. It is not the intention of the book to present a technical treatment of data communications; such a treatment can be found in a number of books, some of which are detailed in the Further Reading and References section at the end of this book. The purpose of the methodology is to lend a systems-oriented approach to the planning and design of information networks rather than a technically oriented approach to what can be a very complex project.

The methodology (which we have termed 'strategic planning for information networks' – SPIN) comprises a comprehensive and flexible set of guidelines that can be modified to match the needs of a particular network project. It is envisaged that analysts and planners will be able to apply generic skills to this kind of project and not be deterred by the technical aspects of communication systems. Clearly, some knowledge of communication systems and services is required. This is provided in the book, but some additional reading will inevitably be required to support the acquisition of technical knowledge. The reader is strongly advised to consult the Further Reading and References section in order to take steps to underpin further the technical aspects of information networks.

The aim of this book is achieved by, firstly, making the reader aware of the need to communicate in business organisations. Secondly, communication requirements are placed in a business and technical context. Thirdly, a range of solutions that meet these requirements is considered. Fourthly, network development is broken down into a number of phases that deal with particular aspects of planning, analysis, design and management. This fourth objective formulates a systems approach to the development and management of information networks.

Structure and contents

The structure of the book follows the progression of the four objectives outlined above. Part One of the book takes as its theme the 'communications environment'. The contents deal, firstly, with the need to communicate and the issues that determine how these needs are changing and, secondly, with solutions that are available to meet communication requirements. Part Two builds upon the awareness of communication requirements and their potential solutions and takes as its theme the 'planning environment'. The contents chart the progress of network development from strategic planning to analysis and design and finally to implementation and network management. Relevant organisational and management issues are raised at appropriate points. Examples and a case study are included to illustrate particular aspects of the planning and design process.

Further reading, by chapter, as well as references cited in the book is included. A number of appendices are provided, including a glossary of terms and abbreviations used in the book.

Target readership

The book will be of use to students of diploma or undergraduate degree courses that include a module or unit on computer networks and their design. It will also be useful to students of M.Sc. conversion courses or similar courses that include an element of analysis and design of information networks. Students of information technology oriented MBAs will also benefit from a study of the book.

The systems development theme of the book will also be useful for systems analysts and consultants who are involved in network development projects. They will be able to familiarise themselves with the background material provided in Part One and make use of the systems approach developed in Part Two. Systems Managers will also find the book useful, in that they will gain awareness of the scope of information networks and the way in which they support business objectives. Systems Managers will also find the management aspects of information networks informative from a practical perspective.

Underpinning knowledge

Familiarity of the technical principles of information networks will be required in order to underpin Part One of this book and some knowledge of systems analysis is needed to underpin Part Two. The Further Reading and References section will provide the reader with references to suitable background reading.

Acknowledgements

We would like to express our gratitude to the many people who have contributed to the preparation of this textbook. Firstly, we would like to thank our wives Annette Etheridge and Herline Simon for enduring sustained periods of absence. Secondly, Rob Moreton and other colleagues at the Polytechnic who provided valuable information. Thirdly, the co-operation of Logica (London, UK), Velec Communications (Chepstow, UK), CCTA (Norwich, UK), US Department of Labor (Washington, DC, USA), UK Government Department of Employment (London, UK). Fourthly, the numerous individuals, who must remain anonymous, who contributed to examples used in the text.

Finally, our thanks to the people at Prentice Hall who worked on this book, in particular the unflagging support of our long-suffering editor Viki Williams.

PART ONE

The communications environment

CHAPTER 1

The communications imperative

1.1 Introduction

The closing decade of the twentieth century is witnessing further advances in the development of free-market economies and the removal of trade barriers between nations. The interrelationships between the economies of Europe, the United States, Japan and those of the Third World and the Pacific Basin will bring new challenges to business organisations that operate in home or overseas markets. Competitive operation in this changing and challenging business environment requires effective management and utilisation of all the resources at the disposal of a business organisation. Irrespective of the nature of the organisation or its market, a vital resource is information; more precisely, the specific information that is required to bring a product or a service to the marketplace.

All organisations make use of human and financial resources in order to operate. Some organisations make use of raw materials or add value to finished or partially finished components in order to manufacture products; other organisations deliver services to their customers. The information content of the process of supplying a product or delivering a service is specific to that product or service. Hence, the acquisition and utilisation of information is regarded as an integral part of the overall management policy of an organisation. In short, information is a valuable resource that can be turned into a powerful asset in an economic climate which demands quality, cost-effectiveness and competitiveness in order to meet market needs.

Consequently, the ability to access and make effective use of information is vital to public or private organisations or business enterprises. Furthermore, it is the ability to make decisions based upon the value and timeliness of information that is the basis of the operation of any organisation. The tasks of storing, processing and communicating information are of fundamental importance and the use of technology to achieve these tasks has meant that information technology (IT) has become the key technology of the closing decades of the twentieth century. Above all, it is the need to communicate information that is vital to the success of an organisation in today's business environment.

This chapter examines the need to communicate and will discuss the problems and

3

requirements that IT-based information networks address. The emphasis will be on communication requirements rather than on ways in which these requirements can be met by technical solutions.

1.2   The role of information networks

Let us begin with an explanation of some of the terms that will be used frequently throughout this book. The term 'information network' is used to describe an IT-based network; a definition follows:

> An information network is that combination of IT-based components that is designed to meet the requirements for communicating a variety of forms of information, such as voice, data, text, image or any combination of these forms, within or between organisations.

In this book, the term information network is interpreted in its broadest sense without any specific reference to the underlying technology required to support the delivery of information. The term 'organisation' is used to refer generally to any public or private body or business enterprise that provides a service or supplies a product to a market.

Therefore, it can be stated that the role of an information network is to meet the need for communicating all forms of information in an organisation. The business activities that can give rise to this need are examined in the next section.

1.3   The scope of information networks

The need to communicate information will emerge as a result of communication-related activities in an organisation. It may be helpful to consider these by taking two views of an organisation and examining the scope for internal and external communication. Figure 1.1 identifies broad activities that give rise to communication problems and requirements.

The business activities identified in Figure 1.1 can be associated with achieving business objectives which are internally oriented or externally oriented. This is summarised in Figure 1.2, which identifies categories of internally and externally oriented business objectives.

The achievement of internally oriented objectives involves the use of information systems that support the work of operational, administrative and managerial staff. An efficiency-oriented objective, for example, gives rise to a requirement to carry out a task correctly and in an agreed period of time. An example of this kind of task is that of producing a sales report at the end of a given period of time. The report must be accurate and produced on time in order to provide the basis for decision-making. The production of such a report depends on the availability of accurate and relevant information; the supporting information system may require communication facilities. An effectiveness-oriented objective, on the other hand, is exemplified by the problem

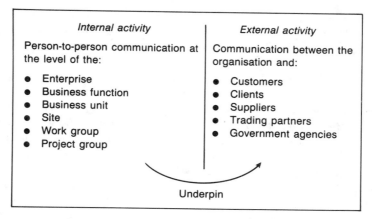

Figure 1.1 Two views of the need to communicate.

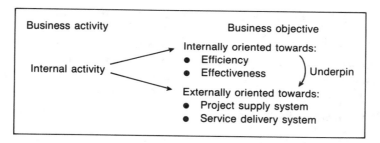

Figure 1.2 Business activities and business objectives.

of increasing the performance of managers. Management by objectives and the establishment and measurement of performance criteria is an important issue in many organisations. The use of management-oriented information systems may contribute to the resolution of this issue and can give rise to communication requirements. Examples of these include person-to-person communication and access to shared information.

The achievement of externally oriented objectives gives rise to communication requirements that underpin product or service delivery systems. Examples of these requirements include the communication facilities underpinning applications such as customer enquiries, customer order processing and inventory control in manufacturing and retail organisations. Others include customer services in banks and other financial services organisations. These applications may be regarded by some organisations as operational; that is, they underpin the product or service delivery system. The perception of these applications is that they are an integral part of the day-to-day operation of the organisation. Other organisations, on the other hand, may perceive some applications as mission critical or strategic; that is, they underpin the business vision of the enterprise. For example, an application that delivers a new

5

service to customers which results in a new market opportunity or a sustainable competitive edge is regarded as strategic. Other strategic applications include those that establish electronic links between an organisation and customers, clients or suppliers.

As shown in Figures 1.1 and 1.2, internally oriented objectives often underpin externally oriented objectives. The existence of this relationship reveals the nature of communication requirements that are linked to business objectives. Furthermore, as illustrated in the examples outlined above, the nature of these requirements is indicative of the scope of information networks. Consequently, an information network can be regarded as the enabling system which meets the requirements of operational or strategic applications, as well as the requirements of internally oriented applications. The business activities that lie within the scope of the business activities of Figure 1.2 will give rise to the need to communicate various forms of information. These are examined in the next section.

1.4   The need to communicate information

The definition of an information network (stated in Section 1.2 above) refers to various forms of information such as voice, data, text and image. The requirements for communicating these forms of information will be examined in turn.

1.4.1   The need to communicate speech

Speech is the most immediate form of human communication; spoken language will therefore continue to play a major role in business activities. Consequently, the telephone will remain an essential communicating device for the foreseeable future.

Surveys have shown that managers spend 5–15 per cent of their time using the telephone, thus underlining its well-established acceptance in the business environment (Data General, 1984). Despite the acceptance of the telephone, a number of problems arise from its use. For example, 'telephone tag' occurs when the recipient of a telephone call is on another telephone, at a meeting or is 'out of the office' for a variety of reasons. When the recipient returns the call, the originator is unavailable and the two parties continue to miss each other. Store-and-retrieve voice mail systems can alleviate this problem to an extent. Voice mail also avoids restrictions imposed by time zones. A survey of European managers by Booz Allen & Hamilton (1984) found that the impact of voice mail systems on productivity was rated as 'high'. Consequently, there is a need for the delayed communication of speech by means of store-and-retrieve systems.

The need to contact people who are not usually in an office environment has been addressed by the development of mobile telephone networks. These systems are used to contact people who are travelling or are working in the field.

These problems and requirements suggest that speech communication will continue to be essential in most organisations.

1.4.2 The need to communicate text

Most organisations generate text-based documents in order to carry out business activities. With the proliferation of personal computers and application software for word-processing, a significant proportion of these documents are created and stored using computer-based systems. Consequently, communication requirements arise from the use of text-processing systems – for example, the need to provide shared access to documents and to communicate documents from person-to-person may be required.

Additional communication requirements arise from the need to provide person-to-person messaging in the form of electronic mail services. The majority of these messages are usually destined for recipients within an organisation, but there may also be a need for external messaging services for the transfer of documents and messages to trading partners, for example.

1.4.3 The need to communicate data

Organisations are becoming increasingly reliant on computer-based information systems to process the data that is generated as a result of business activities. Computer-based information systems are used in a wide range of administrative and financial applications, as well as in product and service delivery systems.

Communications requirements arise from the need to provide on-line access to existing information systems in an organisation. This can include, for example, access to the following:

- Centralised databases in transaction-oriented applications such as order entry and stock control systems.
- On-line reports.
- On-line manuals and other documentation.
- On-line product information such as description, price and so on.

Users of these systems require access to applications and data in order to carry out business activities.

Applications that require new communications facilities can arise as a result of distributing a centralised application. For example, it may be necessary to link several distributed computers together or link them to a central computer in order to bring data together for correlation and summary purposes. A similar requirement may arise as a result of the computerisation of a distributed, manual operation – for example, geographically dispersed sales offices that are interconnected via a computer network in order to exchange information concerning product availability and to facilitate corporate accounting.

Additional communication requirements may arise from the need to interchange business documentation that accompanies the movement of goods between organisations and their suppliers and customers. These include data associated with orders and invoices which are sent from one organisation to another. The electronic

7

transmission of such documentation can be facilitated by using a computer network that links trading partners together. This kind of electronic service is known as electronic data interchange (EDI).

1.4.4 The need to communicate images

There are a number of industrial, scientific and commercial applications that lend themselves to image-processing (IP) techniques. Essentially, an IP system captures and stores an image of the activity, process or environment relating to the application. The image is retrieved for subsequent analysis, manipulation or enhancement purposes, depending on the requirements of the application. Image capture is achieved by a number of techniques such as electronic or optical scanning, or by means of still and moving picture (television) cameras. Image storage and retrieval is achieved by means of high-density storage media and computer systems. The stored images can be viewed using high-definition computer screens.

Image-processing systems provide the means to capture, store and retrieve images appropriate to the application. It may be helpful to summarise some of these applications before communication requirements are discussed. These include, for example, the following:

- Medical imaging – X-rays and X-ray enhancement.
- Analysis of satellite data – mineral exploration, meteorology.
- Making maps, charts, etc.
- Industrial imaging – quality control in production systems.
- Remote sensing, monitoring and measuring.
- Generation of facsimiles of documents.
- Document image processing – archive, management and retrieval of large quantities of documents.
- Creation of compound documents containing a mixture of text, data, graphics and other forms of information.
- Publishing systems.

Other applications require real-time processing or viewing of moving images. These include, for example, the following:

- Security and monitoring systems.
- Videoconferencing – remote meetings and conferences.
- Remote presentations and training.
- Videotelephony.

A third category of applications deal with images that are created on a screen rather than images that are scanned in some way. These applications include, for example, the following:

- Business graphics – graphical output of business data.
- Graphic design.

- Graphics in the arts, entertainment and media.
- Video graphics and animation.
- Computer-aided design.

The requirement to communicate images can arise from the use of IP systems – for example, an engineering company that requires access to a database of drawings and designs which need to be downloaded to engineers' workstations. Transmission of facsimiles of documents or non-textual information may be a requirement for some organisations. Remote security, sensing and monitoring systems may give rise to communication requirements. In addition, business requirements may give rise to the need for videoconferencing.

1.4.5   The need to communicate compound documents

The previous four subsections dealt mainly with the need to communicate one form of information. However, there may be a requirement to create a document that comprises a number of components, each of which may consist of forms of information derived from different sources. Examples of these 'compound documents' include the following:

- Text and data.
- Text and graphics.
- Text, data and graphics.
- Text, graphics and photographic images.
- Image, sound and text.

In practice, a compound document is created by electronic 'cut-and-paste' techniques using the interface facilities between the application software of computer systems. Communication requirements will arise from the need to transfer compound documents.

A richer environment of multiple forms and sources of information is that of hypertext and hypermedia. This technology has emerged recently in order to address the need to add flexible searching facilities to databases of textual and other forms of information. A hypertext system contains richly linked textual information in a storage and retrieval environment such that the links are associative. A hypermedia system extends this concept to include all forms of information that can be encoded digitally and stored and retrieved using computer-based systems. Communication facilities will be required to bring together these various forms of information into the hypermedia system from various sources and provide access to such a system. Whereas current hypermedia technology is typified by stand-alone systems, future systems will be required to operate in a network environment.

1.5   Practical implications

The communications requirements identified in the previous section will have an impact on network design. In order to gain some insight into the practical implications of these requirements, it is appropriate to quantify them approximately. Table 1.1 summarises the requirements to transmit various forms of information.

Table 1.1   Characteristics of different types of network traffic

Information	Capacity	Typical transmission requirements
A sales transaction	Up to a few hundred characters	9.6 kbps
A booking transaction	1000 – 2000 characters	9.6 kbps
An A4 page of text	Up to 5000 characters	24 – 48 kbps
Speech	Varies	A telephone conversation requires 32 – 64 kbps for digital transmission
A video frame	1 – 2 million bits	1 mbps
A screen of graphical information	Several thousand bytes	64 kbps
Document image	Several thousand bytes	64 kbps
Computer-aided design (CAD) file	Several megabits	Several mbps

The table indicates that the requirement to transmit video image information is two or three orders of magnitude greater than that to transmit, for example, a sales transaction. This has implications for the network planner when designing an information network that is capable of transmitting more than one form of information at an acceptable speed. Chapter 3 will discuss network options, where it will be necessary to mention the typical transmission speeds of networks from time to time. The capacity of a given transmission medium to transmit information is often expressed in terms of the number of bits per second (Table 1.1) and is a function of the physical characteristics of the medium. In particular, the parameter known as the *bandwidth* is important in this context. The theory underlying the relationship between the information-carrying capacity of a channel and its bandwidth is outside the scope of this book. However, the reader is strongly advised to consult Appendix B (and the Further Reading section) in order to gain an understanding of the fundamentals of this theory and, in particular, the implications of the concept of the bandwidth of a communication channel.

1.6 Summary

Information networks underpin the achievement of a range of business objectives. These objectives have been categorised as internally oriented or externally oriented in order to indicate the potential scope of the requirements that an information network is designed to address. The achievement of these objectives will involve business activities that require the communication of various forms of information within or between organisations. The need to communicate these forms has been introduced in this chapter.

The next chapter will identify and discuss the primary forces that shape the communications environment in organisations, in order to understand more fully how communications requirements arise.

CHAPTER 2

The communications environment

2.1 Introduction

This chapter will examine the primary forces that shape the communications environment in organisations. The objective of this is to provide an opportunity to gain a fuller understanding of the nature of communications requirements and to understand the environment in which the network planner operates. The focus will be on issues that have an impact on network planning and design.

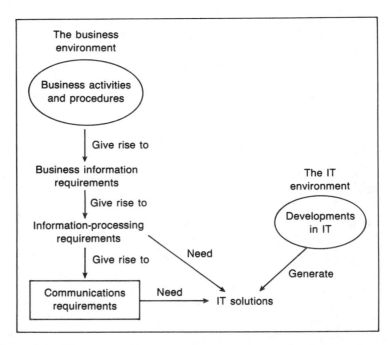

Figure 2.1   The communications environment: communications requirements.

Communications requirements arise from the information processing requirements of an organisation and the way in which IT is used to meet these requirements. Consequently, it is appropriate to examine trends in the way that organisations operate (the business environment) and trends in the use of IT (the IT environment). The context of these trends is illustrated in Figure 2.1. The underlying trends and changes in the business environment and the IT environment will be discussed in the next two sections.

2.2   The business environment

Business organisations operate in a social, political and economic climate and they are often forced to respond to changes in this climate in order to survive. The effect of the oil crisis in the 1970s was felt by most of the world's economies and, subsequently, organisations were forced to become more efficient, accountable and competitive. More recently, the emergence of new markets in Eastern Europe and the development of free-market communities of economies in the European Community, for example, poses both threats and opportunities to today's business enterprises.

Alongside these social, political and economic forces, the last twenty years have witnessed rapid advances in technology. In the last few years, in particular, the business environment has met with rapid advances in manufacturing technology and information technology. In order to continue to operate in a competitive climate, many organisations have invested in technology in order to meet the challenge of today's business environment. Part of this investment is in IT and reflects the growing need to support information processing activities in organisations.

Table 2.1   US labour statistics by occupation
(Entries are in thousands)

Occupation	1983	1985	1987	1989	Increase (%)
Service	68,715	73,524	77,878	82,080	20
Manufacturing	40,467	42,601	44,042	45,033	11

Source: US Department of Labor.

The growing importance of information processing is reflected by the changes in the nature of the occupations of the workforce. Table 2.1 illustrates this by presenting data for the occupation of civilians during the period from 1983 until 1989 in the United States. The table shows that in 1989 there were about twice as many employees in non-manufacturing occupations compared to those in manufacturing occupations. These data also show that between 1983 and 1989, there was a 20 per cent increase in the number of the former, compared to an 11 per cent increase in the latter. In other words, the rate of increase of occupations that involve information processing is approximately twice that for manufacturing occupations.

The growth in information processing can also be seen by examining the nature of the industry sector of the workforce. This is illustrated in Table 2.2 for the workforce in the United States and in Table 2.3 for the United Kingdom. Both tables show the relative number of employees and the rate of growth of service industries compared to non-services industries and illustrate the growing emphasis on the service sector.

Table 2.2 US labour statistics by industry sector
(Entries are in thousands)

Industry	1983	1985	1987	1989	Increase (%)
Service	64,260	68,683	73,238	77,033	20
Manufacturing	31,100	32,690	33,330	34,216	10

Source: US Department of Labor.

Table 2.3 UK labour statistics by industry sector
(Entries are in thousands)

Industry	1983	1985	1987	1989	Increase/decrease (%)
Service	13,169	13,769	14,247	15,322	16 increase
Manufacturing	7,402	7,151	6,833	6,909	7 decrease

Source: UK Department of Employment.

The growth in activities associated with information processing has been mirrored by a growth in the use of IT to support these activities. This has clear implications for the network planner, in that the implementation of IT often requires communication facilities to deliver information-processing services to users of IT-based information systems.

An additional trend that can have an impact on communications requirements concerns changes in the structure of organisations. Some organisations have moved from a centralised to a decentralised structure. This has usually resulted from a review of the way that the organisation operates and responds to market forces. These structural changes can give rise to a number of advantages, including the following:

- Flexibility in the response to changing markets.
- Easier accountability of component parts of the organisation; e.g. the creation of budget centres or profit centres.
- Autonomy of a distributed style of decision-making and management.
- Potential cost savings of decentralisation of human and physical resources.
- Ability to get closer to customers and broaden the market.

Centralised and decentralised structures require different kinds of information systems to support operational and management functions. Consequently, a change in the structure of an organisation can have an impact upon communications requirements. This aspect of the operation of a business organisation is given additional focus when acquisitions, mergers of joint ventures are undertaken. These can have a dramatic impact on information systems and communications requirements and pose a major challenge to the network planner.

2.3   The IT environment

The previous section indicates that investment in IT is a major factor in the way in which organisations respond to changes in the business environment. Information systems are often fundamental to the operation of an organisation and, depending on the type of business, can be regarded as a strategic resource. Consequently, communications facilities play a strategic role as well as a support or operational role, according to the type of business. (The relationship between the type of business and the role of information systems is explored in Chapter 6.) This section will examine the way in which IT is used in organisations in order to highlight factors that affect the provision of communications facilities.

Decisions regarding the development of products or services depend on the availability of information. The value of information which contributes to the development and marketing of products or services depends on effective processing and communication facilities. The technology that delivers these facilities has developed rapidly in the last few years.

Developments in computer technology were dominated by the advent of the mainframe computer in the 1960s and the minicomputer in the 1970s. Both these systems are widely used in many organisations today. It was the emergence of the microcomputer, however, that introduced a new paradigm of computing in the early 1980s. In particular, the subsequent availability of a wide range of application software accelerated their use and gave credibility to the use of a personal computer as a legitimate business tool.

The significance of the development of the personal computer is that computing facilities are brought as close as possible to the user, usually within arm's reach on the desktop. This changed the perception of computing as an operational resource towards the internal, value-added potential of using computers as support tools. Managers, for example, could be provided with powerful business tools in the shape of personal computing facilities.

The penetration of personal computers in organisations has given rise to requirements for communications facilities – for example, there may be a need to interconnect personal computers in order to share files and other resources. In addition, there may be a requirement to provide users of information with access to other resources, such as corporate databases, which reside on local or remote minicomputers or mainframe computer systems.

This advance in computer technology has facilitated the migration of computer resources associated with large, centralised computer systems towards computer systems that are distributed throughout an organisation. In practice, this distributed environment often comprises a range of computer resources. Typically, these include centralised mainframe computers which run corporate applications such as databases. In addition, minicomputers are used to provide processing facilities for individual sites or business functions, and there may be a number of personal computers dispersed throughout the organisation.

In such an environment, computer networks and communications facilities are necessary where there is a need to interconnect distributed computers. This provides users of information with access to application software and other computing resources regardless of where those resources are located within an organisation.

The range of computer applications is increasing steadily. This can result in the existence of 'islands' of computing facilities in an organisation. This diverse IT environment can give rise to additional requirements for communications facilities, where there is a need to link islands together and interface between ISs. This diversity of ISs includes the following principal domains of applications:

- Transaction-oriented systems, e.g. local and remote databases.
- Administrative systems, e.g. accounting.
- Office systems, e.g. text processing and messaging.
- Management support systems, e.g. spreadsheet and other decision support tools.
- Factory systems – those that support design and manufacturing processes.

A requirement to interface between, for example, an order-processing system and an accounting system will determine the communications facilities that will be required to support the integration of these ISs.

As IT penetrates an organisation, users of ISs require integration between applications and access to distributed resources in order to support business activities in the most effective way. The computer network is the enabling technology that supports this environment. Computer networks can be designed to meet the needs of a single site or a multisite organisation and can be used to provide communications links between an organisation and its trading partners. Networks of distributed computers are likely to be the dominant feature of developments in IT for the foreseeable future. These (distributed) systems will eventually provide transparent access to the complete range of services that is required by an information user, so that users will be unaware of where data, application software or computers are located. It should be noted, however, that the goal of a completely transparent distributed system has not yet been achieved. Nevertheless, distributed systems are likely to become the computing paradigm of the 1990s.

One approach to transparent distributed systems that has emerged recently is the 'client–server' architecture. In this environment, computers are regarded as 'service' providers that are attached to a computer network and users access services by means of a personal computer or workstation known as a 'client'. Figure 2.2 illustrates the concept and some of the principles of the client–server architecture. Data access

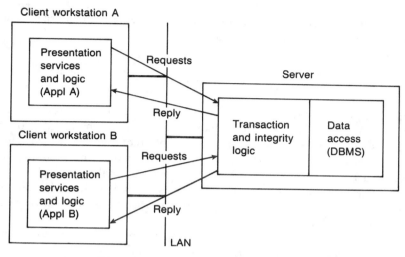

Figure 2.2 Client–server architecture.

functions reside in the server, and application-specific functions reside in the client. Client and server functions can reside in separate computers or can coexist in one computer.

The motivation of the client–server architecture reflects the need to provide users with access to diverse application services in a reliable environment. In the client–server architecture applications are partitioned between client and server devices, so that the components of the application communicate and co-operate with one another. The 'front end' or client component resides on a personal computer or workstation, while the 'back end' or server component resides on anything from a microcomputer to a mainframe computer. Clients and servers will function as independent, logical processors and will co-operate in the client–server environment, as illustrated in Figure 2.2.

The development of distributed architectures such as the client–server architecture will have an impact on network design. Today's network applications may require large volumes of data or entire files to be downloaded from central resources for local processing. In contrast, the client–server architecture determines that computers will co-operate and decide what items are to be downloaded from servers or uploaded to servers. It is important, therefore, for the network planner to assess the network capacity requirements for current and future distributed systems.

Notwithstanding the development of distributed systems, the network planner may be faced with a general demand from users for increased network capacity. The variety of forms of information that can be processed by digital devices has increased the demand for network capacity for the communication of voice and non-voice information. Some observers have suggested that the requirement for the communication of data, text and graphics will approach or even exceed that for voice communications by the end of the 1990s. The overall requirement to provide sufficient

17

network capacity to meet all the communications requirements of an organisation will pose a major challenge to the network designer.

2.4 Summary

This chapter has examined the primary forces in the business environment and the way in which IT is utilised to support information processing activities in organisations. Communications facilities will be required to provide users of information with access to central and distributed computing resources and to exchange data between computers. This is achieved by making use of networks of computers which provide communications services to a single site or building or to a multisite organisation. Specially managed computer networks provide inter-business services between trading partners.

The design of an information network to provide data and non-data communications facilities and services is the responsibility of the network planner; the next chapter will examine the principal options that are available to meet communications requirements.

CHAPTER 3

Communications options

3.1 Introduction

The first two chapters examined the nature of communications requirements; this chapter will examine how these requirements can be met. The principal types of information networks are introduced and their functionality and means of provision discussed. The focus of the discussion is more on network facilities rather than on underlying technical principles, though it is necessary to refer to the latter in order to understand the former.

There exist today many types of network which can be used to deliver communications facilities to users. The technical aspects of computer networks deserve a detailed treatment and there are several excellent books that cover the subject. It is not the intention of this chapter to attempt to cover the subject in depth; the reader is recommended to refer to the Further Reading section for a more comprehensive treatment. It will be necessary, however, to examine different types of networks in sufficient detail in order to give the network analyst an insight into the functionality of the various network options that are available.

This chapter will show that a wide range of network options has emerged in recent years. In the wide area domain, organisations are able to construct private networks or make use of public network services provided by public telecommunications operators (PTOs) or by third-party suppliers. Wide area networks are used for inter-site communications and can provide extensive national or international coverage. Some national regulatory environments have resulted in a limited range of options for public and private wide area networks, whereas others, such as in the United States and the United Kingdom, have encouraged competition in the provision of network services. In the local area domain, a wide range of network options are available for private networking. Local area networks are usually restricted to an area such as a building or a factory site.

It is the objective of this chapter to classify information networks along technical lines and categorise them in terms of their geographic coverage. The network analyst is then able to evaluate network options in the light of the communications requirements of an organisation.

3.2 Components of information networks

The term *information network* has been defined in Section 1.2. This definition can be regarded as embracing a number of network types. For example, a telephone network predominantly carries speech, but may also transmit computer data and facsimiles of documents. A computer network, on the other hand, predominantly carries the data and text that are associated with computer-based applications. In some large, multisite organisations part of the voice network may overlap with that of the computer network and multichannel circuits are configured to carry a mixture of voice and data. In this type of circuit the category of information is not important. The circuit merely carries digital signals, and it is the function of other components of the network to differentiate between the various channels of information.

An information network may comprise several components such as circuits and devices attached to these circuits. The functionality of an information network and its associated communicating devices is, however, based on software which resides in hardware components. Hence, any reference to communicating devices in this section implies that the device usually comprises hardware and software elements. (Chapter 4 discusses aspects of the software associated with network architectures.)

For present purposes, the term *network* will be used to refer to any form of information network. The context of a particular network will imply whether it is a telephone network, a computer network or a network that can carry a mixture of forms of information.

3.2.1 Network structure

In its simplest form, communication of information takes place between two communicating devices that are directly connected by a *point-to-point* transmission path. The practical solution to the interconnection of a population of devices is to attach each to a network. Such a network can be modelled by a *graph*. This is a representation of the network that is independent of the nature of the media that comprise the transmission paths and of the functionality located at the points at which paths connect. Figure 3.1 illustrates this concept for a relatively simple wide area network. In the diagram, the network consists of a number of transmission paths or circuits that interconnect or join at points known as *nodes*. Communicating devices are attached to nodes so that information can be carried from one device to another. For example, if device A wishes to send information to device B, the information is passed along a selected route. For instance, the route with the least number of node-to-node 'hops' would involve nodes 1, 2 and 5. In this network, node 2 does not have any communicating devices attached directly to it; its function is to route information from node 1 to node 5. If the path between node 2 and node 5 was not available, node 2 selects another route via node 4. Node 2 is said to be an *intermediate node*, whereas nodes 1, 3, 4 and 5 are *boundary* nodes with communicating devices attached directly to them. The nodes in the network of Figure 3.1 perform the routeing function between A and B and are capable of *switching* an appropriate end-to-end circuit or path between A

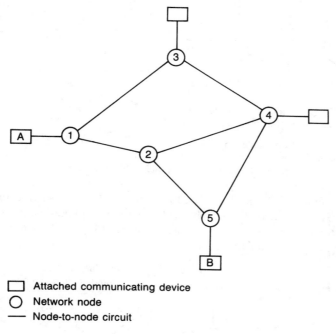

Figure 3.1 A simple information network.

and B. It should be noted, however, that in some networks not all nodes are intelligent and, in particular, do not perform routeing.

The set of nodes that comprise a network of the type shown in Figure 3.1 are capable of selecting a path or route between two end systems that wish to communicate. Consequently, these nodes are intelligent devices, which are usually software controlled. The paths or links between nodes consist of physical circuits that are capable of carrying digital or analogue signals that represent the information being transmitted. A range of media exist that can be used for these links; these include the following:

- Copper cable.
- Fibre-optic cable.
- Microwave and satellite radio links.

In practice, a physical circuit can consist of a number of logical channels, each of which is capable of carrying information. In this way, the capacity of a link can be shared between several pairs of communicating devices. Figure 3.2 illustrates this concept for a circuit that is divided into three logical channels; network nodes have been omitted to simplify the diagram. The technique of making use of a multichannel circuit is known as *multiplexing*; a number of devices that provide multiplexing capability exist.

21

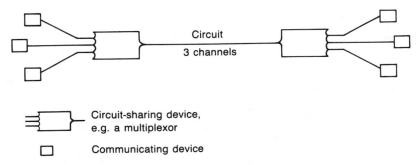

Figure 3.2   Circuits, channels and multiplexing.

The technique of multiplexing is used to optimise the number of communicating devices that can be attached to a physical circuit and makes efficient use of the bandwidth of the circuit. Furthermore, each channel of Figure 3.2 can be subdivided (or submultiplexed) into subchannels.

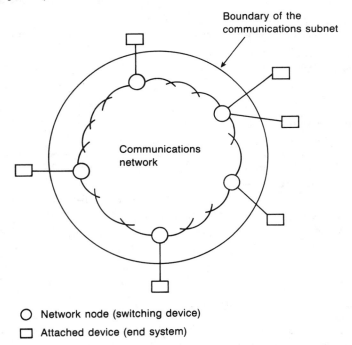

Figure 3.3   A generalized information network.

Figure 3.1 depicts the structure of a relatively simple network of five nodes, with each of the boundary nodes having just one communicating device attached to it. Clearly, most networks are more complex and a generalised representation in their structure is often useful. This is illustrated in Figure 3.3, which shows a few boundary nodes and attached devices. The 'cloud' representation of the network hides the true structure of intermediate nodes and node-to-node links. The generalised structure may be used to simplify the representation of a complex network for illustrative purposes.

The communicating devices that are attached to a network are often known as *end systems*. End systems are telephones, computers, computer terminals or other communicating devices. An end system is attached to a boundary node and end systems are interconnected by the *communications subnetwork* or *subnet* for short. The function of the subnet, shown by the boundary in Figure 3.3, is to carry information from end system to end system. By separating the communications aspects of the subnet from the applications and services associated with communicating end systems, it is possible to separate aspects of network design and simplify the process to some extent.

As Figure 3.1 indicates, node 1, for example, is capable of selecting between two alternative circuits (1 to 3 or 1 to 2). Consequently, the functionality of this node is such that it acts as a *switching* device. The switching function can be performed by devices such as specialised computers, message processors, telephone exchanges, data switches and packet switches. There is no consensus on the terminology used for a switching device, so the term *switching node* is used here to refer to any device that performs the switching function in a network.

3.3   Network classification

There are two main techniques used to transfer information between end systems. This leads to two classifications of networks, each of which can be subclassified as follows:

1.   Switched networks (or point-to-point networks) in the wide area domain:
     ● Circuit-switched networks;
     ● Packet-switched networks.
2.   Broadcast networks in the local area domain:
     ● Local area networks.

Each of these classifications will be discussed in turn.

3.3.1   Switched networks

In a *switched network*, information is transferred from end system to end system by means of a sequence of point-to-point links (see Figure 3.1, for example). The purpose of the boundary nodes and intermediate nodes involved in the transfer is to provide a switching function that will find a route from the sending end system to the receiving end system.

Circuit switching

In a *circuit-switched* network, a communication path is established between the two end systems that wish to communicate. The path may involve a sequence of connected links between nodes such that a logical channel on each link is dedicated to the connection. At each node, incoming information is routed or switched to an appropriate outgoing channel. The two end systems can engage in a communications *session* by establishing an end-to-end connection in this way. When the communications session has been completed, the switching devices release the logical channels so that they become available for other communications sessions. The concept of a circuit switched network is illustrated in Figure 3.4, which shows a circuit between two end systems A and B.

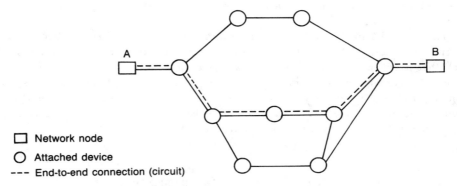

□ Network node
○ Attached device
--- End-to-end connection (circuit)

Figure 3.4　A circuit-switched network.

The principal characteristic of circuit switching is that a dedicated channel provides the minimum delays that are necessary for communication. The most familiar example of a public circuit-switched network is the public switched telephone network (PSTN). When used for speech, each telephone is connected to a local switching exchange (the local node) by a permanent circuit (the local end or local loop). Local exchanges are interconnected by network of main or trunk circuits and exchanges. When used for data communications, computers and computer terminals are connected to the PSTN by means of a device known as a *modem*. The function of this device is to convert digital signals to audio tones which are transmitted via the PSTN. The sending end system dials the number of the receiving end system to establish a connection. Consequently, the use of the PSTN is based on a 'dialup' procedure.

The quality of the PSTN varies from country to country and this is an important factor to take into account when considering this network option. In most of the countries in Europe, for example, telephone networks are at an advanced stage of modernisation and digital signalling is replacing analogue signalling over trunk circuits. The concomitant improvements in quality and capability to transmit computer data will influence the evaluation of the PSTN as a network option.

A number of countries have developed public circuit-switched data networks as part of their telecommunications infrastructure. Deutsche Bundespost Telekom in Germany, for example, operate a data network of this type called Datex-L. The relevance of this to the network analyst has more to do with the cost of using this type of network rather than the technical aspects of this type of switching. Users of public circuit-switched networks are usually charged on the basis of the distance between end systems and the period of time the circuit is in use, rather than on the quantity of information transmitted.

Packet switching

In contrast to a circuit switched network, a quite different approach to switching is used in a *packet-switched* network. In a packet switched network, it is not necessary to dedicate an end-to-end path between end systems. Instead, the sending end system transmits a sequence of blocks of information, each one of which is known as a *packet*. There is intelligence in the sending end system or the boundary node that creates packets from the information required to be transmitted. Similar functionality reassembles packets and reconstructs the original information for the receiving end system. The packets themselves are routed through the network, with different packets taking the same or different routes. As far as the end systems are concerned, end-to-end communication is achieved by reordering packets if necessary.

The nodes in a packet switched network are often called packet-switched exchanges (PSEs). The end systems attached to PSEs can be computers, terminals or devices that are capable of creating packets. For the many end systems and terminal types that do not have this capability, data are processed in a device known as a packet assembler/disassembler (PAD) before being passed to the PSE.

In a packet-switched network, the sending end system sends a packet of information to its nearest (local) PSE where it is stored temporarily. The PSE determines the *address* of the sending and receiving end systems from information contained in the packet. (The address of an end system uniquely identifies it in the network.) The PSE then selects an available route to another PSE, using its stored routeing information, and sends the packet. The packet is again stored temporarily. This process is continued from node to node until the packet arrives at the destination node, which delivers it to the receiving end system. The next packet in the sequence is carried across the network in a similar way and the process is continued until all the packets have been sent and received and the communications session has been completed.

Different packets may take different routes through the network depending on the availability of node-to-node links. It is the responsibility of the subnet to determine the routeing of packets during a communications session. For example, if the network in Figure 3.1 represented a simple, packet-switched network, packets sent by A could be conveyed to B by one of four possible routes, as follows:

- Nodes 1, 2 and 5.
- Nodes 1, 2, 4 and 5.
- Nodes 1, 3, 4 and 5.
- Nodes 1, 3, 4, 2 and 5.

The end systems are not concerned with these aspects of routeing; it is the network nodes that control these aspects of a communications session in a way that is transparent to the user of an end system.

As can be seen from the above discussion of the principles of packet switching, the capacity of the network is used in an entirely different way from circuit switching. Packet switching can achieve better overall utilisation of circuits at the cost of some delay in delivering packets. In circuit-switched networks, a channel may become idle for periods of time while, for example, a user of a computer terminal pauses before pressing the COMMIT or SEND key on their keyboard. In a packet-switched network, individual packets are allocated time slots and can be interleaved with other packets from other end systems attached to the same PSE. The allocation of time slots can contribute to the optimisation of the overall network capacity and is of importance in network performance.

Charging for the use of public packet-switched data networks is primarily based on the quantity of information that is transmitted; in circuit-switched networks, users have to pay for the use of the circuit even when data is not being sent for periods of time. This difference between the charging mechanism for the use of public circuit-switched and public packet-switched data networks is of interest to the network planner when comparing the cost of using public network options. Charging users for the use of a private packet-switched network may also necessitate a similar charging mechanism, based on the quantity of information sent across the organisation's network.

Although utilisation of circuits can be improved, the packet switching approach necessitates a delay by virtue of the *store and forward* nature of end-to-end packet delivery. This delay consists of the time it takes nodes to store a packet, select and seize an outgoing channel and retrieve the packet for retransmission; the time needed to transmit a packet along node-to-node links; and the time that a packet waits in queues at nodes for links to become available. The first two types of delay, node processing time and transmission time, are relatively small compared to the queuing delay. Thus the performance of this type of network depends on the queuing characteristics of the packet switches. Given these characteristics, packet-switched networks are suitable for computer networks. They are less suitable for the immediate transmission of speech. Packetised speech is still the subject of research and development, but the development of a technique known as *fast packet switching* (formally known by the CCITT as Asynchronous Transfer Mode) will eventually enable packet-switching principles to be applied to the transmission of speech and data.

Packet-switched data networks are suitable for high throughput data – for example, the transfer of large files between computers, as well as for low-volume traffic. The latter case is typified by the interactive communication that takes place between a user of a computer terminal and a remote, host computer. Packet-switched networks offer a number of advantages over circuit-switched networks. Since a packet is stored temporarily at each node, its format or speed of transmission can be altered. It can also be retransmitted in the event of corruption or loss. These characteristics provide the public network operators of packet-switched networks with flexibility and control and the means to provide high-quality performance to users.

Furthermore, many public packet-switched networks provide international connections. Interworking standards exist in the domain of public packet switching (see Chapter 4), with the result that national packet-switched networks will interwork for the purposes of international data communications.

Other standards also refer to the interface required to attach an end system to a public packet-switched network. These standards, known as X.25 (see Chapter 4), are supported by most of the major computer manufacturers and allow interworking between computers from different manufacturers as long as they support the same version of the standard. The X.25 standard is also used as the basis of the architecture of multivendor, private packet-switched networks. Organisations such as the clearing banks and major retail organisations are typical users of private packet-switched networks. (In a private wide area network the user organisation owns and manages all components of the network, apart from point-to-point circuits which are leased from PTOs.)

The advantages of the packet-switched approach to data communications means that public circuit-switched data networks become less attractive to users and to the organisations who operate them. It is likely that public circuit-switched data networks will be replaced with a circuit-switched network known as the Integrated Services Digital Network (ISDN), which is capable of carrying data, video and speech. Although many PTOs around the world are in the process of developing ISDN services, packet switching will continue to be offered as a public network service. (Section 3.6.3.1 will discuss the concept of the ISDN.)

Virtual circuits and datagrams

Before leaving the discussion of packet switching, it is important to introduce the two types of service that packet-switched networks support. These are known as *datagram* and *virtual circuit* services. The datagram service is a consequence of what is known as the *connectionless* organisation of the subnet; each packet (known as a datagram) is treated as a self-contained entity and is transmitted through the network independently of other packets. The service is described as connectionless in that there is no requirement to establish an end-to-end logical connection between end systems during the communications session. A route is determined for each packet that is sent. This type of service is analogous to sending a letter using a postal service and is more appropriate for the transfer of short data messages. In the virtual circuit approach, on the other hand, an end-to-end logical connection is established. Communication takes place and the connection is released when the communication session is complete.

An *unacknowledged datagram service* could be used to send packets that do not require an acknowledgement to be sent from the receiving end system to the sending end system. This type of datagram service could be used for applications such as certain kinds of electronic mail or information services, where acknowledgement is not required. For other applications, however, reliability and acknowledgement may be a requirement. In these cases, an *acknowledged datagram service* can be used to provide these facilities. Another service is the *request-reply service*. In this service, the sending end system sends a single datagram that contains a request for a reply; the acknowledged datagram includes the reply. Such a service could be used, for example, for applications such as credit card authorisation and requests for the availability of some kinds of consumer services.

Datagram services are not in wide use in public packet-switched data networks, largely because the work of the standards bodies (in particular the CCITT) has not favoured the connectionless organisation of the subnet. Despite this, some network operators provide a service that can be used for the transmission of short messages. In the United Kingdom, for example, users of British Telecom's public packet switched service (known as PSS) are able to make use a Fast Select service. (This service is made possible with the CCITT X.25 standard for public packet-switched networks.) The packet that requests the establishment of a connection also carries the user's message in the data field of the packet; the packet that confirms the request also contains the responding message and releases the connection. In other words, the phases of connection establishment, data communications and connection release are achieved with one pair of packets. This service lends itself to the applications mentioned above. However, genuine datagram services are only gradually being incorporated into the standards for public packet switched networks.

Despite the apparent lack of enthusiasm for datagram services, particularly in Europe, there are a number of advantages to this approach. The call establishment phase associated with the virtual circuit approach is avoided. This reduces traffic for short data calls. Also, because the datagram approach is fairly primitive, it is more flexible; if congestion develops in a part of the network, datagrams can be routed away from the problem. With the use of virtual circuits, it will be seen later that packets largely follow a predetermined route. In this case, it is more difficult to deal with congestion or overcome the problem of a node failing.

Packet-switched networks that pre-date the development of connection-oriented network standards make use of the datagram approach. For example, the ARPANET in the United States is the creation of DARPA, the Defense Advanced Research Projects Agency of the US Department of Defense, and links academic institutions that are involved in DARPA work around the world. The network began operation in 1969 and has grown to a network of several hundred computers.

For other applications that involve more than a short message to be sent and received, public packet-switched networks provide a *virtual circuit* service. In these cases, a virtual circuit is used where all packets follow a predetermined route and nodes are relieved of the processing that is associated with treating packets as separate entities. This type of service is a consequence of the *connection-oriented* organisation of the subnet in most public packet-switched networks and reflects the approach of standards bodies such as the CCITT and the ISO.

When using this type of service, the sending end system transmits a special packet to its local PSE to request a call. Then, assuming that the request is accepted, an appropriate response packet is returned; a virtual circuit or logical connection is said to exist between the two end systems concerned. Figure 3.5 uses a modification of the

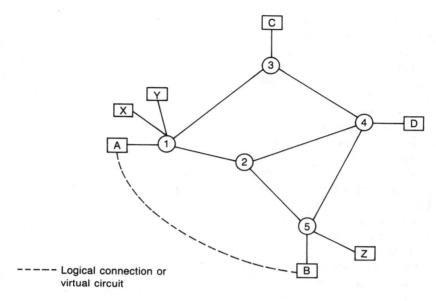

--- --- Logical connection or
virtual circuit

Figure 3.5 Virtual circuit.

network of Figure 3.1 to illustrate the concept of a virtual circuit.

Using Figure 3.5, suppose that A wishes to communicate with B. End system A sends a special packet known as a Call Request packet to node 1, requesting a connection to B. Node 1 routes the request to B via node 2. If B is prepared to accept the connection, it sends a Call Accept packet back to A via, say, node 2. End systems A and B can now exchange data using the logical connection or virtual circuit that has been established. Each packet contains a virtual circuit identifier as well as user data. Each node along the established route knows where to send packets; there are no routeing decisions to be made for each packet as in a datagram service. At the end of the communications session, one of the end systems terminates the session with a Clear Request packet and the virtual circuit is released. An end system can use more than one virtual circuit to another end system and can use virtual circuits to more than one end system.

It may appear that a virtual circuit is similar to a connection that has been established in a circuit-switched network. It should be noted, however, that a virtual circuit is a logical connection. The virtual circuit shown in Figure 3.5 involves nodes 1, 2 and 5. Packets from other communications sessions may be interleaved with those passing between A and B; there may, for example, be sessions between X and Z, X and B, and A and Z as well as other network traffic passing between nodes 1, 2 and 5. It is important, therefore, to treat the virtual circuit connection between end systems as a logical connection.

The significance of the virtual circuit service to the network planner is that users usually pay for the number of virtual circuits they use and for the number of packets that are sent during a data call. Normally, a virtual circuit is released at the end of a session. However, virtual circuits may be provided as *permanent virtual circuits* in situations where two end systems need to be in frequent contact. This could occur, for example, when two computers transfer files between each other on a regular basis. Permanent virtual circuits are usually available within public packet-switched services. As would be expected, users of permanent virtual circuits must pay for this facility on a rental or leased basis.

Most of the public packet-switched networks around the world offer virtual circuit services rather than datagram services. There are historical reasons for this that have more to do with the development of international standards for packet-switched networks than with users' needs or technical limitations of public networks. It remains to be seen whether increased demand for connectionless services will accelerate their inclusion in the range of services that are provided by public network operators.

Our discussion of some of the technical aspects of switched networks is now almost complete. It has been necessary to focus on public networks in order to provide the network planner with an overview of these networks. In practice, the development of private networks has derived from the technology and standards associated with public networks, so an awareness of the latter type is important. It has been necessary to provide an overview of switched services, because most wide area networks (WANs) that interconnect the geographically dispersed sites in an organisation are of the switched type. The next subsection will discuss the relevant characteristics of the second classification of networks, namely broadcast networks.

3.3.2 Broadcast networks

In a broadcast communications network, there are no intermediate switching nodes; a packet or a message sent from an end system is broadcast to and received by all of the other end systems attached to the network. A simple example of this kind of system is a Citizens' Band (CB) radio network. Similar broadcast systems are packet radio networks and satellite networks. In both of these networks, end systems (known as stations) transmit and receive via a radio frequency antenna and all stations share the same channel, based on a particular radio frequency. In a packet radio network, stations broadcast to each other directly. In a satellite network, the transmitting ground station transmits indirectly to all of the receiving ground stations within the footprint of the satellite; the satellite performs the functions of a relay device. A common feature of broadcast systems is that they usually have a single communications channel that is shared by all the stations using the network. Broadcast radio networks are, by definition, not used for point-to-point networks, though line-of-site microwave links or satellite links may be used to form circuits in the latter type of network.

We will mainly be concerned with broadcast networks that are used for computer-to-computer or terminal-to-computer data communications. Most local area networks (LANs) that provide data communications facilities to a single building, site or campus are of this type. A few WANs are of the broadcast type.

An important example of a WAN based on packet radio principles is the terminal-to-computer network at the University of Hawaii. This network, which is known as ALOHA, is important historically because it is the predecessor of the mechanism for controlling the access to the single communications channel in Ethernet LANs, discussed briefly later in this section. The ALOHA system covers several university campuses dispersed throughout the islands of Hawaii and allows computer terminals to access a central computer by radio, without using unreliable telephone lines. The key feature of the system is that frames (or packets) of data are transmitted to and from the central computer using two radio-frequency channels, one for inbound frames and one for outbound frames. The mechanism used to control contention for the use of the inbound channel influenced the development of Ethernet.

Local area networks

A LAN is wholly owned and managed by the user organisation. This classification of network is usually restricted to a private area such as a building or a collection of buildings on a campus or site.

In a LAN, all of the attached devices share the same communications channel. (This contrasts with point-to-point networks, where each end system is assigned either a frequency channel or a time slot on a multichannel circuit.) Packets sent by an attached device contain an address field that specifies the device to which the data is to be sent. When a packet is received by all of the other devices attached to the network, they read the address. If the packet is intended for some other device, the packet is ignored or passed on; otherwise it is copied into memory at the intended device. Typical devices that are attached to LANs include the following:

- File servers, database servers and print servers.
- Microcomputers, personal computers.
- Minicomputers, mainframe computers.
- Factory-based, microprocessor-controlled systems.

It is evident from the list above that LANs are used for data communications. LANs transmit packets of data from one end system to another, usually without the need to establish an end-to-end connection. They are not designed for circuit-switched telephone connections. However, very high-speed LANs based on the Fibre Distributed Data Interface (FDDI) standard are designed to carry data, voice and image.

Although there are several types of LAN on the market, there are two commonly used industry standard types. These are depicted, in simplified form, in Figure 3.6. In a *bus local network* (Figure 3.6a), all attached devices are attached to a length of cable. A transmission of a data packet by an attached device propagates the length of the cable in both directions so that it is received by all attached devices. The contention algorithm operates in such a way that at any instant in time, only one attached device can transmit a packet; all of the other attached devices refrain from transmitting. An arbitration mechanism is used to resolve conflicts when more than one attached device is ready to transmit. It is this contention mechanism that was derived from the work

31

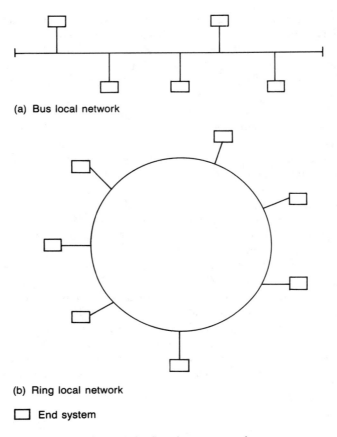

(a) Bus local network

(b) Ring local network

☐ End system

Figure 3.6 Local area networks.

on the ALOHA system and forms the basis of the Ethernet type of industry standard LAN.

Ethernet was originally developed by Xerox in the 1970s and was called Ethernet after the ethereal medium through which scientists once believed that electromagnetic radiation propagated. Ethernet was announced as a product in 1980 and the so-called DIX triumvirate of Digital, Intel and Xerox drew up a standard for a 10 mbps LAN. This *de facto* standard formed the basis of the IEEE 802.3 standard LAN.

The other commonly used industry standard LAN is the *Token Ring local network* (Figure 3.6b). This type of LAN consists of a closed loop, unlike the bus LAN. A packet sent from an attached device circulates around the ring and is received by all other attached devices in turn, until it reaches its destination. Given the topology of the ring LAN, it can be regarded as a special case of a sequence of point-to-point links that form a closed loop, rather than a pure broadcast network. However, the ring LAN is similar to the bus LAN in that they both consist of a single communications channel and packets are received by all attached devices. Where they differ is in the contention algorithm that arbitrates access to the channel. In the ring LAN, packets are circulated rather than broadcast and access to the ring is controlled by a 'token passing' algorithm. The method that is used in IBM's Token Ring LAN product involves a special bit pattern called the token, which circulates around the ring until it is seized by an attached device that wishes to transmit a packet. Upon seizure, the end system transmits data. The token is then released and permission to transmit a packet (by possession of the token) passes to another attached device. All attached devices get an opportunity to transmit in a 'round robin' fashion. Data communication occurs at several megabits per second – a similar speed to the Ethernet LAN discussed earlier.

IBM's Token Ring product formed the basis of the IEEE 802.5 standard for token ring LANs and sits alongside the IEEE 802.3 standard for CSMA/CD LANs mentioned earlier. Although there are other LAN types and standards in existence, it has only been necessary to give an overview of these two standards in this chapter in order to initiate the reader's awareness of some of the basic principles of LANs. (Chapter 4 will give a more complete picture of the LAN standards that are currently in place.)

This concludes our discussion of some of the fundamental technical aspects of broadcast networks in general and LANs in particular. In a book of this type, it has been necessary to minimise and simplify the discussion on LANs. Nevertheless, it is the job of the network planner to evaluate LAN options, and though the basic concepts underlying bus and ring LANs may appear to be relatively straightforward, technical characteristics can be complex. The reader should refer to the Further Reading section for a more detailed treatment of LANs.

Information category	Network classification		
	Packet switched	Circuit switched	Broadcast
Voice	Fast packet switching in the future	Wide area Local area	Some radiotelephone networks
Data	Wide area	Wide area	Local area

Figure 3.7 Summary of the coverage of commonly used networks.

3.3.3 Network classification: summary

So far in this chapter we have examined the nature of information networks and the way in which LANs and WANs transmit information. For non-voice applications, this is achieved by hardware and software components that create special blocks of data known as frames or packets. By processing and transmitting packets, the subnet is able to manage the flow of network traffic, deal with lost or corrupt packets and optimise the utilisation of the available capacity of the network. Voice traffic, on the other hand, does not require quite the same degree of error control as is the case for data traffic; the human brain compensates for minor corruption of speech in telephone conversations. In order to conduct a telephone conversation, an end-to-end connection is usually kept open for the duration of the call. Consequently, voice traffic is usually carried on circuit-switched networks.

Most WANs are circuit switched or packet switched, whereas most LANs can be classified as broadcast. Figure 3.7 brings together these summary points.

3.4   Network topology

This chapter has, so far, examined the topology of network structures in a general way (see, for example, Figures 3.1 – 3.6). However, the design of an information network for a particular organisation has to take into account the geographical location of sites when considering the installation of network nodes and the number of wide area links. For a local network, the physical characteristics of the building or site have to be considered when installing a LAN. In either case, the nature and number of end systems are important factors in network design. For data networks, in particular, the way in which computers are used to run user applications will determine whether the network is centralised or distributed. In other words, there are some constraints on the topologies that are possible for information networks. The next two subsections will examine the topologies for voice and data networks that are commonly used in organisations.

3.4.1   Voice networks

The switching node in a private voice network is a device that is capable of switching voice circuits; a digital private automatic branch exchange (PABX) is used for this purpose. End systems are mainly telephones, though other communicating devices such as facsimile machines may be attached to a PABX. A PABX may also be capable of handling data traffic, though very long data calls may affect its overall performance. Depending on the product, it may be feasible to connect computers and computer terminals to a PABX to provide data communications facilities within a private voice network. (This aspect of using PABXs will be returned to in a later section on integrated networks.) For the present, PABX networks will be discussed from the point of view of voice traffic as the predominant requirement.

A PABX usually has two basic functions: to connect all of the telephones in an organisation to the PSTN, and to interconnect telephones to form an internal telephone network. In its simplest form, a PABX provides facilities for a single building, site or campus; telephone extension cabling runs from the PABX to the

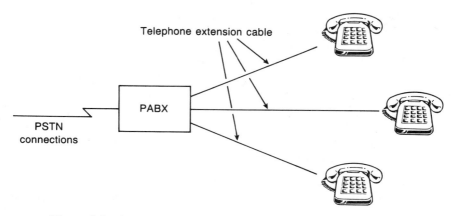

Figure 3.8 A central PABX network (a local area voice network).

telephone sockets dispersed throughout the site. Figure 3.8 illustrates this simple PABX network. Although modern PABXs are digital in operation, most telephones employ analogue signalling for telephone-to-PABX connections. Analogue – digital – analogue conversion is performed within the PABX. Although Figure 3.8 is a single-site network, circuit switching is required in order to connect two telephones together with an end-to-end circuit. Apart from meeting the basic requirements for voice communications, PABXs also offer a number of additional facilities. Typical facilities are summarised in Figure 3.9.

- Direct dial in (DDI) from PSTN
- Call transfer (to another extension)
- Short code dialling
- Group pick-up
- Call park (return to call from a different extension)
- Camp on (automatic call back)
- Three-party conferencing
- Call waiting signal
- Music
- Alarm call
- Voice store-and-retrieve

Figure 3.9 Typical PABX facilities.

Multisite organisations require a more complex voice network topology than the one shown in Figure 3.8. One common solution to the problem of interconnecting a number of sites is to install a switching device at all of the remote sites. These devices, often called remote switching units (RSUs), are PABXs that are used to interconnect extensions at different sites via a central PABX. The topology of this kind of network is shown in Figure 3.10, for an organisation of five sites; the telephone extensions have been omitted to simplify the diagram.

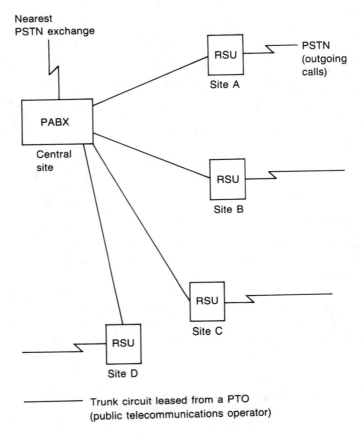

Figure 3.10 A multisite, private PABX network (a wide area voice network).

In the network shown in Figure 3.10, the PABX at site A, for example, processes calls between extensions at that site and may permit direct access to the PSTN for calls outside the organisation. All internal calls are routed via the central PABX, which is typically located at a large site such as the head office of the organisation. If the five PABXs are given the same area exchange number (by the PTO), incoming calls from the PSTN to any telephone in the organisation are routed via the central site. This arrangement is largely a function of where the PTO stores the information about the range of DDI (direct dial-in) extension numbers given to the organisation. In the network shown in Figure 3.10, this information is stored in the nearest PSTN exchange to the central site.

The degree of intelligence residing in RSUs can vary but, in general, it should be noted that to provide telephone facilities in the network of Figure 3.10 will require control information to pass between PABXs in addition to speech. The key to the distribution of intelligence in PABX networks lies in the signalling system that is used to pass this control information. PABXs based on analogue signalling have limited vocabulary for control information, whereas digital signalling based on message passing provides a richer environment for this purpose. Control signals consist of processor-to-processor data messages, allowing precise control of the range of facilities that digital PABXs can provide. Digital technology and message-based signalling allow a degree of distribution of processing in a PABX network. Reliance on a central PABX may be reduced and network topologies can be made more flexible. The standards relating to signalling between PABXs will be discussed briefly in Chapter 4.

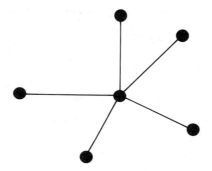

Figure 3.11   A star, point-to-point network.

Returning to the network of Figure 3.10, it should be noted that the network has a central 'hub'; this topology is often referred to as a star network and is shown in a generalised form in Figure 3.11. Despite the existence of four remote PABXs in Figure 3.10, internal voice traffic is routed via the central PABX. A telephone call from site A to site B, for example, involves a circuit to be established from end-to-end and relies on the availability of the central PABX. If this machine goes down, site-to-site voice communication is lost. Another drawback of the star topology is that a site will lose inter-site facilities if a circuit fails, though intra-site facilities remain intact. Despite the drawbacks of star-shaped networks, the main benefit is that the number of circuits that are leased from a PTO is at a minimum; this reduces the overall costs of operating a private voice network. In practice, the network of Figure 3.10 could be provided with back-up inter-site circuits or the PSTN could be used in the event of a failure.

A further point to make about the network of Figure 3.10 is that site-to-site circuits can usually be configured to carry data in addition to speech traffic if, for example, data communications are required between sites. An analysis of the voice and data traffic requirements between sites will assist in determining the most cost-effective configuration of multichannel (voice and data) circuits between sites. This so-called 'integration' of voice and data traffic on a private, multichannel, inter-site circuit is common practice in multisite organisations where there are significant requirements for inter-site voice and data communications and where integrated circuits can be leased from PTOs.

Before moving on to data networks, the main points about the topology of private voice networks are summarised as follows:

- Circuit switched.
- Facilities for one or more sites.
- Digital or analogue inter-site circuits.
- Digital or analogue PABXs.
- Generally uses analogue extension lines.
- Usually star-shaped in topology.
- Can carry voice and data on separate channels on the inter-site circuits.

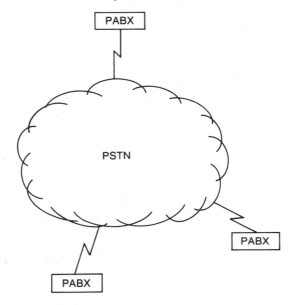

Figure 3.12   Corporate voice network based on PSTN connections.

Finally, it should be noted that the network planner is not concerned with the topology of the PSTN. The points at which a private network interface with it are of interest, however, and these are shown in the example in Figure 3.10. Clearly, there are organisations that cannot justify the implementation of a private voice network. In these cases, the PSTN is used for inter-site traffic and PABXs for intra-site traffic. This type of network is shown in Figure 3.12 for an organisation spread over three sites.

3.4.2   Wide area data networks

For convenience, we refer to any network of computers, computer terminals or workstations as a *data network*. It may carry data, text or image information depending on the nature of the applications that are being used. The configuration of application software depends largely on whether applications and their associated files reside in a single host computer, or whether they are distributed (see Section 2.3). There may be requirements such as file transfer between application processes which reside on separate computers and electronic mail between end users. In broad terms, the topology of a data network is a function of the location of the following:

- Processors that run user applications.
- Application software and their associated files.
- Users of these applications.

Given these requirements, a number of data network topologies are used in organisations.

Centralised data networks

Initially, we will focus on centralised networks in which all applications and files reside in a single host computer system. This system is accessed by computer terminals or personal computers in a number of ways. Some of the methods of access are brought together in the network of Figure 3.13.

Figure 3.13 shows direct links for single terminals and the use of a line-sharing device terminating on a point-to-point link. An alternative cabling configuration is shown by the *multipoint* or *multidrop* line in the diagram. Links to remote sites are achieved by means of public or private data communications links and usually involve a pair of network access devices as shown in the diagram for sites A and B. If links use analogue signalling, this device is a modem. If links use digital signalling, there is usually a requirement for a network access device. This is referred to as a DSU (digital service unit) in the United States and an NTU (network terminating unit) in the United Kingdom, for example. It should be noted that all of the local and remote links in the network of Figure 3.13 are connected to a front-end processor (FEP). This is a special computer that manages all the processing concerned with data communications to and from the host computer.

The data network of Figure 3.13 has a star-shaped topology, rather like the voice networks of Figures 3.8 and 3.10. Data communications takes place between terminals and the host; there is no routeing of data between sites other than to and from the central site. Consequently, there is no switching function associated with the central host computer.

A variation of the network of Figure 3.13 occurs when there are a number of host computers at the central site. A simplified form of this type of network is shown in Figure 3.14, which shows four central computers and a device known as a *data switch*. Most local and all remote terminals are connected to this switch, which allocates a line to a port on whichever host the user requires access. Hence, the data switch is used as a port selection or port contention device and allows a number of users to share ports and hosts.

It can be seen that a centralised computer network supports terminal-to-host connections between the central site and remote sites. This type of network supports communications requirements that rely on a dominant role of the central host

39

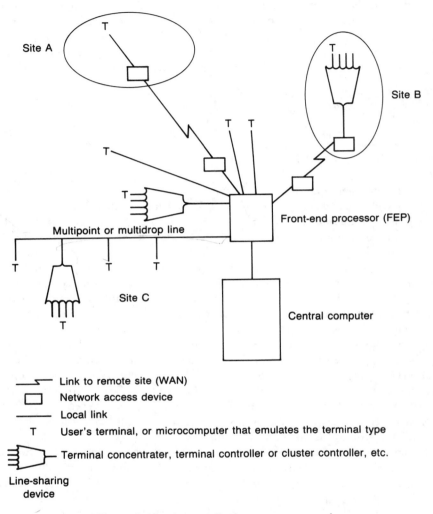

Figure 3.13 A centralised computer network.

computer in the information processing architecture of an organisation.

Distributed data networks

If a computer is installed at a remote site, the network in Figure 3.14 would look like the one shown in Figure 3.15. Furthermore, if there were a number of processors at the remote site, a similar data switch would be required to control access. Consequently, it can be seen that the network would consist of two switching nodes that connect terminals to computers distributed between two sites. This is an example of a relatively simple network of data switches and distributed computers. This type

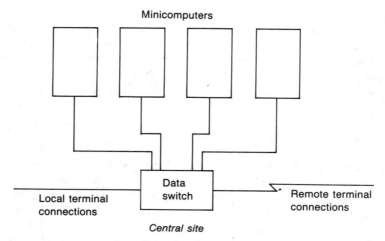

Figure 3.14 The role of a data switch in a centralised computer network.

of network is often more complex and provides users with access to application software that resides on a number of host computers distributed throughout the organisation. Two examples will help to illustrate this type of distributed computer network.

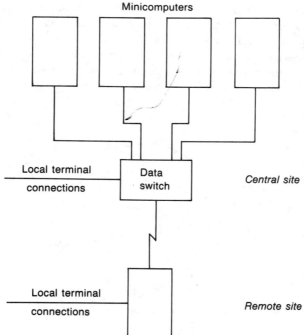

Figure 3.15 The role of a data switch in a distributed computer network.

41

EXAMPLE 1

A software house in the United Kingdom has three sites: one in London and two in a large town about 100 miles away. The three sites are interconnected by data switches in a triangular network. This arrangement provides alternative routeing should one of the inter-node links fail and allows users at any site to login to any host at any of the three sites.

EXAMPLE 2

A consortium of UK and French companies was formed in 1986, under the the name of Transmanche Link (TML), to build a tunnel under the English Channel. The UK part of the consortium built a WAN in the south-east part of England and, by 1989, this network consisted of six nodes (data switches) to interconnect various computer systems associated with the tunnel project. At one of these nodes, there is a gateway to a private PSE which provides access to a number of other computers as well as to a public packet-switched service. The latter connection is used for transferring payroll information to computer systems of banks in the United Kingdom. (The topology of the complete network is relatively complex and will not be shown.)

These two examples illustrate the way in which WANs of distributed computers can be designed using data switches and circuits that are leased from PTOs. These multinode networks are essentially circuit switched in nature (see Section 3.3.1). The networks of Examples 1 and 2 are often described as *mesh* networks, to reflect their irregular topology. A generalised mesh network is shown in Figure 3.16 and illustrates the presence of alternative routes in this type of network. Although this is a major benefit, the price of the resilience of mesh networks is reflected in the extra costs of leasing additional inter-node links. This depends largely on the resilience that is required. The network of Figure 3.16, for example, could have been designed with fewer inter-node links.

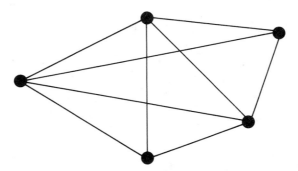

Figure 3.16 A mesh, point-to-point network.

Distributed computer networks are not, however, always mesh-shaped. The requirements of Examples 1 and 2 above resulted in the inclusion of alternative inter-

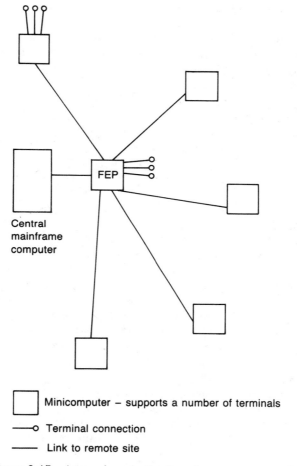

Figure 3.17 A star-shaped, distributed computer network.

node routeing and access to computers located at a number of sites. On the other hand, some distributed computer networks are star-shaped (see Figure 3.11). Such a network can often be found in organisations where distributed computer systems develop from a centralised computer system. Remote terminals are replaced with computers, to provide processing facilities at those sites, and a network such as the one shown in Figure 3.17 evolves. The characteristic of this type of network is that data processing is performed at each site and data communications are required between computers at these sites and the central computer system; there is no requirement for inter-site communication.

This type of computer network supports communications requirements that are largely determined by the need to communicate between an application located at a remote site and an application located at the central site. This is often required for collation and summary purposes; the necessary data is passed to the central site on a regular basis, as determined by business requirements. Similarly, the central host distributes information to each remote site. Data transfer is, essentially, two-way and only takes between each site and the central site of the organisation. This network topology will not support inter-site links unless the central site is equipped with switching functionality.

The type of network shown in Figure 3.17 is found in retail organisations, for example. From time to time, the computer system at each regional sales office transfers files to the central computer system for purposes such as corporate accounting and correlation and summarising of regional sales transactions. The central computer transfers files to regional offices in order to disseminate output from applications running on the central computer; lists of new prices is an example of this. The passing of data to the centre is often found in organisations with a hierarchical management structure and this type of network often develops to support this style of management.

The network of Figure 3.17 does not require any switching capability; there is only one route from each site to the central computer. If there is a requirement for inter-site data communications, however, one solution would be to install a data switch at the central site in order to provide access to any of the other sites. In this solution, the network is dependent on the availability of this central switch for inter-site data communications, and it is for this reason that star networks often evolve into mesh networks in order to provide resilience. Furthermore, as organisations become more distributed in terms of their style of management, there is less dependency on central computer resources. Distributed computer networks often evolve to support this style of management in an organisation.

As an alternative to circuit-switched networks, packet-switched networks are a well-established option for data networks and many organisations operate private packet-switched data networks.

Some examples of packet-switched networks will serve to illustrate their topology and some of the reasons why they are used in organisations.

EXAMPLE 3

A large retail organisation in the United Kingdom operates a private packet-switched network. The network connects over fifty minicomputers and comprises four packet-switching centres or exchanges. (The topology is logically rectangular, and will not be shown.) Ownership of the network is cited as one reason for building a private network, rather than using a public packet-switched service from one of the PTOs.

EXAMPLE 4

One of the United Kingdom's clearing banks operates a private packet-switched network comprising nine switching centres that cover most parts of England. The topology of the network is shown in Figure 3.18 in order to illustrate the mesh topology of this network. The level of control of a private network is a factor in the network strategy of the organisation.

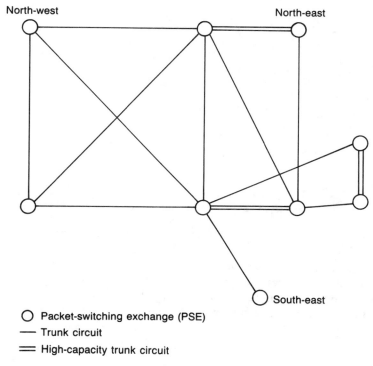

Figure 3.18 Private, packet-switched network for the organisation of Example 4.

EXAMPLE 5

One of the world's major charge card companies makes use of British Telecom's public packet-switched data service in the United Kingdom for authorisation of sales transactions in retail outlets. Sales staff use an authorisation telephone connected to the computer system of the company via the public network. The use of a public network is essential for this type of application; there would be far too many access points to connect to a private network. In practice, the data communications aspects of this type of application would not be possible without the use of a nationwide network service operated by a PTO or a third-party supplier.

These examples show that packet-switched networks can be used for point-to-point networks of distributed computers. Packet-switched networks are often mesh-shaped to meet inter-site communications requirements and provide alternative routeing and resilience. A star-shaped network is possible, with a single PSE at the centre, as in Figure 3.19. This topology is, however, entirely dependent on the central PSE and is not often found in practice for large organisations. Nevertheless, the type of network shown in Figure 3.19 is feasible for an organisation with only a few sites

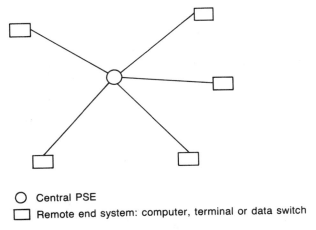

○ Central PSE

☐ Remote end system: computer, terminal or data switch

Figure 3.19 A star-shaped packet-switched network.

and where the cost of additional, alternative routes and PSEs cannot be justified. The examples also illustrate that there are four key elements within any distributed (or centralised) computer system: data, processing power, control and applications. The degree of distribution refers to the extent to which these elements are distributed in a computer network.

3.4.3 Local area data networks

Some of the fundamental characteristics of two industry standard LANs were discussed in Section 3.3.2. Figure 3.6 illustrated the logical topology of these widely used networks. The physical implementation of Ethernet and IBM's Token Ring will illustrate the key aspects of the topology of these networks and how this can be related to the cabling requirements of a local area.

The key to implementing a LAN to meet the data communications requirements of a building, site or campus lies in the choice of cabling and its physical topology. With Ethernet cabling, for example, two types of coaxial cable are commonly used. These are often referred to as 'thick Ethernet' and 'thin Ethernet'. Unshielded twisted pair (UTP) can also be used instead of coaxial cable. These different media give rise to different permitted lengths of cable and performance characteristics of Ethernet LANs. (The choice of media is outside the scope of this book, however, and the reader is recommended to refer to a specialised book on LANs such as those mentioned in the Further Reading section at the end of this book.)

Given that Ethernet is a length of cable rather than a closed loop, there are a number of ways that the logical bus topology can be physically installed. Three of these are shown in Figure 3.20. In Figure 3.20(a), the cable runs from room to room so that attached devices can be connected to the bus. In Figure 3.20(b), a 'backbone' cable runs from the basement to the top floor of a building, with horizontal 'branches'

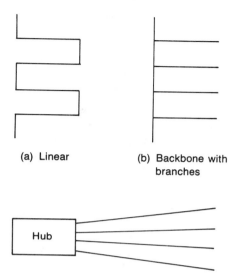

(a) Linear   (b) Backbone with branches

(c) Intelligent hub: physical star and UTP wiring to, for example, end systems located on one floor of a building

Figure 3.20   Ethernet topologies.

serving each floor. In some implementations, the backbone cable is thick Ethernet or fibre-optic cable and the branches are thin Ethernet or UTP. In Figure 3.20(c), the Ethernet bus is shown as a physical star with an intelligent hub. This topology can be implemented with UTP. There are extensions of these topologies in order to provide networking facilities to more than one building on a dispersed site, for example.

In contrast to the Ethernet bus LAN, IBM's Token Ring LAN is a logical ring. The intrinsic disadvantage of a ring topology is that it appears to be susceptible to failure at any point in the ring. This problem has been solved by IBM in their Token Ring product. Each attached device is connected to a device known as a *multi-station access unit* (MAU), so that the LAN is implemented as a physical star which retains its logical ring topology. The physical arrangement for one MAU is shown in a simplified form in Figure 3.21. Cable passes from the MAU to the end system and back again, with packets of data flowing around the network as shown in the diagram. If an end system fails or the cable breaks, the MAU bypasses the problem and the rest of the ring continues to operate. MAUs can be linked together in clusters to form larger rings and, where appropriate, MAUs can be racked together in a conveniently located wiring closet.

Although the logical topologies of Ethernet and IBM's Token Ring are very different, their physical topology can be very similar; both networks can be implemented using intelligent hubs in a physical star arrangement. Consequently, many of the implementation and management issues of these two LANs are similar.

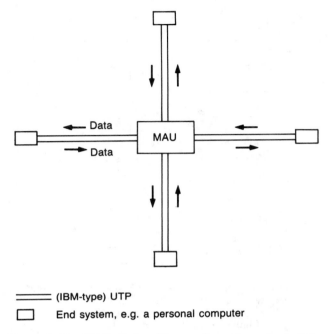

(IBM-type) UTP

End system, e.g. a personal computer

Figure 3.21   IBM's Token Ring configuration; physical star.

Furthermore, the kinds of applications that can be supported are common to both networks. For example, both networks can support connectivity for personal computers and servers so that users can share application software and files.

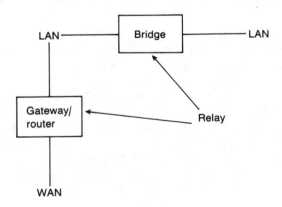

Figure 3.22   Interworking.

A further and very important point to make about LAN topology relates to their interconnectivity. LANs can be linked both locally and remotely to extend the communications facilities by using a device known as a *bridge*. The general use of bridges is shown in Figure 3.22. Users connected to a LAN can also be provided with access to other local and remote computing facilities as shown in the diagram. If these facilities are located in a WAN, a device such as a *gateway* or a *router* is used to interconnect the LAN and the WAN, as shown in Figure 3.22.

3.4.4   Internetworking

The requirements for LAN–LAN and LAN–WAN *internetworking* (or, more simply, interworking) serve to demonstrate the importance of this need. For example, if an organisation operates a number of dispersed LANs, it may be necessary to interconnect these networks by means of a WAN in order to extend communications facilities and services to a number of sites. To complicate matters, the diverse networks operated by the organisation may be incompatible with one another. In this situation, the network planner must analyse these requirements and determine ways in which LANs and WANs can be interconnected to meet the needs of the organisation.

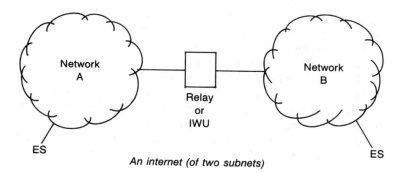

An internet (of two subnets)

Figure 3.23   Interworking. (IWU = interworking unit, also known as a relay.)

In general, when two end systems are in different networks, an end-to-end path must be established so that the end systems are able to inter-operate. In this environment, internetworking is said to take place. Figure 3.23 illustrates this general requirement for the interconnection of two end systems which are attached to different networks connected by a device known as a *relay* or *interworking unit* (IWU).

The function of the IWU is to act as a relay that interconnects two or more subnets to form an *internet*. Typical scenarios that require this function include the following:

- LAN to LAN.
- LAN to WAN (to LAN).
- WAN to WAN.
- Public network to private network, or public network to public network.

A number of different types of IWUs are available, with varying degrees of functionality to meet differing interworking requirements. These can be categorised as follows:

● Repeaters.
● Bridges.
● Routers.
● Brouters.
● Gateways (also knows as protocol converters).

A *repeater* copies individual bits between cable segments. Its function is to extend the maximum length of cable that would normally be permitted in a terminal network or a LAN. A *bridge* stores and forwards frames between similar or dissimilar LAN segments (see Figure 3.22). This creates a single, extended logical network and is used, for example, to interconnect LANs in an organisation that are in separate buildings or at separate sites. In more complex LAN internets, the bridge may have to make routeing decisions to forward a packet. In this case, a device known as a *router* is used. When the functionality of the bridge and router are resident in the same device, it is often known as a 'brouter'.

Routeing is also required when LAN–WAN interworking is required. This is used when LANs at different sites are interconnected via a WAN. In this case, the router IWU stores and forwards packets between the networks concerned.

The function of a *gateway* (also known as a protocol converter) is more complex than a router. The former type of IWU provides interworking at the level of the user applications running over the internet and would be used to convert between the protocols used in dissimilar networks. (Chapter 4 explains the meaning of the term protocol. Here, the term can be interpreted as the rules of communication between end systems.) This would be required, for example, to interconnect a public and a private WAN or to interconnect WANs based on entirely different protocols.

3.4.5 Integrated networks

Before we complete this section on network topologies, we should devote a subsection to 'integrated networks'. Section 3.4.1 mentioned that some PABXs can switch both voice and data calls, and that some circuits in a WAN can carry voice and data in separate channels. Therefore, it is evident that the capacity for 'integration' in network components is a design option that should be considered.

One approach to the concept of integration is to consider 'levels' of integration. This is shown in Figure 3.24, which illustrates the concept for a single node-to-node link; this simplifies the diagram.

Integration is broken down into a number of levels, in Figure 3.24, as follows:

1. Wide area circuit (transmission) level.
2. Switching level.
3. Local area cable (transmission) level.
4. End system (user workstation or terminal) level.

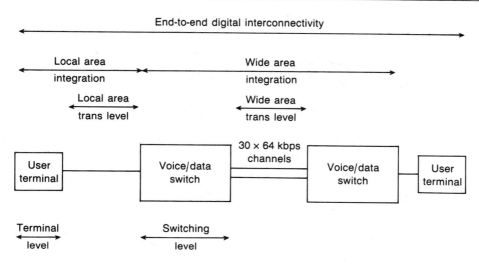

Figure 3.24   Levels of integration.

1   *Wide area circuit level*

As will be seen later, most PTOs provide multichannel circuits that can be leased. These can be used to carry a mixture of, for example, voice and data within a private information network. The circuit is terminated with a suitable multiplexor, which separates the data and voice channels. Generally, the former will be connected to computing devices such as data switches, computers, terminals, etc., and the latter will be connected to a PABX. This is shown in Figure 3.25 for a single network link. Figure 3.26 puts this into a simple network context.

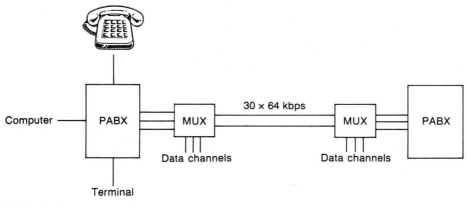

MUX Multiplexor
⸺ Leased line: 2 mbps circuit

Figure 3.25   Integrated based line.

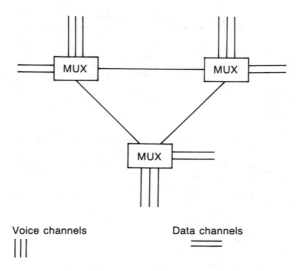

Figure 3.26 High-bandwidth, switching multiplexors.

A public integrated network, known as the Integrated Services Digital Network (ISDN) is available or under development in several countries. This type of network provides a digital interface at the customer's premises, either directly or via a PABX. In the latter case, the PABX is known as an Integrated Services PABX (ISPBX). The ISDN is discussed in Section 3.6.3.1.

Integration of voice and data at the leased line level is very common in multisite organizations where there are sufficient requirements for intersite voice and data traffic.

2 Switching level

Figure 3.24 suggests that the network node can switch voice and data circuits. Some PABXs can provide this functionality, though the network planner must assess products carefully. Although PABXs may claim this functionality, care must be taken in assessing how data calls affect the overall performance of a particular product. In addition, the cost of switching data in this way should be compared with multiplexing voice and data channels in the way illustrated in Figure 3.25. In practice, most organisations that make use of multichannel circuits have opted for the multiplexing approach for the majority of their data traffic, though the PABX may carry some data traffic such as short data calls or relatively infrequent data calls.

Figure 3.27 illustrates the general requirements of an integrated PABX, and Figure 3.28 puts these into a simple network context.

3 Local area cabling level

In practice, almost all organisations have installed separate voice and data networks in the local area domain. Given that LANs are oriented to data communications and

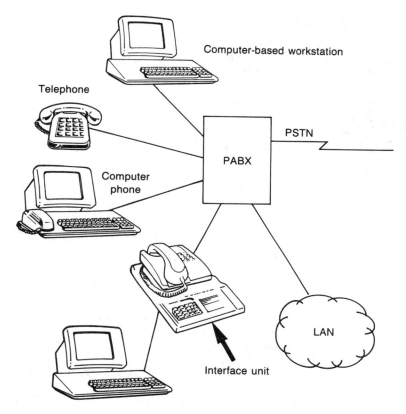

Figure 3.27 The requirement for an integrated voice/data PABX.

are a more recent development than PABXs, they have often been installed in an organisation some time after the internal voice network. For this reason, voice and data networks usually comprise separate cables. In many cases, however, the cables may be incorporated into the same cable sheath, in what is often known as a *structured cabling* environment. In the United Kingdom, however, government regulations specify that the cables that carry voice must be physically separate from those that carry data. The United Kingdom is the only industrialised country that has such a regulation; in other countries, multicore cables are used to carry voice and data in a local network. In this respect, LAN cables do not integrate voice and data.

Integration of voice and data is possible, however, by making use of data over voice equipment (DOVE). Figure 3.27 shows an interface unit which allows a telephone and a computer terminal (or personal computer) to share the same extension cable. This is one approach to DOVE, where voice and data are multiplexed over a single extension cable. However, DOVE approaches enjoy a relatively small market share of the LAN market. In practice, the majority of voice and data connections to a PABX are separate.

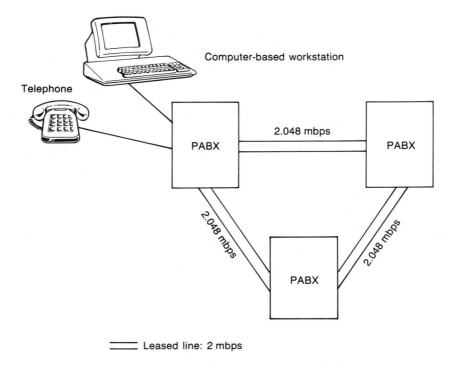

Figure 3.28 The requirement for an integrated voice/data PABX network.

Integration is also possible by means of high-speed LANs based on the FDDI standard. An FDDI LAN is capable of carrying data, voice and image, and facilitates integration where regulations permit.

4 End system level

In practice, most user devices that are attached to networks are single-function devices; these include the following:

● Telephones.
● Computer terminals.
● Personal computers.
● Workstations.
● Multi-user computer systems.
● Facsimile machines.
● Videoconferencing terminals.

Some end systems, however, are multifunctional and will meet particular user requirements. Multifunctional user devices include the following:

● Computer phone, i.e. a personal computer with integral telephone handset (see Figure 3.27).

● Personal computer with integral facsimile board.

To date, multifunctional workstations have not made significant penetration in the end-user market; the vast majority of end-users make use of single-function devices.

3.5 Categories of information networks

We are now able to categorise the networks that are commonly used in organisations in terms of their coverage and the information that they carry. This is shown in Figure 3.29.

Information category	Coverage			
	Intra-site (private)	Inter-site	Off site	Inter-business
Voice	PABX	PABX network PSTN	Mobile telephones	PSTN ISDN (Section 3.6.3.1)
Data	PABX LAN	PABX network Public or private data network	Mobile radio network	PSTN Public data network Third-party networks (Section 3.6.5) ISDN

Figure 3.29 Categories of information networks.

Figure 3.29 indicates that organisations make use of public and private networks for voice and data communications. In private networks, circuits are rented or leased from a PTO in the country concerned. In some countries, there is only one PTO. This is usually the PTT (postal, telephone and telegraph authority) which is the state-owned, monopoly telecommunications authority in that country. In Germany, for example, Deutsche Bundespost Telekom is the sole supplier of telecommunications services. In other countries, the supply of telecommunications services has been liberalised in order to open them to competition. This has occurred in the United Kingdom, the United States, Japan and Australia, where there is more than one PTO.

In a country that has liberalised its telecommunications industry, users can select from more than one supplier of leased circuits and other telecommunications services. Regulation of telecommunications is operated through a government agency in order to regulate service charges and technical standards. For instance, the regulatory body in the United States is the Federal Communications Commission (FCC), and in the United Kingdom it is known as Oftel.

In the United Kingdom, for example, the telecommunications market is regarded as liberal. For instance, it is permissible to resell private network capacity and, effectively, compete with the PTOs. The United Kingdom probably has the most liberal telecommunications market in the world, followed by the United States.

In general, competition has encouraged the provision of a wide range of telecommunication services in some countries, both in the public and private domains. PTOs that are forced to compete have generally become more responsive to user demand for better-quality and higher-capacity circuits for private networks. Consequently, some PTTs have become innovative and progressive, whereas monopoly PTTs or PTOs are less so. (There are exceptions, most notably in France and Germany where the PTTs have been particularly progressive in developing modern telecommunications infrastructures.)

To the extent that the growth of business and the economy of a country depend on the development of telecommunications, the degree of liberalisation of the telecommunications market is an important factor in the availability of public and private network services. Notwithstanding the variations from country to country, there are a wide range of network services available. This may be desirable, but is potentially baffling to the network planner.

It should be noted at this stage that the availability of solutions to network requirements is a function of developments in network technology and the degree of liberalisation of the telecommunications market. A combination of these two forces influences the network options in the wide area domain in particular; LANs are private and are not greatly affected by regulatory arrangements, except where a general licence is required to operate a private network. Figure 3.30 (which extends Figure 2.1) highlights these influences and places network options in the context of the communications environment.

3.6   Network options

The networks that are commonly used in organisations have emerged as a result of rapid developments in network technology and as a result of changes in national telecommunications environments. This has led to a range of network options available to the network planner. In order to provide an overview of these options, the following network options will be summarised briefly:

- LANs.
- Private WANs.
- Public WANs.
- Third-party networks.

3.6.1   Local area networks

These have been discussed elsewhere in this chapter, so little more will be said about LANs at this point, except to make a comment on standards and ownership.

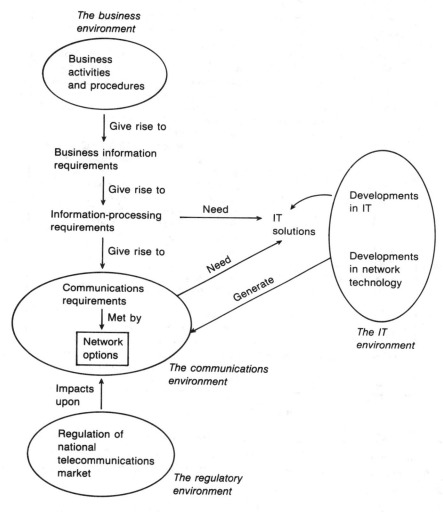

Figure 3.30 The communications environment: communications options.

Chapter 4 will discuss LAN standards, but it will be noted at this point that the development of a local networking strategy should specify adherence to standards. This is an important factor when designing a LAN that is required to support hardware supplied by more than one manufacturer. In addition, LANs may be required to interwork with one another or with a WAN. Interworking requirements are met by the use of appropriate standards and interworking devices.

In practice, LANs are used to provide data communications facilities for a local area such as a building, or a collection of buildings on a dispersed site. Essentially, a LAN is privately owned and operated and is usually confined to land or premises

Country	PTO	Service	Line speed
UK	BT	Keyline	Up to 9.6 kbps
		Kilostream	Up to 64 kbps
		Megastream	Up to 2.048 mbps
US	Any of the Bell operating companies	Voice-grade channels (used for data)	Up to 4800 bps
		Wide-band services	Up to 230.4 kbps
		Digital services	Up to 56 kbps
		2B + D ISDN	2 × 64 kbps
		23B + D ISDN	23 × 64 kbps
		T-1	1.54 mbps
		Satellite services	Up to 1.54 mbps
		Software-defined network (a virtual leased line)	Various
Japan	NTT	A wide range of services for voice, data and video communications	
France	France Telecom	Transfix	Up to 19.2 kbps
		Transcom	Up to 64 kbps

Figure 3.31   Leased line services.

owned by the organisation concerned. Particular requirements, however, may necessitate the extension of a LAN to connect buildings that are separated by areas of public domain such as a road. This can usually be achieved by special arrangement with a PTO.

3.6.2   Private WANs

In this type of network, the user organisation is responsible for the operation of all components of the network. As has been discussed earlier, however, the circuits that make up network links are rented or leased from a PTO; very few organisations actually own any telecommunications circuits apart from the PTOs themselves. Circuits that are rented in this way are often referred to as 'leased lines'. In effect, private circuits are for the exclusive use of the organisation renting them. The PTO provides a circuit that is wired around any trunk-switching equipment that it operates, so that the user organisation can regard leased lines as end-to-end circuits.

The capacity and quality of leased lines varies from PTO to PTO and from country to country. In general, leased lines are analogue or digital and can support single or multiple channels which operate at various speeds. Figure 3.31 summarises selected services from around the world, in order to give an insight into the typical leased line services that are available. By comparing Table 1.1 with Figure 3.31, it can be seen that leased line services can be used for low-speed data communications or can be configured to carry voice and data on multiple channel circuits. Data transmission speeds vary from 9.6 kbps, the speed of a typical modem attached to an analogue circuit, up to 1–2 mbps for a multichannel digital circuit. Higher bandwidth, multimegabit leased lines are also available from some PTOs. These circuits may be required for applications that require high bandwidth transmission, such as image file transfer applications and LAN–LAN interworking.

As Figure 3.31 indicates, there is a wide variety of leased line services available in some countries which provide scope for the design of private networks. In other countries, such as in parts of the Third World and the Pacific Basin, the choice may be limited to using the PSTN for data communications. This often results in an unreliable service. Some of these countries are modernising their telecommunications infrastructure and will be able to provide more reliable public services and leased line services in the near future.

In practice, private networks interconnect computers from more than one manufacturer. Multivendor networking environments give rise to the need for networking standards. These are considered in Chapter 4.

3.6.3 Public WANs

In this type of network the user is responsible for the end systems that access the public network; the PTO is responsible for the network itself. The cost of dial-up services is usually based on the distance and the length of time of the call. In some countries, the PSTN is the only public telecommunications network available for business communications. Data transmission speeds are limited by the available bandwidth of the PSTN and current modem technology. Speeds of 9.6 kbps are typical for data communications via the PSTN, though higher speeds can be achieved with appropriate modems.

In many other countries, the PTOs operate dedicated public data networks. These dial-up networks may be of the circuit-switched type or, more commonly, packet switched. For example, AT&T in the United States offers circuit-switched digital services as part of its ACCUNET family of network services. Switched 56, 64 and 384 kbps services are used for data communications, high-speed facsimile transmission and videoconferencing. The PTT in Germany offer Datex-L circuit-switched services alongside its Datex-P packet-switched service.

Public packet-switched networks are in operation in more than 70 countries. The use of this type of network is more common in Europe than in the United States because many European countries invested in X.25 packet-switched networks earlier than in some other parts of the world. The existence of the X.25 standards raises the possibility of interworking between national networks and provides a solution to meeting the requirements for international data communications based on public

Country	Service
Australia	Austpac
Brazil	Interdata
Canada	Datapac
Germany	Datex-P
France	Transpac
Hong Kong	IDAS
Italy	Euronet
Japan	Venus-P
	DDX-P
Norway	Norpac
Singapore	Telepac
Spain	NTID
Sweden	Telepac
Thailand	Thaipac
USA	Various, including ACCUNET (AT&T) Telenet (GTE) Tymnet (BT)
UK	PSS (BT)

Data transmission speeds are, typically, up to 48, 56 or 64 kbps

Figure 3.32 National public packet-switched services.

networks. Private packet-switched networks can interface with their public counterpart, as was seen in Example 2 on p. 42. This adds to the flexibility of using a combination of public and private packet-switched networks for multinational organisations, for example. Figure 3.32 lists some of the public packet-switched networks available from PTOs around the world. The cost of using this type of network is often independent of distance and is usually based on the quantity of data transmitted and the duration of the data call.

PTOs and PTTs are in the process of developing very high bandwidth, multimegabit, public communications networks. Services that are likely to emerge in the mid-1990s are Metropolitan Area Networks (MANs) and Broadband ISDN (B-ISDN). Both of these networks will provide bandwidths of hundreds of mbps, the former in an urban area and the latter across a region of linked urban areas. This kind of new telecommunications service will meet the requirements of very high bandwidth applications such as those mentioned in Section 3.6.2.

The Integrated Services Digital Network (ISDN)

The ISDN is a relatively new kind of public network and deserves a separate discussion. The ISDN is defined by the CCITT as a set of standard interfaces to a digital network. Basic Rate Interface (BRI) and Primary Rate Interface (PRI) are two of the interfaces that have been specified. BRI specifies two 'bearer' (B) channels of

64 kbps and one 'data' (D) channel of 16 kbps for end systems. The B channels are used for user information and the D channel is used for the common channel signalling (CCS) associated with digital PABX facilities. The BRI is often referred to as '2B + D' and is available in end systems such as telephones and personal computers. To connect a PABX to an ISDN, the PRI specifies multiple B channels and a D channel of 64 kbps. In the United States, the arrangement is 23B + D, whereas in Europe it is 30B + D. Some of the major PABX manufacturers have developed PRI interfaces for their ISPBX products.

Access to AT&T's ISDN in the United States, for example, is by means of a leased line connection (see Figure 3.31), though access may eventually become dial-up. In most other countries that have announced an ISDN service, the basis of using the network is dial-up rather than leased line. Consequently, the ISDN is a dial-up, public circuit-switched network rather like the PSTN or a public data network (PDN). However, the essential difference is that the ISDN is a multiple-channel digital network that terminates at the user's premises. Simultaneous transmission of more than one form of information is achieved via a single access point. This raises the possibility of applications such as simultaneous voice and facsimile transmission or voice and file transfer using two multiplexed channels. Other applications that may require the full bandwidth of two ISDN channels include image communication and videoconferencing. Figure 3.33 shows a schematic representation of the interfaces associated with the ISDN.

The ISDN has been conceived as a replacement of the PSTN. Essentially, the concept embodies a network that offers digital communications of a mixture of forms of information via dial-up access to a public circuit-switched network and has been targeted, initially, at the business market. Several PTOs/PTTs around the world have invested heavily in ISDN development and are making strenuous efforts to attract users to their ISDN services. Commercial services have been announced in the United States, Japan, Singapore, Australia and in several countries in Europe. In France, for instance, France Telecom's Numeris service interfaces with the PSTN and Transpac, France Telecom's public packet-switched network. In Japan, NTT claim over 300 customers for their INS-Net ISDN service.

The ISDN is a relatively new public network and take-up has been cautious. It is unlikely that large organisations with extensive private networks will readily convert to using the ISDN. There will be little advantage in doing so unless it is cheaper than operating a private network. There is, however, some evidence to date that indicates that small and medium-sized organisations are using ISDN as an alternative to leasing private lines. These include organisations that require a high-capacity, circuit-switched service for bulk file transfer, where sufficient capacity is not available on public packet-switched networks. Other organisations using ISDN require communications to a large number of sites, a situation that is not feasible using a private network.

A possible scenario that places the ISDN in the overall communications environment is that dial-up services are eventually dominated by the ISDN and are attractive to small and medium-sized organisations that have not invested heavily in

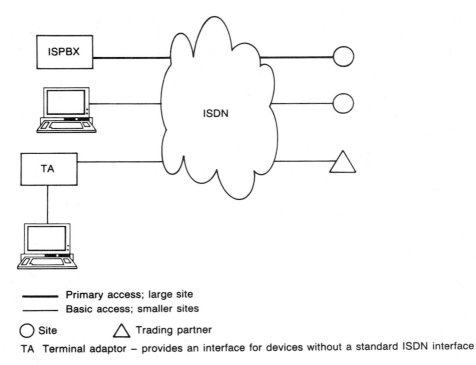

Primary access; large site
Basic access; smaller sites
◯ Site   △ Trading partner
TA Terminal adaptor – provides an interface for devices without a standard ISDN interface

Figure 3.33   Schematic of the public ISDN.

private networks. Large organisations, on the other hand, mostly use the ISDN to communicate at an inter-business level or as a backup service for leased lines.

3.6.4 Private or public networks?

It is evident that many organisations have invested in private networks to meet their requirements. Examples 3 and 4 on p. 44, for instance, suggest that ownership and control are reasons why organisations chose to build private networks rather than rely on dial-up services. Now that private and public networks have been examined, it is worthwhile considering some of the issues that influence the choice between either type of network.

Private networks arose largely as a result of dissatisfaction with the quality and security of dial-up data services provided by the PTTs in the 1970s. Users demanded better quality circuits and an economy of scale that the PTTs were unable or unwilling to provide. Large organisations, in particular, expected preferred customer status and lower charges if they were heavy users of dial-up services. As the number of customers for data communications grew, this created a demand for special treatment by some large organisations. The PTTs responded with the concept of a private leased line and formed the basis of the evolution of the private networks that we know today. To the

PTT, there were a number of advantages. Leased lines decreased demand for data communications on PSTN switching equipment and generated fixed revenue. For the user organisation, on-going costs for leased lines were fixed and could be forecast in annual budgets. Private circuits also provided the opportunity to derive as much usable bandwidth as technology and business hours would allow at a fixed cost. By building a private network, an organisation was in control of resources and was able to respond to changing demand for communication services.

Today, as information networks have become recognised as a strategic resource in many organisations, the operation of a private network gives an organisation greater confidence that it is in control of this vital resource.

Of course, a private network necessitates high initial capital outlay for hardware and software, and the provision of considerable human resources for its continued management and operation. Nevertheless, there is plenty of evidence to suggest that many organisations consider that the cost of implementing and operating a private information network is a necessary investment.

Recently, however, some of the PTTs and PTOs have begun to compete for private network business by announcing services that add value to their normal leased line services. This activity on the part of the operators has been made possible by regulation policies in some countries and the investment in a modern telecommunications infrastructure. These new services include Centrex and Virtual Private Networks.

Centrex provides PABX facilities to users without PABXs. A small organisation or one with several sites in an urban area are potential users of Centrex. Mercury Communications, one of the PTOs in the United Kingdom, offers Centrex services in the London area, for example.

The concept of a Virtual Private Network (VPN) is a relatively new one. It is based on the concept whereby the PTO partitions the public switched network to create a network that appears, to the customer, to be private. Consequently, a VPN provides Centrex-like facilities across a wider area than a Centrex does. Most VPNs feature voice communications at present, and several PTOs and PTTs have announced services. VPNs within the ISDN, on the other hand, will bring virtual, private integrated networks in the future. The advantage of a VPN to a customer would be much lower capital and operating costs than those associated with a private network.

Both Centrex and VPNs are facilitated by the degree of intelligence that resides in public networks. This brings out the concept of the 'intelligent network' (IN), a concept that was coined by Bell Communications Incorporated in the United States in 1985. In an IN, switching is separated from service features; the latter are provided by a separate resource such as a special database. This allows greater flexibility in the provision of network facilities. As the PTOs and PTTs develop INs, Centrex and VPNs will be provided within the IN infrastructure in the future.

Given the range of network options that is available today, the answer to the question 'public or private?' is not easy to determine. The answer may depend on whether an organisation's information network is regarded as a strategic resource, in which case control of the network may not be entrusted to a third party. On the other hand, it may be that the organisation's private network has become inflexible to change and growth; in this case, alternative, public network options may be worth considering. In general, a number of technical, commercial and organisational issues will also influence the outcome.

In some organisations, use is made of both public and private networks for different purposes. A number of possible scenarios present themselves:

1. Private leased lines for all intra-business communications; EDI with trading partners (see Section 3.6.5 for a discussion of EDI and other third party networks); the ISDN (or the PSTN in the meantime) to communicate with everyone else.
2. A mix of public and private networks which satisfy the communications requirements of the organisation.
3. VPNs to replace private leased lines for all intra-business communications; EDI with trading partners; the ISDN (or the PSTN in the meantime) to communicate with everyone else.

Typically, large organisations that have invested heavily in private networks make use of them for the majority of their intra-business communications and use public networks for international communications and for inter-business communications; in other words, something close to scenario 1 above. Depending on how such an organisation develops its information network strategy, there may be some migration towards scenario 2 – in other words, a mix of public and private networks. It is unlikely that such an organisation will migrate fully to scenario 3; this scenario is more likely for small or medium-sized organisations, where investment in private networks cannot be readily justified. Figure 3.34 illustrates intra- and inter-business communications by means of a mixture of public and private networks.

3.6.5   Third-party networks

As we have seen, some governments have encouraged competition in the provision of network services which add value to basic leased line facilities. These services are variously referred to as value-added network services (VANS), value-added data services (VADS) or managed data network services (MDNS). No clear definition of these terms has emerged, since the range of value-added services differs from country to country. Since all of these services are provided by suppliers such as PTOs, PTTs and by other licensed network operators, the term third-party network (TPN) will be used.

The point to make about TPNs is not what they are called, but what kind of service they offer to customers and what added value is provided over and above the basic bit transport of a leased line. The following categories are considered:

- VANS/VADS.
- MDNS.
- EDI applications.

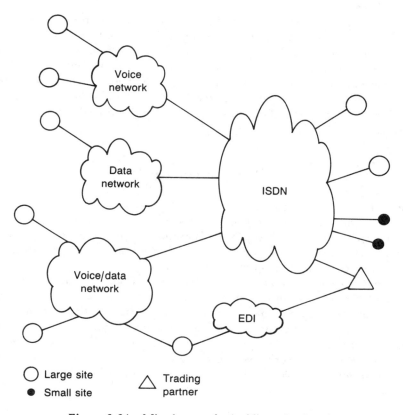

Figure 3.34   Mixed networks (public and private).

VANS or VADS are 'value-added' networks. Typical services are electronic mail (email) and electronic funds transfer (EFT). VANS/VADS generally fall into the category of inter-business communications, whereas a MDNS mainly provides intra-business communications.

A MDNS (or, more simply, a managed network) is facilitated by the use of a TPN to provide full networking and communications facilities for a customer. The supplier provides the circuits, switching and network management; in other words, a complete network service. Organisations considering the use of this kind of service must compare the on-going cost of operating a private network with that of using a managed network. To date, most managed networks in the United Kingdom, for example, are operated by organisations other than the PTOs and PTTs, though the latter have the capability to offer such services. Typical suppliers of managed networks are organisations who themselves operate extensive national or international networks. Electronic Data Systems, for instance, are the suppliers to the multinational company Unilever. GE Information Services is another company that provides managed networks to a number of customers worldwide.

EDI is a rapidly growing inter-business service. EDI is an example of a value added service that runs the applications that are associated with inter-business trading. An EDI supplier will provide a service for the electronic transmission of computer-generated business documents using the supplier's network. Invoices, orders and confirmations of delivery, for example, are transmitted between computer systems of trading partners and replace the paper-based documentation that is associated with trading. For instance, British Coal in the United Kingdom trade with most of their suppliers using an EDI service.

3.7 Summary

We have completed our discussion of a network options. It has been necessary to discuss some of the technical aspects of networks in order to understand how different types of networks can be used to provide communications facilities. The role of the PTOs and other suppliers of network services has been examined to provide an insight into the rapidly changing telecommunications market.

An important concept that has been mentioned from time to time during the discussion of network options is that of network standards. Consequently, it is important that the network analyst understands the implications of the need for standards. The next chapter introduces the concept of a network architecture and examines the standards that comprise an 'open' architecture. The role of standards in LANs and PABX networks will be considered. Chapter 4 will also describe a migration plan for the implementation of open standards.

CHAPTER 4

Information network architectures

4.1 Introduction

When computers exchange data in an information network, the procedures involved can be highly complex. For example, there is an agreement on how data is to be exchanged between one computer and another so that the format of the data is understood by both computers. Also, error detection and recovery are much more critical in data networks than in voice networks and contribute to this complexity. Although communication in voice networks is less complex than that in data networks, it relies on a high degree of co-operation between network components such as PABXs. Consequently, information networks are designed in a highly structured way to reduce as much as possible the complexity of the rules and conventions that are required for the communication of information.

As might be expected, the principles of computer network architecture are complex and require a detailed study. A full treatment is outside the scope of this book and the reader is strongly advised to consult the Further Reading section. This chapter will, however, introduce the key concepts of network architectures in order to provide an insight into the importance and role of architectures in the planning and design of networks.

4.2 Computer network architectures

Many of today's organisations operate in a multivendor environment of computer systems. This may arise as a result of a piecemeal approach to the development of computer systems, either by lack of strategic management or, in decentralised organizations, by managers developing systems that are not compatible with those in other parts of the organisation. On the other hand, the development of a heterogeneous computer system may be a deliberate policy. It is often the most effective solution to the diverse needs of particular organisations.

Multivendor environments can lead to the development of computer networks that may not readily interwork with one another and create problems if the organisation is attempting to develop an enterprise network. Clearly, the requirements of this kind of computing and networking environment cannot be met by proprietary network architectures.

In order to introduce the concept of a computer network architecture, let us consider the example of how two computers exchange a file by means of a computer network. A file transfer program in the sending end system initiates communication of data to a similar program in the receiving end system. What is communicated and how it is communicated without error must conform to some mutually agreed conventions between the file transfer programs resident in each end system. Otherwise, data communications would not be successful and the two computers would not 'understand' each other. The conventions used are called *protocols* which comprise rules that govern the exchange of data between end systems.

To achieve file transfer between the two computers, a number of tasks must be performed, as follows:

1. The sending end system must inform the network of the identity (address) of the receiving end system.
2. The sending end system must ascertain that the receiving end system is ready to receive data.
3. The file transfer program resident in the sending end system must ascertain that there is a user application program resident in the receiving end system that is prepared to accept the file.
4. If the file formats of the two end systems are incompatible, one of the end systems must perform a format conversion.

As can be seen from this set of tasks, it is unlikely that computer-to-computer communications could be performed by a single program; such a program would be extremely complex and unwieldy to design. Instead, the applications-oriented tasks are separated from the network-oriented tasks. Therefore tasks 3 and 4 above would be performed by an application-oriented protocol, implemented in a file transfer program. Task 2 would be performed by a network-oriented protocol implemented in a network services program module and, finally, the network services module would perform task 1 by initiating a network-oriented protocol in order to access the network.

The example outlined above suggests that a hierarchical set of protocols achieve file transfer between two computers. This structured set of protocols is known as the *network architecture*.

In the early days of computer networking, each computer manufacturer developed its own architecture. However, proprietary architectures mean that computers from different manufacturers cannot readily be networked together. Although it is usually possible to develop hardware and software that will solve a particular networking problem, this kind of solution is specific to that problem and will not be flexible enough to be used in a multivendor networking environment.

A networking architecture known as the Internet suite of protocols or TCP/IP (Transmission Control Protocol/Internet Protocol) is supported by a large number of manufacturers and is used in both LANs and WANs. TCP/IP has become a *de facto* standard and is regarded, by some, as the most practical means of interworking multivendor equipment (Rose, 1990). *De jure* standards are the work of the International Organization for Standardization and the International Electrochemical Committee (ISO/IEC, usually abbreviated to ISO). ISO standards are discussed in Section 4.3; TCP/IP is introduced in Section 4.4.

4.3   The Open Systems Interconnection Reference Model

The networking requirements of multivendor environments helped to promote the demand for communication standards that were not specific to any proprietary architecture and led to the evolution of a 'model' for an 'open' architecture. This model is known as the *Reference Model for Open Systems Interconnection (OSI)* and is under development by ISO, an international agency whose members include the designated standards bodies of participating nations. The intention of the OSI Reference Model (OSIRM) is to provide a framework for the development of *de jure* standards which define how computer systems can interchange data via computer networks. In other words, the OSIRM is concerned with the interchange of data at the level of the network and at the level of the user's applications, i.e. with the *interoperability* of computer systems.

The simple example of file transfer, which was outlined earlier, suggested that several protocols are required. In fact, the OSIRM specifies a hierarchy of protocols in seven 'levels' or 'layers'. The reference model is depicted in Figure 4.1. There are well-defined functions associated with each layer of the model; these are summarised as follows:

Layer 7   Provides the user interface to application-oriented services.

Layer 6   Responsible for the conversion between the syntax used for data transfer and that used in the application process in the end systems.

Layer 5   Provides the control of the establishment, management and termination of a logical connection (session) between two co-operating user application programs.

Layer 4   Provides a reliable communication service for higher layers.

Layer 3   Provides upper layers with independence from the technology of the network; responsible for end-to-end routeing and connection.

Layer 2   Provides for the reliable transfer of blocks (frames) of information across each physical link in the network.

Layer 1   Concerned with the transmission of a bit stream across physical links in the network.

Each layer is said to provide a *service* to the layers above it. The service defines what operations the layer performs and the protocol is the implementation of that service. Within the framework of the OSIRM, a number of *standards* have developed to specify the services and protocols of the OSI architecture. The standards have been developed by bodies such as the CCITT and the IEEE and have been published by

69

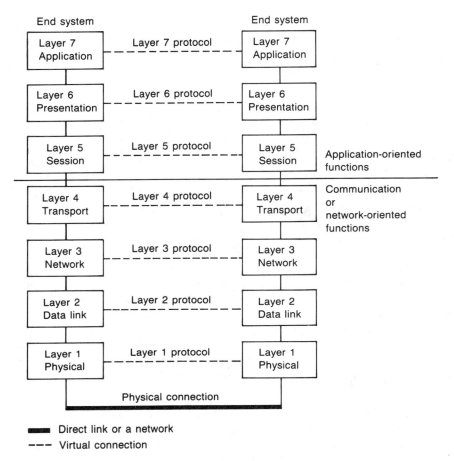

Figure 4.1 The OSI reference model.

the ISO, so that computer manufacturers and software suppliers can develop hardware and software products that conform to OSI.

4.3.1 OSI standards

Standards exist for all seven layers of the OSIRM, the lower layers of which are more mature. The CCITT's X.25 standard for (public) packet-switched networks is the basis of the OSI standard for WANs and embraces the lowest three layers of the OSIRM. Most of the major computer manufacturers (including those with proprietary architectures) support the X.25 interface standard, so that multivendor X.25 networks can be implemented. The IEEE's LAN standards have been adopted by the ISO and embrace the lowest two layers of the OSIRM.

Because of the maturity of LAN and WAN standards, it is useful to draw a distinction between the lower layers of the OSIRM and the higher layers. The former deal with the functionality of the network and the latter deal with that of applications which are designed to run over the network. The lower layers are mature, whereas products that support the higher layers are less so. This is because the design of applications that run over networks is more difficult than for those that reside in a single host computer. However, programming environments for the design of distributed systems are emerging and will lead eventually to mature network applications (Bal, 1990). Standards for layer 7 (the application layer) will take, perhaps, a few more years to reach an acceptable level of stability and interoperability. Nevertheless, it is certain that the next few years will see a great deal of activity in developing products that conform to the standards defined for the upper layers of the OSIRM and, more importantly, that can be demonstrated to interoperate with one another.

Layer 7 standards typically cover applications such as the following:

- File transfer and access across a network.
- Messaging (electronic mail) between end systems.
- Virtual terminal access to hosts.

There are ISO standards for file transfer and electronic messaging; the standards for virtual terminal access are under development.

The advantage of having standards for applications such as those listed above is that bespoke software will be eventually avoided. Clearly, this depends on the availability of layer 7 products that conform to ISO standards and will interoperate between all the end systems in a network. This may seem straightforward in principle. In practice, however, it means that manufacturers that claim conformance to the appropriate layer 7 standard will need to demonstrate the interoperability of products to the satisfaction of the user organisation. This requirement implies rigorous testing of the interoperability of OSI products. In an attempt to meet this requirement, a number of 'conformance testing' centres have been established in countries where there is strong support for OSI. However, these are testing environments; interoperability testing does not necessarily guarantee interoperability in the target network environment.

4.3.2 Support for OSI

Support for OSI has largely been driven by users and governments. Some manufacturers have been less enthusiastic because they have a vested interest in promoting single-vendor environments, though others have been active in the development and promotion of OSI standards. Indeed, several manufacturers have begun to migrate their proprietary architecture towards OSI. In particular, there has been increased recognition of the requirements of multivendor environments recently, with the result that support for OSI is actively promoted in some parts of the world.

Support for OSI is somewhat stronger in Europe than in the United States for the following reasons:

- European vendors got involved in OSI earlier than their counterparts in the United States.
- The European Community (EC) is promoting OSI in the context of the single European Market.
- OSI products are demonstrated frequently at trade fairs around Europe.
- The Internet suite of protocols is well-established in the United States (see Section 4.4).

More importantly, the Telecommunications Decision (87/95/EEC) of the Council of the European Community, which was taken in 1986, states that all public procurements greater than 100,000 ECU within the EC must, with certain exceptions, make use of OSI standards. Under Article 5.2 of this legislation, EC member states are required to ensure that public network operators provide network interfaces on the basis of OSI standards. Also under Article 5, organisations in the public sector are required to make reference to OSI in procurement. In general, this means that public-sector organisations must buy OSI products.

The requirement (by legislation) for procurement of OSI products in the public sector in the countries of the EC has promoted the establishment of agencies and user groups that promote the development and use of OSI products. In particular, a number of OSI conformance testing centres have been established in some of the EC countries. Similar activities are underway in the United States, Canada, Japan and Australia.

4.3.3 Functional standards

Although the OSIRM may appear to be conceptually straightforward, it is designed to allow for a wide range of options for each layer. For two end systems to interoperate, they must both use compatible options at each layer. Thus, although two end systems may claim to be 'OSI-compliant', they might not actually interoperate due to different options present in one or more layers.

A number of interest groups have been formed to represent the views of users and to ensure that standards work and are functional, i.e. standards support interoperability of application services over an OSI network. These *functional standards* define what are known as *functional profiles*, a subset of OSI standards that support particular applications or networking environments. There are two types of functional standards: those oriented towards a wide range of applications and network environments; and those oriented towards a particular industry or business sector.

Functional standards of the first type are known as a government open systems interconnection profile or *GOSIP*. In those countries where there is government support for OSI, a government department or agency is usually identified with the task of promoting OSI standards. In most cases, this agency publishes and promotes a functional profile. Several countries promote GOSIPs, most of which are similar to each other in an effort to ensure that international networks fully interoperate using the standards specified in the GOSIP. GOSIPs have been developed in the United States and in several countries in Europe.

In the United Kingdom, for example, the GOSIP is a procurement guide and informs suppliers of the government's commitment to OSI. The UK GOSIP recognises that the OSIRM is broad in scope and not sufficiently precise enough for suppliers and users. The UK GOSIP (in common with other GOSIPs) selects a profile of OSI standards; these standards are targeted at the public sector, though their wider commercial use is encouraged. A simplified version of the UK GOSIP is shown in Figure 4.2.

As can be seen from the figure, the UK GOSIP specifies standards for LANs and WANs, as well as application-oriented standards at the higher layers of the OSIRM. A GOSIP-conformant protocol 'stack' comprises a vertical slice of the GOSIP and specifies an implementation of all seven layers. GOSIP initiatives in Canada and Australia have, essentially, adopted the UK GOSIP. Similarly, the EC initiative on the adoption of OSI is based on the UK GOSIP and forms the basis of European procurement for OSI products. The US GOSIP is similar in structure to the UK GOSIP, but is oriented more towards connectionless communications than the latter, which is connection-oriented.

Government requirements for OSI mean that suppliers are required to develop products that conform to functional profiles in order to win contracts in the public sector. This pressure on suppliers will benefit the wider commercial market and will encourage the continued development of OSI products. The availability of such products means that a solution to the problem of multivendor environments is, at least, partially in place. As has already been mentioned, many of the large computer manufacturers such as Digital, ICL and NCR are in the process of migrating their architectures towards OSI. IBM are unlikely to do this with SNA, but the company have developed a number of OSI products that provide a gateway between the OSI and SNA environments.

Although network planning and design is the focus of Part Two of this book, it is important for the network planner to understand the principles of network architectures at this stage. This understanding will assist in the assessment of requirements for a network architecture and will help in evaluating OSI products. The examples that follow describe, briefly, how an OSI architecture is used to meet the requirements for data communications in two organisations.

EXAMPLE 1

A large, multinational German company is implementing an OSI strategy in association with an OSI user group. The company recognises that the communications requirements of a multinational organisation imply a need for standards for open communications systems. Heterogeneous computer systems are present in the organisation and it is only open systems that can provide the full functionality with respect to user applications in a distributed computer environment. The company are of the opinion that bespoke

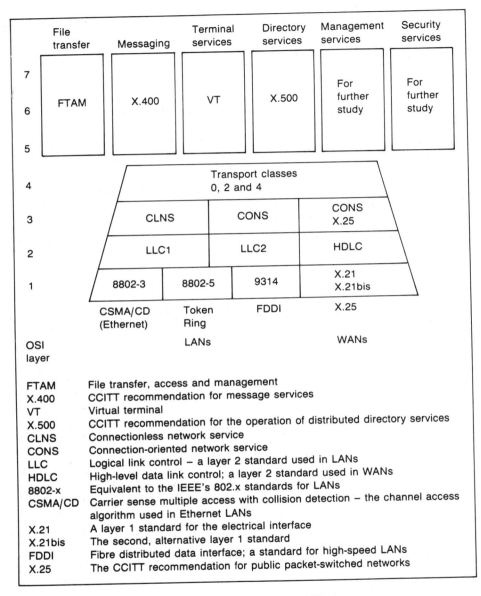

Figure 4.2 The UK GOSIP.

communications software solutions do not stimulate vendors sufficiently to incorporate all the functions that are defined in standard solutions.

Briefly, the company's OSI networking strategy specifies 8802-3 LANs and an X.25 WAN. The company began by connecting together its separate electronic messaging systems by means of the X.400 electronic messaging standard. (Note: X.400 can be found at layer 7 of the UK GOSIP as shown in Figure 4.2.)

EXAMPLE 2

One of England's Regional Health Authorities is implementing an OSI strategy that conforms to the United Kingdom's GOSIP. The implementation is, essentially, a pilot project in which mainframe computers, minicomputers and personal computers are attached to a private packet-switched X.25 network in a multivendor computer network. X.400 products provide data transfer, which is either initiated by the user, for low-volume mail, or is driven automatically by application programs for high-volume mail. Electronic messaging is used to support the transfer of information about patients between different parts of the hospital and between the hospital and a general practitioner. Information such as appointments, admissions and laboratory test results are transmitted using the X.400 systems.

Considerable effort was required to establish interoperability of the various X.400 applications which have been implemented in a number of heterogeneous computer systems.

The next stage of the project is to implement the FTAM standard for file transfer. (Note: FTAM is a layer 7 standard, as shown in Figure 4.2.)

Examples of functional standards of the second type are the Manufacturing Automation Protocol (MAP) and the Technical and Office Protocol (TOP). MAP defines a set of OSI functional standards to support manufacturing applications. It is being developed by a large user group led by General Motors. TOP defines a set of OSI functional standards to support office applications. It is being developed by a large user group led by Boeing.

4.3.4 Migration to OSI

The organisations of Examples 1 and 2 above have specified OSI as their network architecture. In both cases OSI will be the basis of the network infrastructure for the foreseeable future and indicates the strategic direction that both organisations are taking. In this context, the network planner must be able to specify the building blocks of the network architecture and plan its implementation. This is necessary for proprietary or open architectures.

An approach to implementing OSI has been put forward by the Department of Trade and Industry (referred to here as the DTI) in the United Kingdom. In its document ('The Technical Case for OSI'), the DTI presents key issues that should be addressed; these are used here to illustrate the steps that should be taken in the migration of current systems to OSI-based systems.

The approach is summarised by highlighting three principal steps:

- Requirements analysis.
- OSI architecture.
- Migration plan.

Requirements analysis

Requirements analysis identifies communications requirements in terms of two sets of services: application services and transport services. Application services are provided by OSI layers 5 – 7. They are specified in terms of file transfer, message processing and terminal access to hosts. The strategy phase of SPIN (Chapter 6) describes how communications requirements are identified. Transport services enable communication between applications to take place; they are provided by OSI layers 1 – 4. To specify the transport service requirements, it is necessary to identify the location of information-processing facilities and their users. To support transport service requirements, appropriate LAN and WAN solutions are evaluated (see Chapter 3).

OSI architecture

Communications requirements are translated into an OSI architecture by identifying standards for application and transport services. In order to specify the architecture, the availability of OSI products must be investigated. Documentation associated with some of the functional profiles includes procurement advice; the UK GOSIP is an example. It should then be possible to present the architecture as a set of OSI layers, annotated with functional standards at each layer. This set is regarded as the OSI 'map' of the organisation.

Migration plan

The migration plan identifies benefits, costs and risks; it also includes the implementation plan. The benefits of migrating to an open, multivendor networking environment are identified and compared with the costs of procuring OSI hardware and software. Risks arise from the possibility that the interoperability of layer 7 products may not have been demonstrated.

In the organisation of Example 2 above, a number of X.400 products have been implemented; at the time of writing, the implementation of FTAM is underway. Each supplier had interpreted the X.400 standard in a slightly different way in its product, according to the options set out in the standard specification. Although each product could be said to be 'OSI-compliant', significant effort was required to ensure that each X.400 implementation could interoperate. Experience such as this shows that there is no substitute for interoperability testing on the target hardware; it is the only guarantee that open systems will work in the user's application environment.

The statement of benefits, costs and risks establishes the business case for OSI. (A formal, structured approach to this is the subject of another UK DTI document: 'Making the Business Case for OSI'.) The business case should establish whether it is feasible to migrate current systems to OSI-based systems, in terms of costs and benefits. If migration is feasible, a phased approach to implementation is advisable. An attempt to implement every OSI level all at once increases the risk of something going wrong, so it is likely that implementation will proceed in two broad phases:

1. The design and installation of a network that will provide an OSI foundation and support the OSI transport service. This will be based on appropriate LANs and WANs.

2. The implementation of interoperable application services, based on standards such as FTAM, X.400, etc.

The organisation in Example 2 implemented an X.25 WAN to support the subsequent implementation of X.400 and FTAM application services.

The advantages of this approach are as follows:

- Transport services are more mature, both in terms of standards and technology and can be implemented first.
- As each phase is completed, the experience of the implementation team will benefit the next phase.
- Migration can proceed application by application, site by site, or by some other appropriate means that suits the organisation concerned.
- Interoperability of application services can proceed in a phased manner, providing an opportunity for controlled testing of program code from different suppliers.

The planning and scheduling of implementation is also part of the migration plan. The implementation of an information network is the subject of phase 5 of SPIN. The reader should refer to Chapter 10 for guidance on this aspect of the migration plan.

4.4   The Internet suite of protocols

The Internet suite of protocols is commonly known as TCP/IP (Transmission Control Protocol/Internet Protocol). Work on this network architecture was originally sponsored by the US Department of Defense and grew out of research associated with the Defense Advanced Projects Agency (DARPA). The work was motivated by a need to provide reliable networking over potentially unreliable means of transmission, such as public data networks. In addition, Internet offered internetwork interoperability. Today, the technical body that oversees the development of Internet is the Internet Activities Board (IAB).

The emphasis of Internet is internetworking of diverse WAN and LAN technologies; it is regarded as the only *de facto*, open network architecture (Rose, 1990). Internet is generally based on protocols that are known to work before standardisation occurs. Consequently, it is regarded by many as more technically sound than OSI. Furthermore, Internet is more readily available than OSI as it is often bundled with the Unix operating system.

Given the practical basis of Internet, its importance has grown and its installed base has become significant. However, the installed base is much greater in the United

States than in Europe, where there is greater support for OSI.

The Internet protocols are based on the following:

- A connection-oriented (CO) transport service, provided by the Transmission Control Protocol (TCP).
- A connectionless (CL) network service, provided by the Internet Protocol (IP).

Application services are, primarily the following:

- Simple Mail Transfer Protocol (SMTP).
- File Transfer Protocol (FTP).
- TELENET – virtual terminal access to host computers.

(These services can be compared with OSI applications mentioned earlier.)

Figure 4.3 illustrates the Internet suite of protocols. (This figure can be compared with Figure 4.1, the OSI suite of protocols.) Figure 4.3 shows that Internet comprises four conceptual layers (of software) built on to a fifth layer of network hardware. The functionality of each layer is summarised as follows:

- The application layer – provides application programs with access to services across a TCP/IP internet.
- The transport layer – reliable communication from application to application in different end systems; provided by the connection-oriented TCP.
- The Internet layer – provides routeing of datagrams through the internet to a specified end system; provided by the connectionless Internet protocol.
- The network interface layer – makes use of data link protocols, e.g. LLC in LANs and HDLC in WANs.
- The physical layer – the electrical interface to a network.

(This functionality can be compared with that of OSI mentioned earlier.)

4.4.1 Migration of Internet to OSI

Whether and when OSI will replace Internet is open to question (Rose, 1990). Internet is widely available and is supported by a large number of manufacturers, and it seems therefore likely that there will be a period spanning several years when both protocol suites coexist.

One of the current problems with OSI is that it does not readily provide effective interworking between LANs and WANs. LANs are generally connectionless and are oriented to the transmission of datagrams. WANs, on the other hand, are connection-oriented, particularly in public data networks that support X.25. This creates problems when interconnecting LANs via WANs. However, the ISO have recognised this and have published a connectionless network protocol based on the Internet IP protocol. Nevertheless, OSI handles interworking less well than Internet.

It is clear that OSI enjoys government support in the form of GOSIPs, for example. Given that Internet is well-established, however, the question remains as to what will force users of Internet to migrate to OSI. This is a problem for the network

End system	End system	Equivalent OSI layer
Application layer	Application layer	5–7
Transport layer	Transport layer	4
Internet layer	Internet layer	3
Network interface layer*	Network interface layer*	2
Physical layer	Physical layer	1

Physical connection

* Also known as the data link layer

Figure 4.3   The Internet suite of protocols.

planner; users are much more interested in applications than protocols!

4.5   LAN architectures

Figure 4.2 indicates that a GOSIP embraces LAN standards as well as those for WANs. The inclusion of the former suggests that the OSIRM is applicable to both LANs and WANs; this is indeed the case and the ISO has adopted the IEEE 802 family of standards for LANs.

Figure 4.2 appears to show that LAN standards correspond to layer 1 of the OSIRM. This is because of the way in which the structure of the UK GOSIP is depicted in government documents. In fact, LAN standards embrace the lowest two layers of the OSIRM. In a LAN, there is a one route between end systems, and the routeing function associated with layer 3 is redundant. Consequently, the services normally associated with the lowest three layers of the OSIRM are implemented in layers 1 and 2 in LANs.

In a LAN, layer 2 comprises two sublayers: the Medium Access Control (MAC) sublayer and the Logical Link Control (LLC) sublayer. The former is specific to the type of LAN (e.g. Ethernet or Token Ring) and the latter is common to all MAC

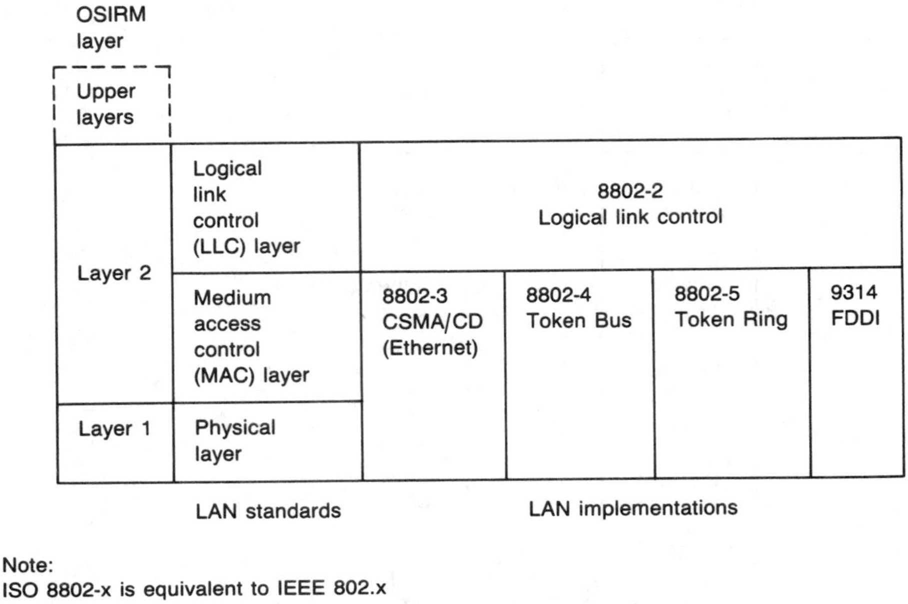
OSIRM layer
Upper layers
Layer 2
Logical link control (LLC) layer
8802-2 Logical link control
Medium access control (MAC) layer
8802-3 CSMA/CD (Ethernet)
8802-4 Token Bus
8802-5 Token Ring
9314 FDDI
Layer 1
Physical layer
LAN standards
LAN implementations
Note:
ISO 8802-x is equivalent to IEEE 802.x

Figure 4.4 LAN standards.

implementations. The relationship between LAN standards and the OSIRM is shown in Figure 4.4.

The existence of LAN standards means that the network planner must incorporate these into the LAN strategy of the organisation. This also has implications when it comes to meeting the internetworking requirements in the organisation, either between LANs or between LANs and WANs.

4.6 Internetworking architectures

Section 3.4.4 introduced some of the fundamental concepts of internetworking. Interworking devices operate at different layers in the OSIRM, and this is summarised in Figure 4.5.

A *repeater* copies bits between cable segments. The functionality of this device resides in the physical layer. A *bridge* is used to interwork between subnets with the same layers 1 and 2. Consequently, bridges operate at layer 2 as shown in Figure 4.6. It is possible to connect similar or dissimilar LANs by means of a bridge – for example, 8802-x to 8802-x or 8802-x to 8802-y. *Routers* connect subnets with the same transport layer but with dissimilar network layers. Routers operate at the network layer, as shown in Figure 4.7. A *gateway* (GW) is used to connect dissimilar networks, when one network may not be OSI. A gateway may be required to operate up to the application layer, as shown in Figure 4.8.

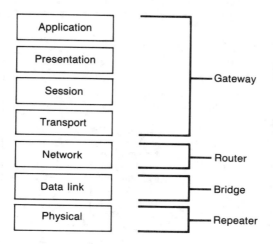

Figure 4.5 Internetworking devices and the OSIRM.

In general, the function of the IWU in Figures 4.6–4.8 is to convert between different protocols. This functionality can be specified by knowing the nature of the protocols used in the subnets that make up the internet. In this way, an Internet architecture can be built up from the architectures of the subnets.

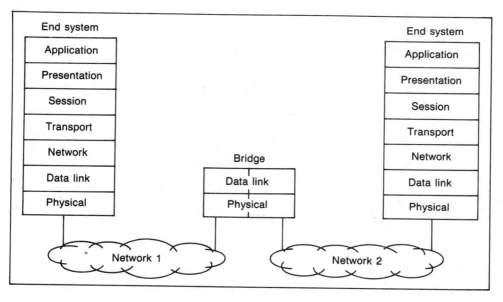

Figure 4.6 An OSI model of a bridge.

81

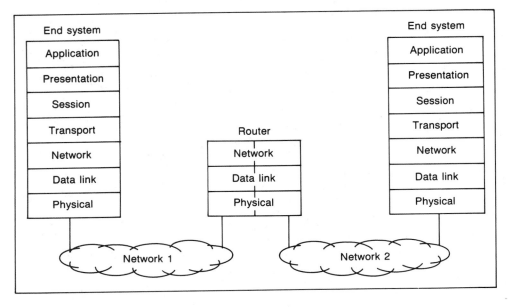

Figure 4.7 An OSI model of a router.

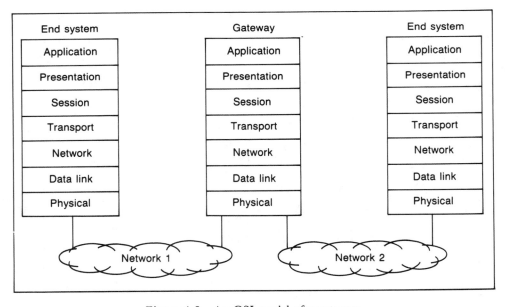

Figure 4.8 An OSI model of a gateway.

4.7   Voice network architectures

Inter-PABX signalling (referred to in Section 3.4.1) is required to transfer control and supervisory messages between PABXs or ISPBXs in a private network and between a private network and the PSTN or the ISDN. Control messages contain all the necessary information required to establish and release a voice call and request PABX/ISPBX services in private and public networks. Digital circuits enable these messages to be assigned to a dedicated channel, which is separate from other channels. The signalling system that is used to convey the control messages that are associated with PABX networks is known as Common Channel Signalling (CCS). The role of CCS in a private network is shown in Figure 4.9.

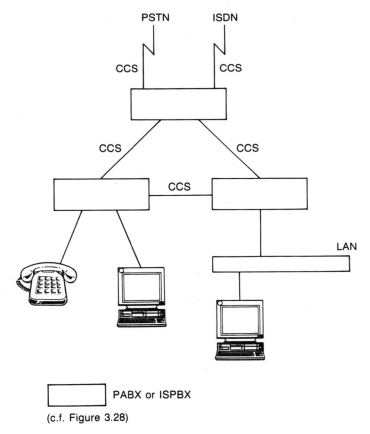

Figure 4.9   The role of CCS in a private network.

The architecture for the interchange of CCS information is structured in a similar way to the lower part of the OSIRM. This 'three-layer' structure is shown in Figure 4.10. The lower two layers are entirely similar in function to the lower two

83

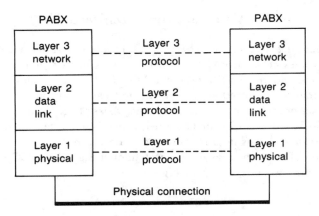

Figure 4.10   An architecture for common channel signalling.

layers of the OSIRM, whereas layer 3 is concerned with the meaning and interpretation of the inter-PABX messages.

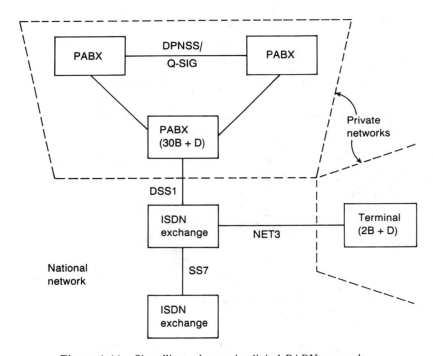

Figure 4.11   Signalling schemes in digital PABX networks.

To date, inter-PABX standards have been mainly proprietary. Consequently, voice networks usually have to be designed with PABXs from a single manufacturer.

Some *de facto* CCS standards, on the other hand, are supported by a number of manufacturers. For example, British Telecom initiated a standard known as DPNSS (Digital Private Network Signalling System) that is supported by a number of manufacturers in Europe. Work on *de jure* CCS standards is on-going, but the emergence of ISDNs has progressed the development of CCS standards for private and public networks. Figure 4.11 summarises the inter-PABX standards that are important in a private network that interfaces to a public network. A brief description of each CCS standard follows:

O-SIG   Developed by ETSI (European Telecommunications Standards Institute); based on the CCITT's Q.931 standard.

NET3   ETSI's Normes Europeenes de Telecommunications No. 3; used for ISDN 2B + D access.

DSS1   Digital Signalling System No. 1; based on the CCITT's Q.931 standard.

SS7   CCITT's Signalling System No. 7; used for inter-exchange signalling.

The development of CCS standards means that it will be possible to design private networks with PABXs/ISPBXs from more than one manufacturer and migrate towards open networks. There is still some way to go before open PABX networks are practical, but in the meantime the network planner should be aware of PABX/ISPBX standards and should investigate whether suppliers are committed to the implementation of *de jure* standards, such as those identified in Figure 4.11.

4.8   Summary

This chapter has discussed the fundamental aspects of network architectures, so that the network planner is able to specify the standards that will be required to be implemented in a private information network. The role of standards in computer networks and PABX networks has been introduced from the point of view of the development of open networks; in this context the work of standards bodies such as ISO, IAB, IEEE, CCITT and others has been introduced in this chapter.

PART TWO

The planning environment

CHAPTER 5

Strategic planning for information networks (SPIN): a planning framework

5.1 Introduction

Part One examined communications requirements and the network options that meet these requirements. Part Two considers how requirements and options can be brought together; i.e. how communications requirements are identified and how an information network can be designed to meet these requirements. This will be achieved by describing a planning framework that enables the network planner to utilise analytical skills in a structured and effective way.

Despite the existence of a range of public and managed networks (see Chapter 3), many organisations will continue to operate private networks for the foreseeable future. In recognition of the undoubted existence of private information networks and their strategic importance to many organisations, it is imperative to use a structured approach to the development and management of private network resources. This planning approach should be flexible enough to incorporate changes in technology or changes in business requirements. Such a planning framework, known as SPIN (strategic planning for information networks) will be outlined and placed in context in this chapter; the remaining chapters will describe each phase of SPIN in detail.

5.2 What is strategic planning?

The word 'strategy' derives from the Greek word 'strategos', which means a general or a person who directs military forces to win a battle in a war. Put simply, a strategy in the business context enables an organisation to stay ahead of the competition and achieve its business mission. In this context, 'planning' means exercising influence and control over future events and 'strategy' – borrowing from the military context – means a high-level activity whose importance influences the overall direction of the organisation. Strategic planning, therefore, can be described as the process of choosing long-term objectives (the business mission) and deciding how to achieve them.

Strategic planning can enable an organisation to respond to changes in markets and to evaluate technologies that are relevant to business operations. The need for strategic planning has increased in recent years as the business environment has become more competitive and as IT has generated opportunities to improve business performance.

5.3 Strategic information systems planning (SISP)

Strategic planning as applied to information systems (ISs) is often referred to as SISP. Given the fundamental necessity of ISs to an organisation, SISP brings IT closer to the business planning cycle and enables IT to be exploited effectively in an organisation. The basis of SISP is that it should be business-driven rather than technology-driven, with the initial focus on *what* should be achieved rather than *how* to achieve it.

The key issue of SISP is the link between the business strategy of an organisation and its IS strategy. The SISP process must work from a starting point of either assuming that the business strategy exists or that one will be developed as a precursor to SISP. Given this assumption, an on-going review of the goals and objectives of the organisation is an integral component of SISP. This review should evaluate how the use of IT can redefine business activities from a strategic position. This will ensure that ISs support strategic business objectives. As business objectives become more innovative, more complex technology is required to support information-processing needs. The increasing technical content of ISs reinforces the need to recognise and establish the link between business objectives and IS planning. Figure 5.1 highlights this link and emphasises the role of SISP.

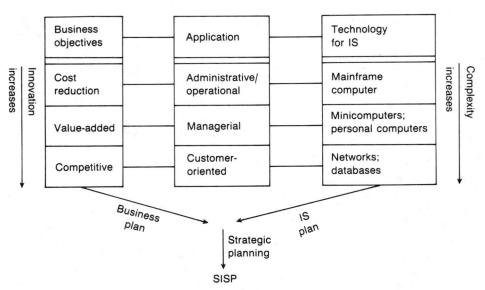

Figure 5.1 The line between key business objectives and key technologies.

90

5.4   Why use SISP?

The use of SISP techniques has increased in recent years in response to competitive business environments and opportunities for exploiting IT. Some reasons for adopting a SISP approach are as follows:

- It forces managers to consider the impact of external forces such as threats upon business operation and performance.
- It provides an opportunity to examine strengths and weaknesses in business operation and performance.
- It identifies key areas of performance that are critical to the success of the organisation.
- It provides a basis for allocating resources to these critical areas.
- It provides a forum for evaluating new business opportunities which require significant underpinning with IT.

Strategic planning, in general, can give business managers a sense of direction and, hopefully, motivation to work for the achievement of corporate objectives. SISP, in particular, can raise the profile of IS planning and management and emphasises the need to recognise the strategic nature of today's ISs. Above all, SISP will provide an on-going review of resource allocation and the value of ISs in an organisation. The financial component of this analysis provides the organisation with an on-going measurement of the performance of IT systems; this is particularly important in demonstrating 'value for money' from investment in IT.

5.5   Strategic planning for information networks (SPIN)

Figure 5.1 illustrates the key point that IS planning is a component of the overall strategic planning in an organisation. Consequently, an IS strategy is seen as more than just a plan for computing and telecommunications in that it is concerned with the long-term development of ISs which support the overall, strategic direction of the organisation.

The outcome of SISP is often a number of sub-strategies that embrace the scope of the ISs used in an organisation. The following example illustrates this point:

EXAMPLE 1

The IT strategy of one of the United Kingdom's utility companies comprises a number of sub-strategies, including data processing, personal computers, office systems, data communications and telemetry.

The overall IT strategy is in line with the corporate business strategy (which is formally defined in a brief document) and sets out to meet the information requirements of the company. The strategy also identifies stages of development of the sub-strategies and recommends ways in which IT resources should be managed.

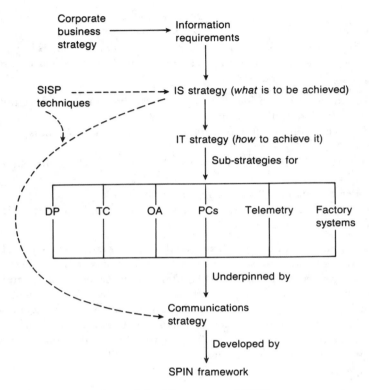

Figure 5.2   The context of SPIN.

Figure 5.2 illustrates how a communications strategy underpins an IT strategy and emphasises that communications systems underpin the implementation of ISs. Communications systems provide essential links between users of information and sources of information and form the basis of the IS infrastructure where there is a need to transfer information between source and user. Consequently, communications systems planning is a key outcome of IS planning, as shown in Figure 5.2.

However, the communications strategy can never be a complete statement of the information network infrastructure of an organisation, because there will always be a degree of uncertainty about future network technology, services, regulations and standards. Nevertheless, the strategy will act as a signpost which points the way towards the development of an information network and is flexible enough to recognise and incorporate any changes that result from these uncertainties. The approach to the development of a corporate communications strategy, which is described in this part of the book, is known as SPIN (strategic planning for information networks); its context is shown in Figure 5.2.

5.5.1 The objective of SPIN

The overall objective of SPIN is to ensure that planning for communications systems is interpreted in terms of the business needs associated with the transmission of all forms of information. This implies a need to define a corporate information network that meets the communications requirements of the organisation and identifies milestones for the development of the network. This means that SPIN will provide a framework for tactical planning; that is, SPIN will encompass the implementation and management of the corporate communications network as well as its design.

In order for SPIN to complement systems development methods, the SPIN framework must meet a number of objectives. These are summarised as follows:

- The framework should be flexible enough to be tailored to a given project; it should not be perceived or used as a rigid method.
- The framework should be broad in scope and should embrace LANs and WANs.
- The framework should be subject to QA procedures.
- The framework should lend itself to project management procedures.
- The framework should interface with SISP techniques where appropriate.
- The framework should interface with structured systems analysis methods where appropriate.
- The framework should identify phases and links between phases; tasks within phases and links between tasks; deliverables; review and decision points.

With the last objective in mind, it can be seen that SPIN sets out to provide a phased approach to the development of information networks.

5.5.2 An overview of SPIN

The SPIN framework has been expanded into two main stages and six phases. These are summarised in Figure 5.3; the figure also notes which chapter will describe each phase. An overview of each phase follows.

Strategy

This phase is concerned with identifying applications and their qualitative communications requirements. Requirements are reviewed for current applications and are identified for new applications. The outcome of this phase includes documentation which refers to qualitative communications requirements. The required information-processing architecture (IPA) of the organisation is also produced during this phase. The IPA shows the location of processing and storage elements in relation to company sites and gives an indication of the links between these elements.

Feasibility

This phase makes use of the qualitative communications requirements that were identified in the strategy phase, in order to develop a business case for network

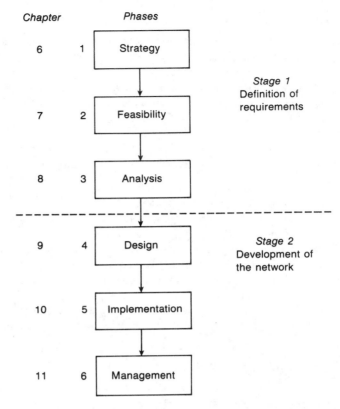

Figure 5.3 The phases of SPIN.

development. This involves carrying out some initial quantification of the communications requirements in order to estimate bandwidth requirements and, hence, calculate approximate costs of private networks. The outcome of this phase includes an initial costs and benefits analysis and a business plan. The objective of these outcomes is to define a decision point which will focus the attention of senior management as to whether further analysis and design should be carried out and to identify adequate resources for this purpose.

Analysis
This phase is concerned with translating the broad communications requirements, which will have been identified in the strategy phase, into detailed requirements. The analysis phase then seeks to quantify these detailed requirements, using appropriate metrics, in order to provide data for network capacity planning purposes.

Design
This phase is concerned with modelling the information network. Quantitative requirements from the analysis phase and the IPA from the strategy phase are used

to generate the network configuration. Network modelling will also provide data such as costs of private circuits and estimates of network performance.

Implementation

This phase is concerned with implementing the communications strategy, i.e. with planning the practicalities of network development in terms of timescale, procurement and installation.

Management

This phase is concerned with the on-going management of the information network. Network management functions are identified and tools and standards are introduced.

Network planning and management can be a lengthy and complex process. SPIN breaks down this process into six manageable phases so that its use realises a number of benefits:

- The evolution of a network infrastructure that underpins strategic and other applications, thus ensuring the explicit link between the IT strategy and the business strategy.
- Better control of network planning and management.
- Better co-ordination of human resources through well-defined tasks and links between tasks.

5.6 Moving towards the strategic IS organisation

Merely to postulate the use of strategic planning does not guarantee the realisation of the benefits outlined above; a number of organisational and management issues should be addressed as precursors to the SPIN process. The success of any strategic planning exercise is dependent on obtaining approval and support from top management, whose commitment will enable an organisation to establish a cohesive link between business objectives and the strategy for ISs. This will ensure that the communications strategy is driven by business needs and the desire to exploit opportunities to improve business performance. In order for strategic planning to be successful, top management must foster a climate in which the creativity that leads to strategic thinking and innovation can develop. In short, strategic vision must originate from and be encouraged by the most senior management in an organisation.

A lack of commitment at the highest level can result in a failure to exploit IT successfully and a loss of opportunities to improve business performance. The reasons for this lack of commitment may stem from a limited perception of the role of IT in an organisation or from the way in which IT is managed.

5.6.1 Awareness of IT in the organisation

The use of IT in an organisation will not succeed unless there is a sufficient level of awareness of the potential of IT as an operational resource and as a strategic weapon.

This awareness must be evident from the most senior management level downwards, if the development of ISs is to succeed. For example, one of the United Kingdom's oil companies initiated an awareness programme in the mid-1980s. The programme was suggested by senior managers and was used to explain the company's IT strategy to over 2500 managers and other staff who took part in the scheme.

5.6.2 Management of ISs

The management of ISs varies from one organisation to another. For instance, in some organisations the management of ISs is not co-ordinated. For present purposes, this will be referred to as 'traditional' management; it is often characterised by the following responsibilities:

- The systems department handles data processing and data communications.
- A separate department has responsibility for voice communications.
- An information centre or end-user computing department has responsibility for personal computers and LANs.

Traditional management can give rise to problems such as the following:

- The responsibility for IT and reporting to management is dispersed throughout the organisation.
- A lack of an overall perspective of communications requirements and facilities.
- A lack of co-ordinated control of resources.
- A lack of co-ordinated and long-term planning.

This type of management of ISs can result in a fragmented approach to the development of information networks and often leads to a reactive rather than a proactive approach to planning.

In order to co-ordinate network development effectively and proactively, it is appropriate to co-ordinate the management of ISs and develop an 'integrated' style of management. The following examples will illustrate this principle in practice.

EXAMPLE 2

The approach of one of the United Kingdom's largest manufacturing groups of companies has been to create a group-wide management services function whose role is the stewardship of IT throughout the group of companies. The director of IT manages this function and formulates policies and strategies for computing and telecommunications. Although the group of companies operates as a federation of semi-autonomous businesses, the management of computing and telecommunications has been centralised in order to facilitate the effective management of this function.

EXAMPLE 3

One of the United Kingdom's retail organisations has appointed a director of IT who sits on the board of directors of the company. This management function brings together all aspects of IT under a single management umbrella. The director of IT sees his position from the perspective of setting targets rather than receiving them from someone else. In this respect, this individual sees clear advantages in his role of director, compared to that of a senior manager who would report to a director.

These examples suggest that an integrated management structure can create the climate for more effective management procedures compared to traditional management. Integrated management co-ordinates the responsibility for ISs and is represented by a single business function, whose director sits on the board of directors of the organisation. This means that there is a mechanism that can be used to emphasise the strategic nature of information networks and obtain top management support for network development. The provision of communications facilities can be rationalised and management effort can be steered towards the development of a communications strategy that supports the needs of individual business units and those of the organisation as a whole. An integrated management function is in a much better position to identify these needs and should be able to avoid the problems of a fragmented approach to the development of communications facilities.

5.7   Summary

This chapter has identified the need for SISP in general and SPIN in particular. The phases of SPIN have been summarised and some of the management requirements for the SPIN process have been discussed. The remaining chapters will describe each phase of SPIN in detail.

CHAPTER 6

The strategy phase

6.1 Introduction

This chapter is concerned with the strategy phase of the SPIN. This is the first and most critical phase of SPIN, since it involves thinking strategically about information requirements in an effort to identify communications requirements.

This chapter will focus on the following:

- Objectives of the strategy phase;
- Techniques to be used.
- Deliverables for this phase.

A fictitious case study will be used to illustrate some of the activities involved in this phase. The case study will be supplemented with examples of some of these activities used in practice. Any discussion that refers to the case study will be indented.

6.2 The strategy phase in outline

The principal objectives of the strategy phase are as follows:

- To review existing information-processing applications.
- To identify new information-processing applications and new business opportunities.
- To specify qualitative communications requirements for retained and new applications.
- To develop a high-level network configuration; this shows the location of: company sites; data-processing elements and associated application software and data-storage elements; users of data/information; links between the above.

The above objectives give an overview of the tasks that should be performed in this phase. A number of SISP (strategic information systems planning) techniques are used to assist in the development of the application portfolio (retained and new applications). This is used to generate matrices of communications requirements. Modelling techniques are used to develop network configurations.

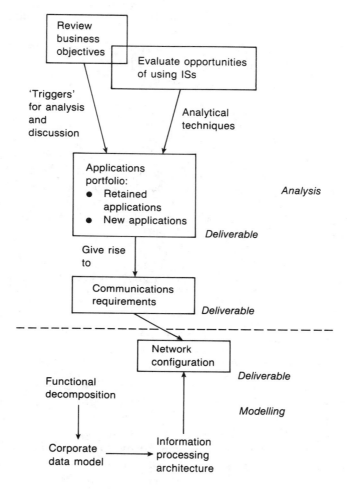

Figure 6.1 Overview of strategy phase.

Since the strategy phase relies on the involvement of senior management, relatively straightforward techniques of analysis and modelling should be employed by analysts in this phase. In order to maintain the commitment of senior management, it is critical to avoid excessive detail in the strategy phase. An important principle, therefore, is to keep analysis relatively straightforward in an effort to maintain the interest of senior managers in the task at hand.

The main deliverables from the strategy phase are as follows:

- The application portfolio.
- Communications requirements matrices (qualitative).
- A high-level network configuration.

99

The overall shape of the strategy phase is illustrated in Figure 6.1, which summarises the approach to this phase.

Prior to describing how the deliverables are developed, the next section will present the background information to the case study.

6.3   The case study

Scandania is a fictitious company. The company is a manufacturer of processed food products and distributes its products to customers in the United Kingdom and in mainland Europe. The business activity of Scandania is kept relatively straightforward in order to simplify analysis and modelling tasks. To achieve this, it is necessary to concentrate on the UK operation to illustrate the generation of deliverables. This will make it easier to present the outcome of tasks and keep diagrams straightforward, while illustrating aspects of the strategy phase. In practice, these tasks may be more complex and generate much more detail than is the case for Scandania. Nevertheless, the case study is intended to indicate the scope of the analysis required and the documentation that is produced for the deliverables.

Scandania

Background information

Scandania (UK) is a manufacturer of packet and tinned foods and a wide range of chilled and frozen, ready-to-cook meals. The company supplies directly to several of the major supermarket chains in the United Kingdom and in mainland Europe, as well as to hotel chains. Scandania (UK) is a subsidiary of a large Anglo-American company. The parent company is a federated organisation, which means that Scandania (UK) operates as an independent company in the group. Business strategy is the responsibility of the management team in the United Kingdom.

Scandania's UK manufacturing operation is based at a large split site in the central region of England, known as the West Midlands, from where products are distributed to the company's regional distribution centres in four other locations throughout the United Kingdom and to France, Belgium and The Netherlands. Customers are supplied from their nearest regional centre. Orders can be placed with sales personnel when they make regular visits to customers, or placed directly by telephoning the nearest regional centre.

In the United Kingdom the company operates a sales team that is distributed throughout the four regions. Most of the sales team work from home, but are attached to one of the regional centres and report to the regional sales manager. Usually, a salesperson spends the equivalent of one day a week in the office (at the regional centre); the other four days are spent in the field, dealing with customers and developing prospects for new customers.

The company has considerable expertise in the production and packaging of ready-to-cook meals and other 'convenience' foods. The company also leads the field in responding to consumer trends and demands for quality food that is free of additives such as colouring and preservatives. This means that many of Scandania's newer products have a shorter shelf-life than most of the company's well-established packet and tinned products. The majority of Scandania's newer products have been highly successful; it is this market that is growing steadily.

Scandania has achieved a high degree of automation in its food manufacturing plant; it intends to continue the development and implementation of automated control of production.

Current operations

Current business operations at the company's manufacturing headquarters comprise two sites, which are about 5 km apart. One site consists of a large manufacturing plant, research laboratories and kitchens, and a large refrigerated warehouse. The second site consists of the administration function and the mainframe computer facility. The company have occupied these sites for almost twenty-five years and have invested in factory automation and computing since the late 1960s.

The administration function handles all dealings with suppliers of raw materials or other goods. The main stock file of the company's range of products is held on the mainframe computer. Additional files reflect stock levels in each regional distribution centre; these are updated on a regular basis, usually once per day.

Currently, there are four regional distribution centres in the United Kingdom. These comprise warehouse and office facilities. Each regional centre holds supplies of Scandania's products and serve customers in that region. Each regional centre employs personnel in addition to the regional sales team. These are employed in accounts, stock control and transport. The company also operates a number of distribution centres in mainland Europe.

Customers are able to order any of Scandania's products from their nearest regional centre, though this does not necessarily mean that each regional centre will carry every item of the company's product line. Items that may be unavailable temporarily can be obtained either from headquarters or from one of the other regional centres. Customers do not usually experience any delays in delivery under such circumstances. Customers such as supermarkets usually expect deliveries two or three times per week. Regional sales reports are transmitted twice per week by the

101

mainframe computer to each regional centre for printing. Regional stock position is reflected in regional stock files, which can be examined by accessing the mainframe computer.

Normal replenishment of regional stock is carried out by making requests for deliveries of stock from headquarters. This is done by accessing the mainframe computer from one of the terminals in the regional office. A regional centre is equipped with a printer and about five terminals, with national or international dial-up links to the mainframe computer.

Scandania operates its own fleet of delivery vehicles. These transport supplies from the company's headquarters to regional centres and from these centres to customers. Normally, two trips are made each week to transport large amounts of stock from headquarters to each regional centre.

Current applications at the main sites
Administration
The accounting and supplier order processing systems are based on a mainframe computer, which supports a number of terminals. Regional account reports are sent to regional centres once per week, usually during an overnight period over dial-up lines. Other regional reports are also transmitted in the same way. Central and regional stock control is also handled by the mainframe computer system. Regional stock reports are transmitted to regional centres by the start of each working day. A number of 'stand-alone' personal computers are used in the administration departments; applications include spreadsheets and word-processing.

Scandania has established a mature management development and technical training function; this is the responsibility of the Computer Services Division of the company. Computer Services is in a position to become a profit centre. This will enable it to sell facilities management (FM), consultancy and training services to customers outside Scandania.

Production
Much of the food-manufacturing equipment is microprocessor controlled. Production planning is carried out by personnel who collect data periodically from this equipment.

Short-term requirements

The company has acquired a plot of land next to its manufacturing facility and is planning to move the administrative and computing departments from its other site. This will give the company the opportunity to rationalise its UK operations and develop a single site for manufacturing and administration. A new office block and a new computer centre will be built.

At the same time, the company is taking the opportunity to review its information systems requirements. Initial discussions have generated the following issues, which will be included in the scope of the review:

● Communication between all departments at the expanded site.
● Communication between headquarters and regional offices.
● Regional centres to be responsible for their own sales and stock control information.
● The accounting systems (mainframe computer software).
● Automating the production planning and purchasing procedures.
● Integrating production planning, purchasing and stock control.

No decisions have been taken on these issues; their scope has been agreed, in principle, by a senior management team which includes the manager of Computer Services.

6.4   Development of the applications portfolio

Figure 6.1 indicates that the applications portfolio comprises retained and proposed, new applications of information-processing systems. The applications portfolio is developed from two perspectives: firstly, by reviewing business objectives, and, secondly, by evaluating opportunities of using ISs in the organisation. SISP techniques are used to assist in this task and will provide a forum for discussion, review and the generation of ideas. Although there may be some overlap between these perspectives (as suggested by Figure 6.2), they are dealt with separately in order to describe a number of SISP techniques in context.

6.4.1   Review business objectives

The underlying assumption of the strategy phase is that the business strategy exists in some form; if not, this is a good opportunity to review and articulate formally the business strategy of the organisation as a prerequisite for SPIN. The formulation of business strategies is outside the scope of this book, so it is sufficient to point out here that the business strategy of an organisation may exist in the shape of a formal document. For example, an international bank drew up such a document in the form of a twenty-page 'vision paper' which included statements that referred to the bank's business strategy (Keen, 1988). On the other hand, the business strategy of an organisation may not exist in written form; it may only be said to exist as part of the culture of the organisation and could be expressed verbally by any of the senior managers. Obviously, a formal business strategy is a preferred starting-point for SPIN.

Scandania's business strategy underlines the desire to increase profitability. The strategy is summarised by the following business objectives:

1. Increase market share; competitors are threatening the company's position.

2. Respond to new competitors by
   - developing additional regional centres in the UK within two years;
   - establishing manufacturing plant in Belgium within two years;
   - increasing the range of chilled food products.
3. Decentralise the control of distribution within one year; regional centres are to be made responsible for sales, accounting and stock control for their own regions.
4. Provide a shorter delivery time for customers, i.e. within 24 hours of orders being placed.
5. Speed up trading with suppliers.
6. Make it easier for major customers to place orders.
7. Permit Computer Services to offer facilities for management, consultancy and training to customers in the United Kingdom and Europe.
8. Expand the side of the business that sells packaging materials to other food manufacturers and other companies that require specialised packaging for their products.
9. Develop a database of research and development information that is relevant to the industry; sell this information to pharmaceutical companies, government departments, academic institutions and so on.

   The company drew up the list during a half-day brainstorming session involving senior management. A discussion paper was circulated among other management staff and the list was reviewed and formalised. The list of objectives represents a summary of the business strategy for the next 3—5 years. It will be reviewed every 12 months.

It is evident that Scandania's strategic thrust tends towards that of providing an improved service to their customers and the development of new business opportunities, in an effort to sustain competitive advantage over their nearest competitors. The business strategy of Scandania is expected to influence the profitability and competitive position of the company. This type of strategic thrust does not, however, apply to all organisations, so it is instructive to be able to say something about the strategic thrust of a given organisation as part of the review of business objectives.

Broad categories of strategic thrust are summarised in Figure 6.2. It can be seen that although Scandania is a manufacturing company, its business strategy is a combination of the first and third categories. The nature of the strategic thrust of an organisation is a valuable starting point in the review of business objectives.

The process of reviewing business objectives is a creative exercise; it means creating a vision of the future direction of the organisation. The process can generate ideas for new business opportunities in response to changes in the market. The process also provides an opportunity to evaluate current business operations and performance. Indeed, this is an ideal opportunity to undertake a critical examination of what is currently happening in the organisation.

However, the exercise may require a 'trigger' to help get it underway. One

Sector	Strategic thrust	Orientation of business objectives
Service	Sustained competitive advantage	Enhanced service provision to customers, clients, suppliers
		Develop new business opportunities
Public	Efficiency	Drive down costs; maintain quality of service to customers and clients
Manufacturing	Efficiency	Drive down unit costs; increase productivity
		Enhance service provision to customers and clients

Figure 6.2 The strategic thrust of an organisation.

example of such a trigger is to identify the strengths and weaknesses of the organisation and identify opportunities and threats. This kind of analysis is often referred to as SWOT (strengths, weaknesses, opportunities and threats) analysis. Another is known as critical success factors (CSFs) analysis. These techniques are discussed below.

SWOT analysis

SWOT analysis provides an opportunity to evaluate what an organisation is good at and what it is not so good at. The analysis should also compare these aspects of the organisation's operation, performance and competitive position with competitors; this in not an easy task but will yield valuable information if carried out.

SWOT analysis begins by asking a number of questions for the organisation concerned; typical questions that should be addressed are as follows:

Strengths
- What is the organisation good at; what gives it special competence and potential advantage?
- What do customers and suppliers see as the strengths of the organisation?
- How can the organisation build upon these strengths?

105

Weaknesses
- What is the organisation not so good at, in the opinion of employees, customers and suppliers?
- What is the risk of ignoring any weaknesses that may be identified?

Opportunities
- What changes are evident in the organisation's markets which can be viewed as providing an opportunity to generate new business or increase market share?
- What opportunities are provided by the use of new technology (in manufacturing and in information processing)?
- How are competitors using technology?
- Does market regulation provide opportunities?
- Will joint ventures or collaborations provide new business opportunities?

Threats
- Of new entrants in the organization's markets.
- Is the industry sector vulnerable to new entrants; is there room?

SWOT analysis for Scandania resulted in the following conclusions:

Strengths

- Long-established reputation for quality; this should be capitalised upon in future marketing.
- Leader in the field of producing new products of the frozen and chilled variety; this position must be maintained.
- A mature information systems function; this function is to be used to develop new business opportunities.

Weaknesses

- In the recent past, the company have tended to rely on their reputation and have tended to 'rest on their laurels'; this has led to a reluctance to innovate and a failure to recognise that competitors are beginning to pose a threat to their business position.

Opportunities

- To capture a significant share of the market provided by new chains of supermarkets that are opening in the United Kingdom.
- Expand upon the sale of packaging products and materials; this is a new business opportunity.
- Offer facilities management, consultancy and training to customers in the United Kingdom and Europe; this is another new business opportunity.

Threats

● Recognise that Scandania's leading market share is continually under threat; there are several food manufacturers competing in this market sector.

Essentially, SWOT analysis will help to evaluate the competitive position of an organisation. Knowledge of the underlying sources of competitive pressure will highlight the strengths and weaknesses and will help to review business objectives.

Critical success factors analysis

In order to translate the review of business objectives into entries in the applications portfolio, the information needs that support key business objectives must be identified. A powerful and proven technique for doing this is known as critical success factors (CSFs) analysis. The CSF process was developed by John F. Rockart, who defined CSFs as 'those few critical areas where things must go right for the business to flourish' (Rockart, 1979). The CSF process is summarised in Figure 6.3.

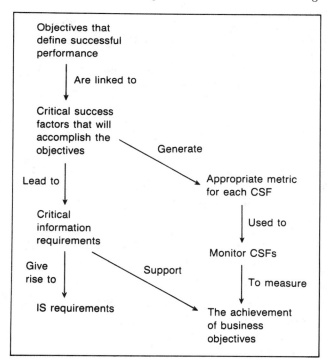

Figure 6.3 The critical success factors process.

Rockart originally developed the CSF process as a means to understand the information needs of chief executives. The process has subsequently been applied to organisations as a whole and has been extended into a broader planning method. When used in planning, CSF analysis is an enabling vehicle in the process of rethinking the way in which an organisation operates and performs. The outcome of the analysis identifies the key performance indicators of the organisation.

When used in practice, CSF analysis helps senior managers to focus on those aspects of the business that will determine its success in the future, i.e. it focuses on the vision for the next 5-10 years. Key business objectives that will realise this vision are identified, along with the CSFs that will achieve these objectives. A CSF is usually associated with an appropriate metric so that it can be monitored effectively.

Some CSFs are 'monitoring' CSFs and some are 'building' CSFs. The former are associated with current procedures and the latter with changing the way that the business operates by, for example, developing new products or new business opportunities. Both categories of CSFs may change over time, so the CSF process must be regarded as iterative to some extent. CSFs are often associated with particular business functional areas in order to assist in the monitoring process.

EXAMPLE 1

After examining several methodologies for identifying strategic IT opportunities, one of the United Kingdom's largest manufacturing companies selected CSF analysis and used it successfully with many business units. Most of the business executives involved found the technique an excellent process for identifying those areas where action plans were critically necessary (Earl, 1988).

CSF analysis within Scandania will help to illustrate some of these points.

The same group of managers that drew up the business strategy were involved in a number of interviews that were conducted by consultants who were skilled in CSF analysis. The outcome of the analysis is summarised as follows:

CSF 1:   Increase market share by 10 per cent within three years.
Functions: R&D, Marketing, Sales.
Metric: Estimates of market share.

CSF 2:   Increase revenue from sales of packaging to 25 per cent of overall sales within three years.
Functions: Production, Marketing, Accounting.
Metric: Sales revenues.

CSF 3:   Continue to introduce new food products.
Functions: R&D, Marketing.
Metric: Not possible to quantify, given that the range and number of products changes as a function of market trends.

CSF 4:   Provide a 24-hour delivery time to customers.
Functions: Regional Distribution Centres.
Metric: Delivery time, as expressed by customers.

CSF 5:   Develop facilities management, consultancy and training so
           that Computer Services generates significant revenue.
Function: Computer Services.
Metric: The target revenue has not been quantified at this stage.

The critical information requirements for Scandania are as follows:

CSF 1:   Marketing information; access to market research, sales
           histories and forecasts.
CSF 2:   Access to up-to-date revenue information; analysis by product,
           by customer, by region, etc.
CSF 3:   Support for marketing function to document and analyse
           results from surveys of pilot sales of new products.
CSF 4:   Access to a rapid and responsive ordering system in each
           regional centre; information held will be on customers,
           accounts and stock position.
CSF 5:   Access to a booking system to reserve places on training courses
           and make other enquiries about courses.

Essentially, the outcome of CSF analysis is to identify critical information requirements. Finally, the CSF process should identify how CSFs are to be delivered. This involves evaluating the opportunities of using ISs in the organisation. This is discussed in the next subsection.

6.4.2 Evaluate opportunities of using information systems

Figure 6.1 shows that a second, complementary analysis contributes to the development of the applications portfolio. This analysis can be conducted in parallel with that of the review of business objectives and involves an evaluation of the opportunities of using ISs in an organisation. There are a number of techniques that can assist in this; the most relevant of which are as follows:

- Technology impact analysis (TIA).
- IT investment analysis.
- Value chain analysis.
- Competitive advantage analysis.
- Using information networks strategically.

The development of the Applications Portfolio does not depend on the use of all of these techniques. It is left to the judgement of the analyst to decide which of the techniques discussed here should be used in the strategy phase of SPIN for a particular organisation. Before discussing the techniques in turn, however, a few points about the role of ISs in organisations will be made. This discussion can be used as a trigger or starting-point for the evaluation of opportunities of using ISs.

The role of information systems in organisations

The degree to which ISs are able to play a strategic role in an organisation depends, to some extent, on the business sector in which the organisation operates. In some organisations, ISs play a support role and are not critical to the delivery of the organisation's products or services. In other organisations, ISs play a strategic role in supporting the competitive position of the organisation. The work of McFarlan and McKenney provides a generic method which places an organisation into one of four categories of IS roles (McFarlan and McKenney, 1983).

McFarlan and McKenney's method comprises, essentially, a classification of ISs which assists in understanding the role of ISs in an organisation. The classification can be applied to the organisation as a whole or to its constituent business units. The method identifies four IS environments (the examples are the authors'):

1. Support (e.g. a brick-making company)
   - Information-processing applications are not crucial to the strategic direction of the organisation.
   - IT is used in administrative systems.
   - The organisation can still operate in the event of operational difficulties in ISs of the order of half a day.
   - Return on investment in IT is relatively low.
   - The attention of senior management in matters of IT is only necessary occasionally.
2. Turnaround (e.g. a supermarket chain)
   - Considerable IT operational support.
   - Considerable investment in IT.
   - IT is becoming strategic and critical to the growth of the business.
   - IT is being 'turned round' from a low profile activity towards a strategic one.
3. Factory (e.g. a car-manufacturing company)
   - Depends heavily on IT support for current operations and their management; a disruption of IS services impairs the smooth operation of the business.
   - ISs are not necessarily at the heart of the organisation's strategic development.
4. Strategic (e.g. a major bank)
   - Critically dependent on IT.
   - ISs planning and management is directed from board level.
   - ISs are crucial to the delivery of new products and services.
   - IT investment is likely to be the company's highest capital budget.

A particular organisation (or business unit) is positioned in the matrix of Figure 6.4.

Two principal forces drive an organisation from one part of the matrix to another. Firstly, there is the link between the potential of IT and the business objectives of the organisation. This results from the potential to exploit IT to support the achievement

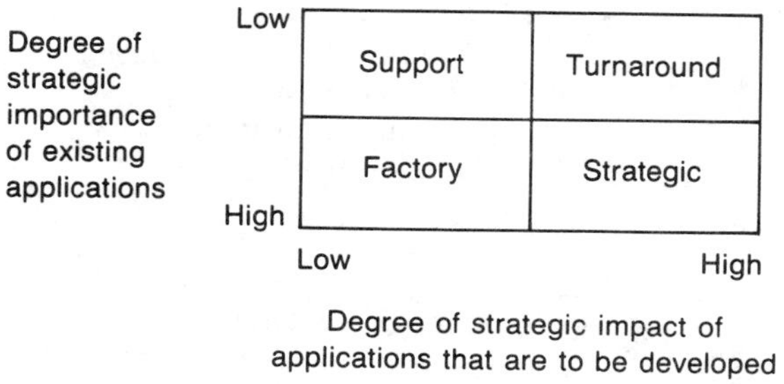

Figure 6.4   IS environment grid.

of business objectives. Secondly, there are the changes that are unfolding in the organisation's competitive environment. The actions of customers, suppliers or competitors may push the organisation into or through the turnaround quadrant of the matrix.

The implications of this analysis are that senior managers must assess the current and future importance of ISs and evaluate the potential opportunities of using ISs; the grid of Figure 6.4 is a useful starting-point in this analysis. However, in order to take this analysis further and understand more fully the potential impact of ISs, it is necessary to employ techniques such as those highlighted at the beginning of Section 6.4.2. These techniques will be described in the following subsections.

Technology impact analysis

Technology impact analysis (TIA) is used in a methodology known as information engineering as a relatively quick means of identifying new business opportunities arising from the use of ISs (Martin, 1986). TIA is concerned with the opportunities and threats created by the use of IT and maps a taxonomy of changes and developments in IT against business opportunities for new products or services. TIA makes the assumption that senior management are often not fully aware of the implications of advances in IT and that this can result in lost opportunities or threats from competitors. Therefore, TIA attempts to identify these opportunities and threats. TIA (as used in information engineering) will be described briefly and modified to some extent for the purposes of SPIN.

The first step in TIA is to develop a taxonomy of IT developments, including those in information networks (see Chapter 3). This will have to be carried out by someone who has sufficient knowledge of IT and its applications. The taxonomy of IT developments is represented by an action diagram. A form of this type of diagram is shown in Figure 6.5, which shows examples of entries for developments in information networks.

The next step is to develop an action diagram of business opportunities arising from the use of IT. The organisation should develop its own list of business opportunities by asking themselves a number of questions which will generate

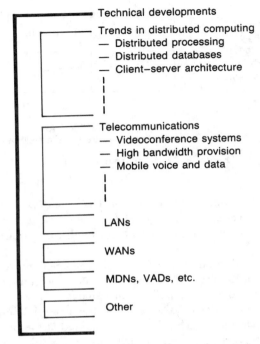

Figure 6.5 Action diagram of technical developments.

discussion and ideas. These include the following:

- Can the organisation benefit from the development of electronic lines of communication to suppliers or customers?
- Can the organisation improve market intelligence by employing appropriate ISs?
- Can IT reduce product lead times?
- Can IT impact upon the manufacturing process?
- Can IT impact upon training?
- Can IT improve support for managers?
- Can the organisation reduce order-delivery times?
- Can ISs underpin the delivery of new services to customers or clients?

This list of questions (which may, of course, be extended) will provide an opportunity for what could be a wide-ranging discussion about the use of IT in the organisation. At the same time, the way in which IT is used by competitors should be assessed in an attempt to identify threats to the organisation and the risks of not responding to the activity of competitors. The outcome of a discussion of this nature is an action diagram of business opportunities; a form of this diagram is shown in Figure 6.6, in which the entries are applications of IT in each functional area of the organisation.

Finally, the action diagram of technical developments is mapped onto the action diagram of business opportunities. This generates a matrix of entries which may either

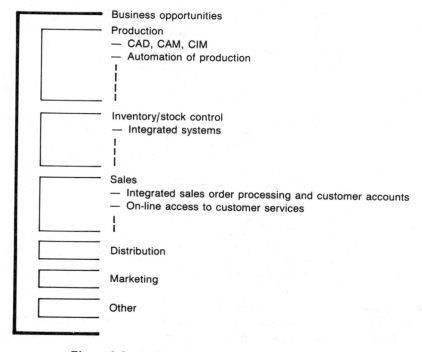

Business opportunities
Production
— CAD, CAM, CIM
— Automation of production

Inventory/stock control
— Integrated systems

Sales
— Integrated sales order processing and customer accounts
— On-line access to customer services

Distribution

Marketing

Other

Figure 6.6   Action diagram of business opportunities.

be a tick or an indication of priority such as 'critical', 'desirable' and so on. This step of TIA is shown in Figure 6.7.

TIA is not highly rigorous but can be carried out relatively quickly. It provides an opportunity to analyse the opportunities of using IT and information networks in the functional areas of an organisation and may be used to prioritise developments in the application of these technologies.

Information technology investment analysis

IT investment analysis is concerned with targeting IT at the appropriate functional area of an organisation. IT budgets are, generally, increasing and IT should therefore be regarded as an investment in a growth area rather than merely a necessary expense. Consequently, it is important to evaluate whether current and future IT spending is allocated to where it is most needed and where it will realise the maximum value to the organisation. The analysis is approached within SPIN by posing a number of questions:

1. What is the profit potential of the business?
2. How appropriate is IT spending?
3. How risky is IT investment?
4. How is the performance of IT measured?

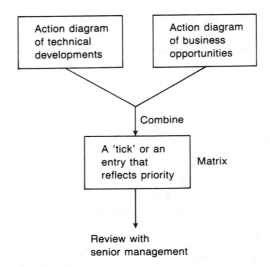

Figure 6.7 The final step of TIA.

1   What is the profit potential of the business?
A matrix is used to categorise business areas according to current and future profit
potential. This is illustrated in Figure 6.8 and is intended for use as a guide to directing
IT investment.

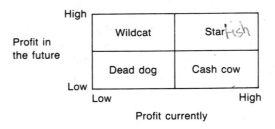

Figure 6.8 Profit potential matrix.

- *Dead dogs* are the business or product areas that provide little contribution
  currently and are not expected to provide future growth in revenue. IT should
  only be considered as a short-term measure and directed towards reducing costs
  or moving the area into a more profitable category.
- *Cash cows* are those areas that are the current high revenue areas and a major
  source of funding for future business developments. Cash cows are, however,
  relatively short-term; they are not expected to provide significant future revenue.
  For this category, use of IT should be directed towards increasing profitability,
  increasing the life of the cash cow or moving it into a more profitable category.
- *Stars* are the areas that provide significant income currently and are expected to

114

continue to do so in the future. In this category, an organisation may wish to increase profitability or extend the life of the star by the judicious use of IT.

- *Wildcats* are those areas that an organisation expects to be the stars and cash cows of the future. They are usually business areas, products or services that are still under development and do not contribute significantly to current profitability. IT should be directed in this category with caution. Once the risks are understood, IT investment should be directed to ensure that wildcats are more likely to turn into profitable categories.

This analysis will give a clear indication of the nature of the business or of its component units, products or services. It also serves to help to understand which of these is regarded as profitable and, therefore, will assist in making informed decisions concerning IT investment.

2   How appropriate is IT spending

One way to approach this question is to compare the overall costs of running the business with the costs of ISs. A much-simplified comparison is illustrated in Figure 6.9 for a hypothetical manufacturing company. The diagram shows that a relatively high proportion of IT investment is targeted at a low-cost area of the business. This area may indeed require ISs to support business activities, but the comparison indicates that other, high-cost areas of the business, which have a much greater impact on profitability, do not enjoy IT investment. By considering IT investment in high-cost areas, it may be possible to identify ways in which costs can be reduced and profitability increased.

It is useful to consider the following questions when evaluating how IT investment can have an impact on functional areas:

- Does IT impact upon efficiency, i.e. reduce the time it takes to perform business activities and reduce costs?
- Does IT impact upon effectiveness, i.e. add value to decision-making and other management procedures?
- Does IT help to overcome geographical and time-zone constraints in managing a dispersed organization?
- Does IT target particular CSFs, i.e. is IT allocated to functional areas that are responsible for the delivery of a CSF?

The answers to questions such as these will help to gain an insight into the nature of IT investment in functional areas of the organisation. It is important to know whether IT is directed to efficiency objectives or whether its use adds value or is innovative. This knowledge contributes to an understanding of the value of IT in an organisation and the way in which this value is perceived by senior managers.

3   How risky is IT investment?

Network technology is advancing rapidly. A new business venture based on new technology may involve an element of risk. Innovation via network technology can lead to success, but a number of organisations have experienced failure by misjudging

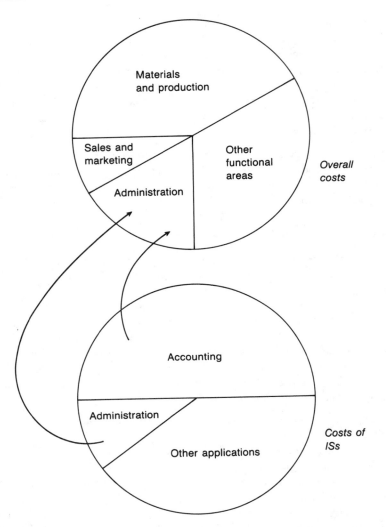

Figure 6.9 Comparison of overall costs with costs of information systems.

the market for network-based services (Keen, 1988, pp. 13–14). It is important, therefore, to assess carefully the risk of being an innovator in the use of network technology to deliver new services to users and customers. On the other hand, an organisation may be forced to follow competitors in implementing network services to maintain competitive position. In this case, it is necessary to assess the risk of not following the leaders.

4 How is the performance of IT measured?
Finally, to evaluate fully the potential of IT investment, it is necessary to identify and

116

monitor performance metrics for ISs. This is not an easy task, but should be attempted in order to evaluate the impact of investment in IT on the overall performance of the organisation.

In order to quantify the performance of ISs, a number of criteria present themselves. These include quantification of the following:

- Increase/decrease in sales revenue.
- Increase/decrease in market share.
- Increase/decrease in profitability.
- Increase/decrease in lead times for products/services.
- Increase/decrease in unit costs.
- Increase/decrease in business transaction costs.
- Increase/decrease in manufacturing/production errors.
- Increase/decrease in administrative errors.
- Increase/decrease in stockholding.

This will help to identify performance metrics. These are associated with the use of information systems and monitored over time.

IT investment analysis can make a contribution to the development of the application portfolio by measuring the value of existing and planned IT applications. Where possible, the former should be measured on an on-going basis and the latter should be estimated in an attempt to evaluate their value and justify their inclusion in the applications portfolio.

Value chain analysis

Porter and Miller's value chain analysis is an analytical tool that can assist in identifying options for using IT strategically. The analysis focuses on competitiveness and the role of technology in the activities and processes associated with an organisation's products or service delivery systems (Porter and Miller, 1985).

The value chain analysis examines an organisation's activities in terms of the scope for utilising IT within and between activities. The distinct activities are called 'value activities' because they add value to the product or service that buyers are willing to pay for. A business is profitable if the value it creates by selling a product or service exceeds the cost of performing the value activities. Consequently, it is important to identify ways in which each value activity uses information and, therefore, identify the potential impact of IT on value activities.

The typical primary and support value activities are represented in what Porter and Miller call the 'value chain'. The value chain for a typical manufacturing company is shown in Figure 6.10. The value chain shown in the diagram is a system of interdependent activities: the primary activities are those associated with the production, marketing, distribution and after-sales support or service of a product; the support activities are those that allow the primary activities to take place. Figure 6.10 also indicates examples of links between activities and shows external links.

Figure 6.10 also includes examples of the role of IT applications in an activity. IT can either apply directly to an activity or to the links between activities. In the latter

117

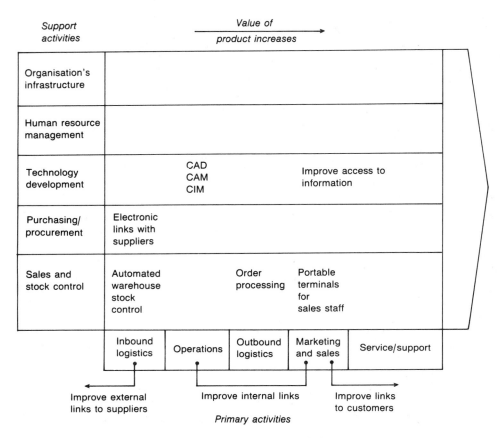

Figure 6.10 The value chain.

case, links extend beyond the organisation to suppliers and customers. Consequently, the value chain of a supplier is linked to that of the organisation, which, in turn, is linked to the value chain of a customer. Porter and Miller refer to this 'stream' of linked value chains with the term 'value system'. This concept is illustrated in Figure 6.11, for a number of suppliers and customers. The importance of understanding the value system is that the points at which value chains meet are potential areas for the exploitation of IT. For example, the feasibility of providing electronic links to major customers and suppliers could be investigated.

The outcome of value chain analysis (i.e. an understanding of the organisation's value system) provides no more than a high-level checklist of IT applications, a similar outcome to TIA (p. 112–14). However, the technique can be used to promote a strategic perspective and will provide an opportunity to calculate the cost and value of current and planned applications of IT. The other strength of the technique is that it focuses on internal and external links. This focus is important in the context of

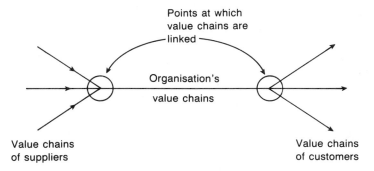

Figure 6.11 A value system.

information networks in that it begins to focus on the communications requirements of applications of IT that are associated with these links.

Information technology and competitive advantage

An approach that overlaps the two uppermost 'boxes' of Figure 6.1 focuses on the strategic posture of an organisation. It also begins to suggest where IT can bring advantage. Porter's model of five competitive forces has its place here (Porter, 1980). The model can be used to clarify business strategy and identify where IT applications may potentially yield competitive advantage in terms of defending the organisation against industry forces or influencing them in its favour. The five forces are as follows:

- The bargaining power of suppliers.
- The bargaining power of customers.
- The threat of new entrants.
- The threat of substitute products or services.
- The intensity of rivalry amongst competitors.

To gain and sustain competitive advantage over its rivals, an organisation must either perform its value activities at a lower cost than its rivals or perform them in a way that leads to product or service differentiation at a premium price. In order to achieve this, an organisation must assess its competitive position and assess how IT applications can create the potential for competitive advantage.

A first step in this analysis is to understand the implications of the five forces on the organisation concerned. This is summarised as follows:

Bargaining power of suppliers
- Threat of suppliers' power to increase prices.
- Costs involved in switching to another supplier.
- Degree of competition amongst suppliers.

Bargaining power of customers
- Power of customers to demand lower prices and improved services.
- Ease with which a customer can switch to another organisation to purchase products or services.

Threat of new entrants
- Presence of barriers to new entrants in terms of costs involved in becoming a competitor.
- Ease with which new entrants can bring lower cost products or services to market or differentiate products or services.

Threat of substitute products or services
- Ease with which customers can switch to substitutes.
- Nature of differentiation of substitutes.
- Relative cost of substitutes.

The intensity of rivalry amongst competitors
- The diversity of competitors
- Product differences amongst competitors
- Scope for competition on price
- Scope for competition on after-sales service or support.

Next, the organisation should assess how IT applications change the nature of competition. Porter (1985) suggests that IT does this in three ways:

1. IT changes the industry structure.
2. IT creates competitive advantage.
3. IT spawns new business.

According to Porter, these three effects are critical in understanding the impact of IT in a value system.

Changing industry structure
The structure of an industry sector is embodied by Porter's five forces (Figure 6.12). IT can alter each of the five forces in a number of ways. For example, organisations that have established electronic links between themselves and their larger suppliers and customers can 'lock in' trading partners into a business network. This practice alters the nature of competition among customers and suppliers by making it less easy and more costly to switch to another trading partner.

A defensive strategy to limit new entrants in a market is to erect barriers to entry. IT can, for example, increase economies of scale; raise the capital costs of entry; make pre-emptive strikes in a market which are difficult to imitate quickly or cheaply. Conversely, IT can be exploited effectively to break down barriers to entry by altering the traditional economies of scale by the exploitation of specialised or flexible technologies.

EXAMPLE 2

The building societies in the United Kingdom are able, as a result of legislation, to provide customer services previously associated with the major clearing banks. IT has played a major role in this move towards retail banking operations and helped the societies to compete effectively with banks.

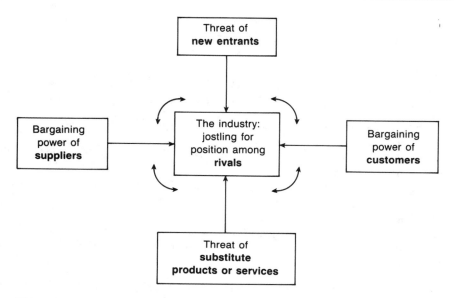

Figure 6.12 Porter's five forces of industry competition. (Source: Porter, 1985.)

IT has become a source of innovation; it can be built into new products and services and can add value to them, thereby generating substitutes in the market. A value-added service often helps to differentiate an organisation from its rivals and attracts customers to its products.

EXAMPLE 3

> Electronic databases are substituting for literature search and consultancy firms. Subscribers to databases can search for references, patents, company information and products, and so on without resort to a specialist research consultant. Subscribers avoid the cost of consultants and reduce the time taken to conduct searches.

Responding to rivalry amongst competitors boils down to one of two mechanisms: either compete or collaborate. IT can be used aggressively as a competitive weapon or it can become the basis for collaboration in order to reduce rivalry. In the former case, IT can be used to establish a service that is costly for rivals to imitate, and the organisation that takes this lead often sustains a competitive advantage for some considerable time. On the other hand, collaboration may be suggested by the availability of communications networks to share the delivery of, for example, financial services.

EXAMPLE 4

> Some banks and building societies in the United Kingdom share telecommunications and automatic teller machine (ATM) facilities as

121

distribution channels for their services. This collaboration shares costs and resources and is attractive to customers.

Creating competitive advantage

According to Porter (1985), it is likely that IT will play a strategic role in an industry that is characterised by one or both of the following factors:

1. High information intensity in the value chain. For example:
   ● a large number of customers or suppliers;
   ● a product that requires a large quantity of information to market and sell;
   ● a product line with many varieties;
   ● a product composed of many parts;
   ● a large number of steps involved in the manufacturing process.
2. High information intensity in the product. For example:
   ● a product that mainly provides information (i.e. an information service);
   ● a product whose operation or use requires the buyer to process a substantial amount of information.

In order to create competitive advantage, it is the task of the organisation to assess the existing and potential information intensity of the value chain activities and products associated with its competitive position. Activities that represent a significant proportion of cost or that are critical to differentiation bear close scrutiny, particularly if they are supported by significant information processing. In addition to a close examination of its value chain, the organisation should consider how IT might permit a change in competitive scope. In essence, the organisation should assess how IT applications can do the following:

● Help to lower costs.
● Enhance product differentiation.
● Change competitive scope to move into new markets.

Spawning new business

IT has given birth to new business opportunities and services. New services are technologically feasible through the use of computing and telecommunications systems; electronic messaging and information services are examples of such opportunities. IT can create new business opportunities from existing operations. Organisations with excess computing and telecommunications capacity embedded in their value chain have generated revenue by selling this capacity and providing services to customers outside their traditional markets.

Some organisations are also able to sell information and expertise that is a by-product of their existing operations.

Scandania are developing the business activities of its Computer Services Division. These activities will generate a new source of revenue. Scandania are also evaluating the feasibility of establishing a database of information

relating to research and development which is relevant to its industry sector. This information will be sold to interested parties.

In summary, identifying new ways to spawn new business opportunities and revenue requires asking questions such as the following:

- What information generated (or potentially generated) could the organisation sell?
- What excess or spare information-processing and telecommunications capacity is available for the purpose of delivering services on behalf of customers?

Although numerous case studies have demonstrated the contribution that IT has made towards achieving and sustaining competitive advantage, they tend not to go into detail about how this is achieved in practice. It is not IT that is the catalyst; other factors associated with the management style and culture of the organisation are necessary prerequisites for the effective exploitation of IT. Organisations that claim competitive advantage through the use of IT have often made pre-emptive strikes and have pursued their business vision with vigour. Competitors may take some time to imitate and catch up with the leaders. Nevertheless, competitive advantage often becomes a strategic necessity. For example, the leaders in the implementation of ATM networks enjoyed competitive advantage for a period of time; however, both large and medium-sized banks and building societies (in the United Kingdom) operate ATM networks. This application of IT is of strategic necessity rather than competitive advantage. A similar example is evidenced by the use of scanning devices at supermarket checkouts; almost all supermarket chains in the United Kingdom have installed this technology, essentially as a matter of necessity.

The analytical technique discussed in this subsection indicates when IT can be deployed to strategic advantage or to strategic effect. Used at the highest level in an organisation, the technique is a powerful aid to thinking strategically and will help to generate key entries to the applications portfolio.

Using information networks strategically

We are almost at the point in the strategy phase of SPIN when we can generate the applications portfolio (see Figure 6.1). Before doing so, however, it is worthwhile reiterating that Figure 6.1 also shows that the next deliverable is the set of communications requirements which arise from the entries in the applications portfolio. This underlines the important point that communications facilities are the delivery vehicle for the entries in the applications portfolio and form an integral, underpinning component of these applications.

Therefore, it is important to carry out an analysis of the strategic use of information networks in conjunction with the SISP techniques that have been discussed in the previous subsections of Section 6.4. This analysis will form the framework within which to focus on those applications that emerge as candidates for the applications portfolio and require communications facilities for their delivery. This subsection, therefore, brings together and summarises the principal ways in which information networks underpin applications of IT. Most of these applications of information networks have been mentioned already in this chapter but it is worthwhile summarising them here. This will be achieved by considering four perspectives:

- Time compression.
- Geographic restrictions.
- Relationship with trading partners.
- New business opportunities.

Time compression

This includes applications and associated benefits such as the following:

- Access to and transmission of information internally; improved internal communication.
- Reduced time in carrying out business transactions; reduced costs.
- Electronic ordering of parts for production; reduced stockholding and just-in-time (JIT) manufacturing.
- Information services to trading partners (suppliers, customers, clients); improved services.
- EDI with trading partners; improved cash flow and shorter order-delivery times.

Geographic restrictions

These are largely associated with the degree of centralisation or decentralisation of the organisational structure and management style of an organisation. A number of issues present themselves:

- An enterprise-wide information network can lead to greater control over dispersed sites or business units.
- Integration of dispersed business units will realise benefits of decentralised management by using an information network to monitor distributed business units.
- The organisational structure of the organisation can be changed; distributed operations can be combined with centralised management; an information network can facilitate lines of reporting to the centre.
- A distributed organisation can get closer to its customers and create effective distribution channels; an information network is a necessary facility to underpin this policy.

Relationship with trading partners

These can be changed dramatically by the use of information networks in the following ways:

- Electronic links improve access to the organisation for suppliers and customers.
- 'Lock in' of trading partners to the organisation's order-processing system.
- EDI of business documents.

New business opportunities
These arise, essentially, as a result of using an information network as the delivery vehicle to deliver new services and generate new revenue. This is achieved by providing services to customers such as organisations that do not operate a network but whose services depend on one.

Clearly, these opportunities will only arise as a result of the availability of sufficient capacity in an organisation's information network, over and above that which is needed to deliver existing communications facilities.

The issues raised under the four headings above will help to think strategically about information networks and will contribute to the identification of communications requirements of candidates for the applications portfolio.

6.5   The applications portfolio

The applications portfolio is the first deliverable in the strategy phase of SPIN (Figure 6.1). Essentially, it is a checklist of retained and new applications that has been developed as a result of the review of business objectives and an evaluation of opportunities of using ISs (Section 6.4). It should, however, be thought of as more than just a checklist; each entry will have been arrived at after careful consideration as to its contribution to the business strategy of the organisation. In essence, the inclusion of a retained application or the justification of a new application will be based on one or more of the following factors:

- Whether it is a strategic application.
- Whether it is a support or operational application.
- The cost of supporting the application.
- The value or benefit of the application to the organisation.
- Its inclusion as part of the business vision of the organisation with little or no cost – benefit analysis.
- A strong case has been argued that the application is a strategic necessity.

The candidate applications for the applications portfolio are documented by using a template such as the one shown in Figure 6.13. Applications are classified by site, by business unit or by any other appropriate or useful means. Level 3 merely states what the application is and level 4 (not shown in the diagram) provides a detailed description of each application. The template forms a useful reference for anyone wishing to see, at a glance, an overview of the organisation's applications. To be of continued use in this respect, the applications portfolio template must, of course, be kept up to date.

The concept of templates used in the context of network planning was first introduced by Clemons, Keen and Kimbrough. The template of Figure 6.13 is derived from this concept (Clemons *et al.*, 1984).

The applications portfolio for Scandania is shown in Figure 6.14(a) and (b).

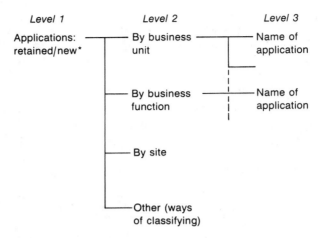

* A separate template is required for retained applications and for new applications

Figure 6.13 The applications portfolio template. (Note: level 4 is not shown in this figure.)

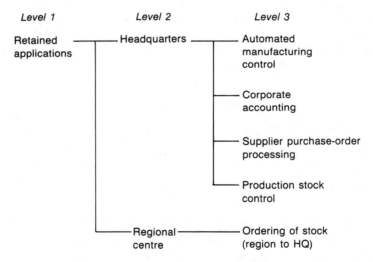

Figure 6.14(a) The applications portfolio for Scandania: retained applications.

6.6 Communications requirements

The next deliverable is the qualitative communications requirements (see Figure 6.1). These are documented by means of a high-level matrix such as the one shown in Figure 6.15. The entries in the matrix are qualitative – either a tick to register that the requirement is necessary or an entry such as 'mandatory' or 'desirable' to indicate

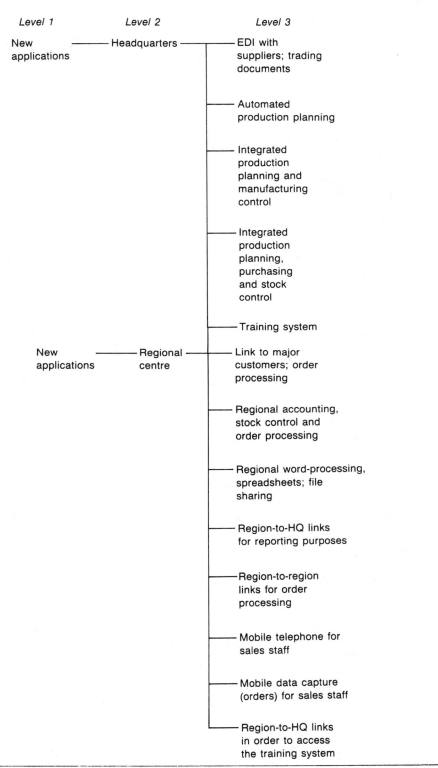

	Level 1	Level 2	Level 3

Level 1   Level 2   Level 3

New applications —— Headquarters —— EDI with suppliers; trading documents

—— Automated production planning

—— Integrated production planning and manufacturing control

—— Integrated production planning, purchasing and stock control

—— Training system

New applications —— Regional centre —— Link to major customers; order processing

—— Regional accounting, stock control and order processing

—— Regional word-processing, spreadsheets; file sharing

—— Region-to-HQ links for reporting purposes

—— Region-to-region links for order processing

—— Mobile telephone for sales staff

—— Mobile data capture (orders) for sales staff

—— Region-to-HQ links in order to access the training system

Figure 6.14(b)   The applications portfolio for Scandania: new applications.

Information	Requirement			
	Intra-site	Inter-site	Mobile	Inter-business
Data (all applications) Transaction processing ● Enquiry ● Update File transfer File sharing				
Text Telex Electronic mail Document transfer				
Voice Telephony Store and retrieve				
Fixed image Facsimile Graphics file				
Moving image Full motion TV Slow-scan TV Freeze-frame TV				

Figure 6.15   The high-level communications requirements matrix.

a priority rating. The high-level matrix is completed in order to indicate the overall scope of communications requirements arising from the applications portfolio and from voice requirements.

EXAMPLE 5

An insurance company, based in the south of the United Kingdom, used a high level requirements matrix to identify network resources to meet the organisation's communications requirements. The matrix provided a vehicle for discussion and provided a framework within which the development of a communications strategy took place. Entries in the matrix were indicative of the priority and effort required to commit resources.

The high-level matrix for Scandania is shown in Figure 6.16.

In the analysis phase (Chapter 8), the high-level matrix is decomposed into as many low-level matrices as required. The purpose of this is to permit the

128

Category of information	Requirement					
	Intra-site		Inter-site		Mobile	Inter-business
	HQ	Region	HQ–Region	Region–Region		
Data (all apps) Terminal access:						
— Local	✓	✓	NA	NA		
— Remote	✓	✓	✓	✓		
Transaction:						
— Enquiry	✓	✓	✓	✓		
— Update	✓	✓	✓	✓		
File transfer	✓	✓	✓			✓
File sharing	✓	✓				
Voice telephony	✓	✓	✓		✓	

NA, not applicable

Figure 6.16   The high-level communications requirements matrix for Scandania.

documentation of detailed communications requirements for each application in the applications portfolio on the basis of, for example, the following:

● Intra-site requirements, for each site.
● Inter-site requirements, for each site-to-site link.
● Inter-business, for each link to each trading partner.

It is necessary to quantify the data category, in particular, during the analysis phase for *each* application in the applications portfolio in order to document communications requirements.

6.7   High-level network configuration

The lower part of Figure 6.1 indicates that modelling techniques are used to generate the final deliverable of the strategy phase: the (first cut) high-level network configuration. This provides a high-level view of the organisation in terms of the information flows between sites and between the main processes. It is used, subsequently, in the design phase of SPIN to assist in identifying where network links and nodes are required. An overview of the steps involved in developing the network configuration is shown in Figure 6.17.

Modelling is used as an effective way of gaining an organisation-wide view of the information flow across functional boundaries and between sites. The organisation is described in terms of narrative and diagrams which cover the following:

● The organisation – showing where main business functions are carried out.
● Data – showing data associated with main processes.

129

- Processes – showing main processes within the organisation.
- Information flow – showing the links by which information flows internally and externally between processes, functions, sites and users.

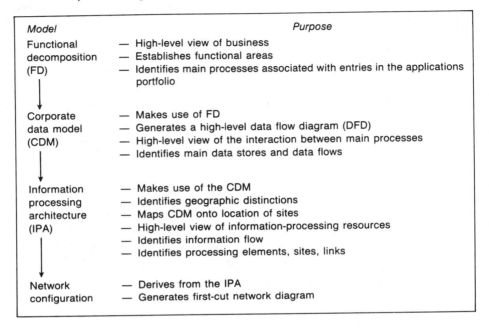

Model	Purpose
Functional decomposition (FD)	— High-level view of business — Establishes functional areas — Identifies main processes associated with entries in the applications portfolio
Corporate data model (CDM)	— Makes use of FD — Generates a high-level data flow diagram (DFD) — High-level view of the interaction between main processes — Identifies main data stores and data flows
Information processing architecture (IPA)	— Makes use of the CDM — Identifies geographic distinctions — Maps CDM onto location of sites — High-level view of information-processing resources — Identifies information flow — Identifies processing elements, sites, links
Network configuration	— Derives from the IPA — Generates first-cut network diagram

Figure 6.17 Modelling techniques.

Each of the techniques in Figure 6.17 will be discussed in turn, with examples of their use where appropriate. Scandania will be used as a straightforward illustration of the modelling process used to generate the deliverable. In practice, the diagrams associated with modelling of this kind can be highly detailed and more complex than those associated with Scandania.

6.7.1 Functional decomposition

Functional decomposition (FD) is a proven technique for providing a model of the functions and processes within an organisation. When used in strategic planning, the organisation's functional areas are decomposed until all the processes that make up each business activity are revealed. The outcome is a list of all the processes and a description of each one.

EXAMPLE 6

As part of a data-modelling exercise at one of the United Kingdom's higher education establishments, functional decomposition was carried out to establish the processes performed by each administrative department. Five main functions were identified, each of which was decomposed into its main processes. Each main process was, in turn, decomposed into subprocesses. The outcome was a list of several dozen subprocesses, each of which formed the basis of program design.

In the strategy phase of SPIN, FD is used to identify the functional areas of the organisation and the main processes associated with the entries in the applications portfolio.

Functional area	*Main processes*
Production	Planning Manufacturing
Finance	Corporate accounting Regional accounting
Sales (wholesale customers)	Regional sales order processing
Stock control	Production stock control Regional stock control and replenishment
Purchasing	Supplier purchase orders
Computer services	Includes provision of training both internally and to external customers

Figure 6.18   Functional decomposition: Scandania.

The main processes for Scandania are summarised in Figure 6.18.

6.7.2   The corporate data model

A corporate data model (CDM) provides a high level Data Flow Diagram (DFD) of an organisation. It shows the main processes and data flows between them.

EXAMPLE 7

The organisation of Example 6 (above) generated a CDM as part of the data-modelling exercise. This showed a high-level view of the data flow between seven major systems (processes) and eight sources or recipients (external entities) of information. The purpose of the CDM was to assist in gaining a corporate-wide view of information access requirements across functional boundaries. The CDM formed part of the input to database design for the organisation.

131

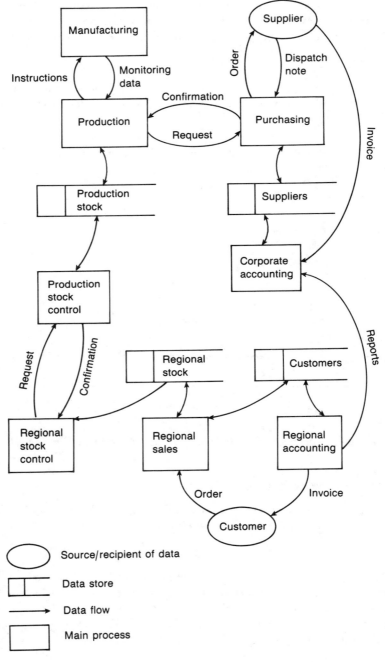

Figure 6.19 Corporate data model: Scandania.

EXAMPLE 8

One of the (formerly public) utilities in the United Kingdom conducted an IT strategy study, with the objective of reviewing how IT should continue to support its corporate business strategy. This was a wide-ranging study, part of which examined overall information requirements. A CDM was developed in order to provide a comprehensive, integrated view of the organisation's information requirements. The set of DFDs helped to identify functional boundaries and geographic groupings and distinctions, the latter showing the occurrence of centrally held data and divisionally held (distributed) data.

The CDM for Scandania is shown in Figure 6.19.

6.7.3 The information-processing architecture

The information-processing architecture (IPA) maps the CDM onto the given and desired geographic distinctions, i.e. it identifies information flows within and between sites and to trading partners.

EXAMPLE 9

As part of the IT strategy study in the organisation of Example 8, the IPA was developed. The purpose of this was to present an organisation-wide view of the distribution of IT facilities. The IPA identifies the logical relationships and data flow between elements of the CDM and maps these onto the location of users (business functions). The IPA includes current and planned IT facilities.

The IPA for Scandania is shown in Figure 6.20.

6.7.4 The high-level network configuration

The high-level network configuration is a first-cut network diagram derived from the IPA. It shows the location of sites; data-processing elements; and intra-site, inter-site and inter-business links.

The high-level network configuration for Scandania is shown in Figure 6.21. The figure shows the first-cut network diagram for the data network associated with headquarters; only one regional centre is shown. It is proposed to consider the feasibility of designing a private network to facilitate data communications from region-to-region and region-to-headquarters.

In addition to data communications, a private voice network is proposed. Integrated voice and data inter-site circuits will be considered at the design stage. Mobile telephony (using one of the public operators in the United Kingdom) is required for sales staff in most regions.

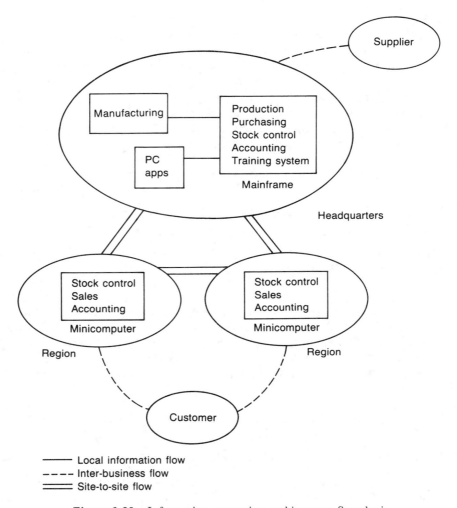

Figure 6.20 Information-processing architecture: Scandania.

EDI will be evaluated for trading with suppliers. Dial-up access to the regional order-processing systems will be implemented for several of the larger customers in each region.

Reference to Figure 6.1 will indicate that all the deliverables of the Strategy Phase have now been generated, namely:

● The applications portfolio.
● Communications requirements (qualitative).
● The high-level network configuration.

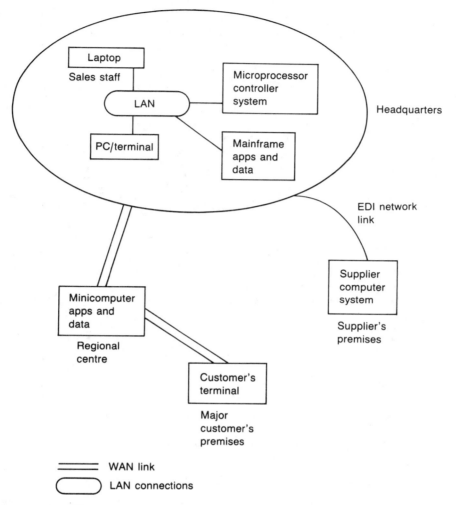

Figure 6.21   High-level network configuration: Scandania.

Each of these deliverables is used in subsequent phases of SPIN. The applications portfolio is used to guide the analyst during the data-gathering stage of the analysis phase; the communications requirements matrix is expanded and quantified in the analysis phase; the network configuration is used to assist in the design of the network in the design phase.

6.8   Summary

This chapter has described the techniques used in the strategy phase of SPIN. Three deliverables have been identified and a case study has been used to illustrate the kind of documentation that is required for each deliverable. The purpose of each deliverable has been identified. The next chapter describes the feasibility phase of SPIN.

CHAPTER 7

The feasibility phase

7.1 Preamble

This chapter can be read out of sequence. The reader may study the chapters on the analysis, design, implementation and management phases of SPIN and then return to the feasibility phase after Chapter 11. This will give the reader an insight into phases 3–6 before considering the tasks involved in the feasibility phase.

In an information network project, the feasibility phase takes place after the strategy phase and before the analysis phase (see Figure 5.3). Therefore, the sequence of the SPIN phases is preserved in the order of the chapters.

The tasks involved in the feasibility phase of SPIN closely resemble those required for the feasibility phase or preliminary investigation phase of any information systems development project. The reader should consult the Further Reading section for references to suitable books on systems analysis.

7.2 Introduction

The scope of a feasibility study varies from project to project. It will depend on the scope of the applications in the applications portfolio and the way in which these are justified in the strategy phase (Section 6.5). Therefore, the network planner should apply the principles of feasibility judiciously. This chapter describes a framework for a feasibility study; it is not the intention here to be prescriptive about how a feasibility study should be carried out or how much detail to include at this stage of the project.

Feasibility is particularly appropriate for information network developments that have the following characteristics:

- Require high investment.
- Require long timescales.
- Are high risk, i.e. rigorous justification is necessary.
- Are innovative or strategic.

Feasibility starts with the deliverables from the strategy phase. These are as follows:

- The applications portfolio (Section 6.5) – the value of each entry is assessed as part of the strategy phase.
- Communications requirements matrices (Section 6.6) – these are qualitative.
- The high-level network configuration (Section 6.7) – this identifies local and wide area network links.

The principal deliverable of the feasibility phase is the feasibility report.

7.3 Objectives of the feasibility phase

There are two main objectives of the feasibility phase:

1. To develop and present a business case for the project, i.e. justify the commitment of resources to the remaining phases of the project.
2. To examine the technical, organisational and financial feasibility of the information network project, i.e. examine the feasibility of the scope of the information network before detailed analysis and design is undertaken.

The following sections of this chapter describe how these objectives are achieved.

7.4 The business case

The business case involves gathering information to enable the organisational, technical and financial feasibility of the information network project to be assessed. The findings are presented to senior management (in the form of a report) to inform them of the costs, benefits and risks of the project.

7.4.1 Organisational feasibility

Organisational feasibility determines the requirements associated with the implementation and management of network resources. These include the following:

- Management procedures to implement and manage network resources (Section 5.6.2).
- Skills and tools to manage the network on a day-to-day basis (Chapter 11).
- Recruitment and training.

These requirements should be matched with existing information systems management in the organisation and any deficiencies highlighted.

7.4.2 Technical feasibility

Technical feasibility considers the communications requirements associated with the applications portfolio and estimates the network capacity required. This involves

138

estimating network traffic and evaluating network options in the light of these estimates.

Data gathering is undertaken for applications that are likely to require significant network capacity. For retained applications, peak network traffic is estimated. Sources of data include the following:

- Users: the number of transactions during, for example, the busiest hour in a given period is estimated; given the size of each transaction (in bytes), network traffic is quantified.
- Network management tools (Chapter 11): some of these tools provide statistics on network traffic in both WANs and LANs.
- Other, specialised monitoring systems are often used in host computers to measure transactions between terminals and the host.

(Section 8.5 describes, in detail, how communications requirements are quantified.)

In voice networks, call-logging systems monitor network traffic.

In addition to these 'snapshots' of current network traffic, it is essential to estimate its growth. This requires knowledge of business trends associated with retained applications. This task is made easier if historical data is available. In the absence of these data, advice should be sought from senior management in an attempt to forecast growth in business activities that are associated with retained applications.

Estimating network traffic for new applications in the applications portfolio can be difficult. Nevertheless, this should be attempted in order to estimate the capacity requirements of the network. Experience of similar applications in the organisation may be helpful. In the absence of these data, estimates will have to rely on projections of business activity and market research.

In order to evaluate network options, a number of issues present themselves for investigation:

- Does the current network provide sufficient scope for growth, given the new communications requirements?
- Will a new network have to be designed and installed?
- Do current public/private circuits/services offer sufficient capacity for retained and new communications requirements?
- Do network software, hardware and standards exist to support communications requirements?
- What network technology are competitors using; how much did it cost them and how long did it take them to implement their networks?
- What are the technical risks, i.e. is the proposed network solution proven or new technology?
- What are the risks of overestimating network capacity and creating spare capacity?
- What are the risks of underestimating network capacity and not meeting growth in demand for additional network capacity?

The results of this investigation assist in evaluating network options in the light of the network capacity requirements and the high-level network configuration.

7.4.3 Financial feasibility

It is insufficient to refer vaguely to 'productivity' or 'competitive edge', when justifying the cost of implementing network facilities. It is more effective to focus on benefits and value to the business, even though this may be difficult to quantify. Therefore, financial feasibility concentrates on the benefits, risks and costs of the information network project.

The value of each entry in the applications portfolio is assessed in the strategy phase (pp. 114–17). The criteria for this assessment, which are reiterated here, are as follows:

- Impact on revenue.
- Reduced cost of delivering products/services.
- Reduced business transaction costs.
- Reduced unit production costs.
- Improved customer service; difficult to quantify, but could be translated into increased sales revenue.
- A response to market trends or new business opportunities; expressed in increased revenue.

This assessment will form the basis of the quantification of benefits associated with the entries in the Application Portfolio.

The outcome of technical feasibility (Section 7.4.2) assists in estimating the overall costs of implementing the components of the high-level network configuration. The scope of costs includes the following:

- Capital costs of hardware and software.
- On-going costs of network services supplied by PTOs in the case of WANs (difficult to predict future costs).
- On-going costs of supporting and managing network facilities.

Finally, it should be possible to compare overall costs with benefits using the information gathered and draw appropriate conclusions about the overall feasibility of the project.

7.5 The feasibility report

The feasibility report formalises the business case. It can be handed over to senior management during a presentation, the purpose of which is to summarise the findings of the Feasibility Phase. This provides a decision point in SPIN, before full analysis and design are undertaken.

A suggested structure for the report follows:

1. Management summary:
   - a brief synopsis of the report.
2. Statement of the business objectives:
   - available from the Strategy Phase.

3. Statement of the deliverables from the strategy phase:
   - the applications portfolio;
   - communications requirements matrices;
   - high-level network configuration.
4. The business case:
   - Technical feasibility – refer to the high-level network configuration; estimates of network capacity; evaluation of network options.
   - Organisational feasibility – network management (NM) requirements; human resources and NM tools (Chapter 11).
   - Financial feasibility – benefits, costs and risks (the latter reiterated from the strategy phase (Section 6.4.2)).
5. Resource requirements for the analysis and design phases:
   - human resources;
   - hardware and software support.

7.6 Summary

This chapter has presented a formal framework for carrying out a feasibility study within SPIN. The framework highlights the information that is gathered, without specifying the depth and level of detail. The latter will depend on the scope of the project; the network analyst should apply analytical skills accordingly.

If this chapter has been read out of sequence, the reader is reminded to return to the Postscript, which follows Chapter 11.

CHAPTER 8

The analysis phase

8.1 Introduction

Systems analysis and design is a necessary aspect of any development project, whether the project is to develop a car, information system or a communications network. Systems analysis and design is concerned with the establishment of a system to process existing statistics and gather information in order to formulate proposals and recommendations, allowing management to make more informed decisions. This involves the following main functions:

- The review and evaluation of existing systems.
- The specification of new requirements.
- The design and specification of new systems to meet the stated requirements.

A successful project to develop a communications network satisfies not only the functional requirements identified by application workloads (e.g. access requirements), but also service-level requirements such as response times, throughput, extensibility and cost. As with information systems development projects, the future maintenance and management implications of a particular design must also be considered.

Typically, network analysts tend to adopt a technology-oriented approach to enhancing the network without due regard to the user and the interface through which the user gains access to network services. This issue is becoming more important due to the trend towards organisations allowing customers to access on-line applications. Network analysts are responsible for designing the total network environment including security, and the user interface to the network. Consequently it is important to adopt a systems approach to the design of a communications network to ensure that all functional and non-functional requirements are considered. The old adage 'a problem well stated is half solved' is particularly applicable to network analysis and design.

In this chapter we will focus on the analysis phase of SPIN. It is difficult to separate the processes of analysis and design as many passes through these phases are necessary in order to arrive at the correct system architecture and topology. The

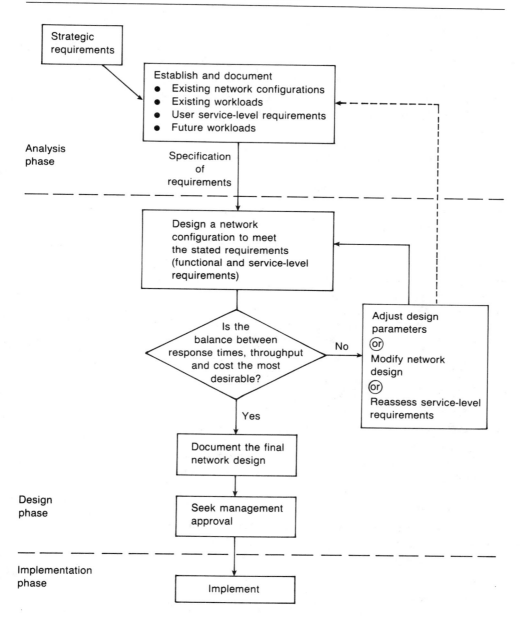

Figure 8.1(a) A network analysis as design methodology.

correctness of a particular design is measured by achieving an appropriate balance between network functionality, service levels and cost. Arriving at an agreed compromise will clearly involve an iterative process as illustrated in Figure 8.1(a).

143

A fictitious case study will be used to illustrate some of the activities involved in this phase. Although fictitious, it is based on a real-life environment with which the authors are familiar. The case study is used for illustrative purposes to highlight the process of network analysis and design. Consequently it concentrates on a particular new application: the Scandania Training booking system. The principles and procedures illustrated apply to any new application being developed.

8.2   The analysis phase in outline

The objectives of the network planner are as follows:

- To provide the network services necessary to facilitate achievement of the business goals of the enterprise.
- To deliver responsive, high-quality and secure network services at an affordable cost to end users.

It is therefore essential to formulate a detailed specification of how well the network is expected to function. The principle objective of the analysis phase is to formulate these detailed requirements, using appropriate volumetrics, to provide data for the design phase of SPIN. Any systems design approach is reliant on the availability of meaningful input data. The GIGO (garbage in/garbage out) adage still applies and, if one is not careful, an analysis and design exercise will produce believable but meaningless results.

The major pieces of information to be determined are as follows:

- An accurate description of the existing communications network.
- Traffic flow and workload during the busy hour for the existing network configuration.
- The adequacy (or not) of the present communications network.
- Future growth projections and new workload demand for network services.
- Future service-level requirements.
- Budget constraints.

These requirements must be clearly stated and understood to ensure that the design phase is successful. Requirements analysis can be viewed from two perspectives, as illustrated in Figure 8.1(b):

1. A 'top-down' requirements analysis. This perspective looks at the communications infrastructure required to underpin the organisation's high-priority or strategic applications. These requirements have already been identified in the strategic phase of SPIN.
2. A 'bottom-up' requirements analysis. This perspective looks at the infrastructure requirements for the existing application workloads.

We identify future growth trends, present deficiencies in the level of service offered, and other factors that generate a demand for additional network resources.

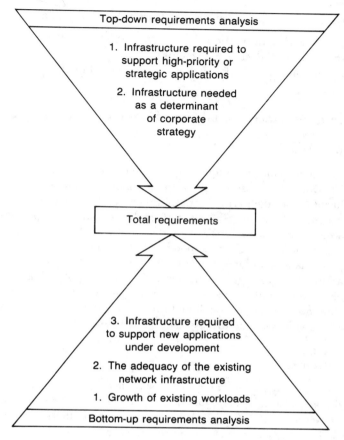

Figure 8.1(b)   Analysis of requirements.

Although collecting these data may take a long time and require a great deal of effort, the effort is well worth it. In the case where an existing network is to be enhanced, much of the data should exist as part of the network inventory. With existing, large networks, network management tools should be in regular use providing additional data on the current capacity and performance level of the network. With appropriate use of naming conventions and data structuring, the very detailed network performance database can be used to extract and summarise data for the purposes of planning network capacity.

It is important to maintain regularly updated performance and capacity management databases so that both short-term and long-term planning needs are met. Both databases should be established from the same data sources. There are many software products on the market that provide the tools and procedures for establishing and maintaining these databases.

The following are the main deliverables from the analysis phase:

- A summary of traffic information.
- A summary of service-level requirements.
- A more detailed network configuration containing volumetric data.

8.3   The quantitative analysis of communications networks

8.3.1   Introduction

The network planner aims to design a communications network to meet certain requirements. It would be irresponsible of the planner to propose a solution without assessing the likelihood of the particular design meeting the stated requirements. This assessment requires a quantitative analysis of the behaviour of the proposed network under given workloads. Three types of models are used for quantitative analysis: measurement, analytic and simulation models. The key factor that determines which is the most appropriate technique to use is the current position within the life-cycle of the application of concern (i.e. whether it is a new application or an existing application being significantly modified). In most cases validation is usefully carried out by employing more than one modelling technique in an evaluation exercise (if time permits). The following sections discuss each model type.

8.3.2   Measurement

Measurement of a system under evaluation is possible only if a previous version of the system, or a similar existing system, can be used to generate measurement data. The advantage of measurement is that it is more convincing to others than simulation or analytical modelling. Measurement requires the use of hardware and software resources and an upredictable amount of time to capture the necessary data. The use of measurement can be just as error prone as other methods, and the analyst should therefore interpret measurement data carefully and use the correct analytical tools. As with all evaluation techniques, measurement results should be validated against expert intuition and other criteria. The accuracy and cost of a measurement exercise depend on how closely the system being measured matches the system of concern in the real world.

8.3.3   Analytic models

This type of model makes use of mathematical equations to describe the behaviour of the communication network and to predict the performance of the network. The analytic models inevitably are simplified by use of an agreed set of simplifying assumptions. These assumptions mean that only an approximate solution to the real-world system results. The accuracy of the model therefore depends, among other factors, on how well the assumptions reflect the real-world situation.

146

Analytic models relevant to communication networks usually adopt a probabilistic approach which recognises the existence of random variation and chance elements in the real world. Queuing theory is usually the foundation of any analytic model used. The queueing system is described using the following components:

- The arrival process describing how messages or calls arrive in the system from the outside world.
- The service process describing the length of time that a server (e.g. a communications line) will be occupied by the message or call (this is a function of the expected message length and length distribution).
- The number of servers and the service rate.
- The queue discipline for deciding which messages or calls to serve next.
- Whether or not there is a limit to the number of messages or calls waiting to be serviced.

The above components determine the data that need to be collected by the network analyst during the analysis phase.

8.3.4 Simulation models

Simulation models represent the communication network characteristics as a set of computer models (implemented as computer programs) of the network. A simulation exercise systematically builds a model, produces benchmark data, alters the model adding more realism, and so on until the simulation model accurately reflects the network performance described by the various benchmark data. The baseline simulation model is then used to predict the performance levels of the network due to future workloads.

The advantage of simulation models over analytic models is that potentially any network feature can be modelled and to any level of detail. The more detail that is included in the model, however, the more complex the data-gathering exercise and the more cumbersome and costly the model construction exercise. A change in any one parameter usually means re-running the entire simulation. Simplifying assumptions therefore are equally applicable to simulation models. The data required for a simulation model depend on the design of the model itself and are therefore product specific.

In practice, both analytic and simulation models have their use in modelling a communication network. Analytic modelling is very useful in a scoping exercise to reduce the number of design options to be considered. Once a narrow set of options are determined, simulation and analytic models can be used to model each option at a detailed level. Potentially, simulation models can produce a higher level of accuracy if they have been constructed to model the real-world network more closely than is achievable using an analytic model.

8.3.5 Identifying workloads to be modelled

The analysis phase of SPIN identifies the requirements to be serviced by the communications network. The existing and new workloads that will make use of the network are too numerous to engage in detailed modelling of every workload. Therefore, the network analyst must decide which workloads are important enough to be worth establishing detailed requirements and subsequent modelling. Each workload selected will be later converted into a workload model at the design phase of SPIN using appropriate network-modelling software.

The Pareto 80/20 rule suggests that 80 per cent of the network load is generated by only 20 per cent of the workloads being serviced by the network. The selection of the 20 per cent requires judgement and experience on the part of the network analyst, combined with data on existing usage of the network and strategic requirements as identified by the strategic phase of SPIN. Each workload selected requires a detailed analysis of requirements, such as the following:

- How quickly is each transaction (corresponding to a single message pair) expected to provide the user with a response?
- What is the expected arrival rate of each transaction?
- What is the average time and variability required for receiving a dial tone on the voice network after going off-hook?
- What is the average time and variability required to make a connection across the voice network?

For existing workloads, these data should already be known and documented in the form of a service-level agreement (SLA). For new workloads, some of these data may have been captured during the development of the application.

8.4   Defining service-level requirements

Measures of how well a network should function differ depending on whether the analyst is designing a voice or non-voice network. The following sections identify the principle measures of service-level requirements likely to influence the design of the network architecture and topology. These measures define the parameters against which the quality of the service delivered to end-users can be measured.

8.4.1   Response time requirements

Data networks
For on-line and interactive workloads, the total response time is usually defined as the average elapsed time from the moment the terminal is ready to transmit (i.e. the user presses 'Enter' at the keyboard after the last character of the input message) to the time the *entire* response (i.e. the last character of the message) is received. This most accurately reflects applications in which the complete output message is accepted into the terminal's receive buffer and checked for accuracy before the entire message is displayed on the screen.

For streams of batched requests (batch jobs), response time is alternatively known as *turnaround time*, which is defined as the time between the submission of a batch job and the completion of its output (this includes the time to read the input).

The total response time will consist of the sum of the network response time and the host response time. The host response time consists of the activity required in satisfying the request, including field editing, message routeing, message interpretation, data manipulation and calculation, and database access. It is important to realise that the delay due to the network is only one component of the total response time. Therefore host and network capacity planning must be an integrated exercise to ensure a balance between optimising network response times and other components of the total response time. It is usually necessary to model the host response time to begin with since this normally represents the largest component of the total response time.

For slow terminals working at, say, 1200 bps, a message could take 5 seconds to be displayed on the screen. In this case an alternative definition of response time is the average elapsed time from the moment the terminal is ready to transmit to the time the *first* character is received and displayed. Throughout this book we will use the former definition.

Ideally, any response time requirement should ideally be specified in terms of both the average response time and variability of the response time. This is because they relate to user expectation. Numerous studies have shown that consistency of response time is much more important than a reasonable average response time. The user can adjust working practices around a consistently 'slow' (but not too slow!) response time. However, highly variable response times frustrate users and cause dissatisfaction due to the resulting disruption to working practices.

Variability of the response time can be specified either as a standard deviation or as a percentile (e.g. a 95th percentile value). For example, a response time requirement might be expressed as a 2 second average response time, with a 4 second 95th percentile. This means that the average response time will be 2 seconds and that 95 per cent of the response times observed will be 4 seconds or less.

Response time requirements need to be specified with great care since the cost of producing a network is particularly sensitive to this design parameter. The end-user is often prone to overstate response time requirements and will almost certainly specify a very low average response time requirement. When the user is presented with the costs of achieving such a requirement, however, it tends to move the user to accept a more affordable service-level requirement – particularly if the user has to pay directly for it!

Measuring overall response time (i.e. host response time plus network response time) can be difficult. Performance monitoring software typically estimate the response time from a related statistic such as line utilisation. The only accurate measure – the stop-watch – is impractical. An alternative is to employ a hardware monitor which achieves a high level of accuracy, but this is an expensive option.

A microcomputer attached to the network can provide the facility to execute periodically a predefined script which simulates important transactions. The script would automatically record response time data for later analysis. A reasonable level of accuracy can be achieved using this method, and a number of different transaction profiles can be developed to simulate various application workloads.

Voice networks

For PABX-based voice networks the main response time requirement is the time required to make a connection. The connection time is the sum of the times required to find a route and make the switching connections to establish the physical links between switching exchanges. The call connection time can be expressed in probabilistic terms using an average and deviation value.

The response time design parameters are the statistical distribution of the following:

- The system response time (elapsed time between the user going off-hook to the moment the dial tone is heard).
- The call connection time (elapsed time between last digit dialled and call connected).

The total call set-up time is therefore equal to the sum of the system response time, the call connect time and the time to dial all digits.

8.4.2 Throughput requirements

Data networks

The throughput of a data network is usually defined as the number of messages or packets handled per unit time. The throughput is a function of the speed of the communication links, the CPU speed of the switching nodes (e.g. packet-switching nodes), the amount of memory available for temporarily storing messages in transit, and the software overhead imposed by the protocol stack.

Voice networks

The throughput of a voice network is simply the number of calls handled by the network per unit time (usually the busy hour). A 'call' could be measured as a call attempt (which is either successful or blocked) or a call in progress. The throughput of the entire voice network is also measured in terms of the maximum number of calls that can be handled concurrently during the busy hour. Typical throughput measures are the following:

- The maximum number of simultaneous calls that may be carried.
- The maximum number of calls that can be set-up during any 10-second period.
- The maximum sustainable number of busy hour call attempts;

The calling rate (measured in Erlangs) is the usual throughput measure. The standard measure of the density of voice traffic is an Erlang, after the great Danish engineer A. K. Erlang, who first studied the traffic performance of telephone systems using a statistical approach in the early part of the twentieth century, and is regarded as the foremost pioneer of queuing theory. Generally, 1 Erlang is defined as one circuit in continuous use for 1 hour. Below is an example of specifying throughput objectives for a PABX that supports both analogue and digital connections:

- 0.18 Erlangs per analogue extension.
- 0.5 Erlangs per digital extension.
- 0.8 Erlangs per ISDN channel.
- 1.0 Erlangs per digital private circuit channel or analogue private circuit.

8.4.3 Reliability and availability requirements

Organisations are demanding ever-more reliable communication networks as their dependence on the network increases. The larger the network the wider is the scale of impact of network failure. This is particularly true of 'strategic' organisations that have implemented 'mission-critical' business applications. Reliability is defined as the probability that a system will continue to function within a given timescale, whereas *availability* is defined as the extent to which the system is operable when a system user requires it, specified as a percentage of the time that a system should be available. The network planner must take full account of the need to ensure maximum reliability and network uptime (i.e. availability).

Data networks

For data networks supporting critical workloads, reliability and availability may be key service-level requirements. Most data network architectures deliver messages with a high probability that the message is error-free. However, the network topology must be designed to provide the desired resilience to component failure. This increases the cost of the network due to the need to configure switches and links in addition to those required to meet throughput and response time requirements. The aim is to configure the network with redundant common components to guarantee system performance in the event of a single switch, link or local access network component failure. The mode of operation of the additional components could be parallel, load sharing, hot standby, etc. The following are typical reliability and availability measures:

Bit-error-rates (BER)   the number of bits received in a transmission that are in error, relative to a specific number of bits transmitted; usually quoted as a proportion of a power of 10, e.g a BER of 1 bit in 10^9.

Mean time between failures (MTBF)   the average period of time that a component will operate before failing; usually quoted in hours.

Mean time to repair (MTTR)   the average amount of time required for a failed component to be back in service.

Reliability measures the stability of the network and the error profile of the network components. The MTBF is a direct measure of reliability, but some errors do not cause outright failure of a component (e.g. slow response times due to excessive errors on the communication link). A failed component can cause down time and

151

reduced availability unless alternative components are used to provide a back-up facility.

The reliability of a component reduces over time and can therefore be modelled using the following probability density function which expresses the probability that a component will not fail within time interval (t) (Nickel, 1978):

$$R(t) = e^{-at} \qquad \text{where } a = 1/\text{MTBF}$$

Thus for an MTBF of 2500 hours, then over the week (assuming an 8 hour day) from installation the reliability is $e^{-(1/2500)(40)} = 0.984$ (i.e. 98.4 per cent reliability).

Reliability of multiple components

The total system reliability is obtained by calculating the product of of the reliability of each of its components. Thus if each of the seven components of the link between a user and the host processor has a reliability of 0.95, then the total reliability is $0.95^7 = 0.698$.

The reliability can be improved by installing back-up components, particularly at points where the component reliability is low. Communication links are a frequent candidate for back-up links. Nickel (1978) gives the following formula to calculate the effect on the reliability of a component of adding a back-up component:

$$R_{\text{backup}} = 1 - (1 - R_{\text{no backup}})^2$$

Thus if a component has a reliability of 0.95, then adding a back-up component would increase the reliability to $[1 - (1 - 0.95)^2] = 0.9975$. A significant increase in reliability (there is a small probability that both components fail at the same time).

The availability (A) of a component (n) is usually defined as:

$$A = \frac{\text{MTBF}}{\text{MTBF} + \text{MTTR}}$$

For example, a component has a MTBF of 2500 hours and a MTTR of 0.5 hours. The availability is therefore 2500/2500.5, i.e 0.9998. Thus on average we would expect the component to be unavailable two times in every 10,000 tries.

Nickel has shown that for a specific time interval (t), availability can be defined as

$$A(t) = \frac{b}{a+b} + \frac{a}{a+b} \, e^{-(a+b)t}$$

where $a = 1/\text{MTBF}$ and $b = 1/\text{MTTR}$. Thus for the example above, the availability for an 8-hour day is ($a = 0.0004$ and $b = 2$):

$$A(8) = \frac{2}{2 + 0.0004} + \frac{0.004 e^{-(2 + 0.0004)8}}{2 + 0.0004}$$

$$= \frac{2}{2.0004} + \frac{0.0004 \times 0.0000001122}{2.0004}$$

$$= 0.9998 + (2.2 \times 10^{-11})$$

$$= 0.9998$$

Availability of multiple components

The link between user and application consists of multiple components. All components must be available to make the system available to the user. System availability is calculated by obtaining the product of the availability of the individual components. Thus if the processing path consists of eight components each with an availability of 0.991, then the system availability seen by the user is $0.991^8 = 0.93$.

Voice networks

The quality-of-service (QOS) criteria generally deal with transmission quality, quality of voice reproduction at the receiver end, and system reliability and availability, as measured by MTBF and MTTR. Typical categories of failure are:

- Catastrophic failure of the system.
- Complete loss of service.
- Major loss of service – a high proportion of calls are not being processed.
- Five per cent or more of extensions out of order.
- Mishandled calls.

The same techniques as described for data networks are used in the case of voice network components.

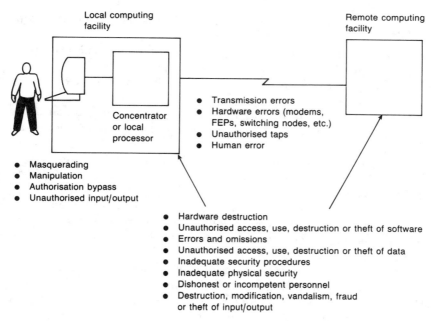

Figure 8.2(a)   Example breaches of security.

8.4.4   Network security and control

The IT infrastructure, like any important asset within a business, requires protection from accidental and unauthorised damage, and unauthorised access and use. The

153

emphasis is on prevention, detection and correction through appropriate security controls. The network analyst must identify the security *control points* (points at which security controls must be established) and implement controls appropriate to the use to which each network component being put. There are four main control activities:

1. Minimise the probability of accidents or intrusions.
2. Detect any breach of security as soon as possible.
3. Return to a previously valid state.
4. Minimise the extent of any loss or damage.

Example breaches of security is illustrated in Figure 8.2(a). Typical security control points are identified in Figure 8.2(b); the control points are as follows:

Control point	Example security controls
1	Access control mechanisms and error controls to prevent unauthorised access and accidental or malicious errors by internal and external persons.
2	Physical and access control mechanisms at the user input/output device level.
3	Physical security of all wiring and associated equipment to prevent breaks or malicious tapping.
4	Physical security, backup and access control mechanisms at the cluster controller, PABX and LAN gateway level.
5	Security of messages using encryption and other equivalent techniques.
6	Physical security, electrical and other back-up equipment, use of automatic call-back units and other techniques at the modem and line sharing equipment level.
7	Security at the local loop level (e.g. vulnerability to tapping).
8	Physical security and back-up facilities of switching equipment (both public and private).
9	Physical security and back-up of the communication link.
10	Physical security and back-up of the communications processor. The logging of message and transaction flows at this level for network monitoring and control.
11	Physical security and back-up of the host processing facility. The logging of message flows and transaction activity using appropriate software and hardware mechanisms provided by the operating system, transaction-processing monitor, network management and other systems. The provision of security control mechanisms.
12	Logging of message flows and transaction flows, and provision of security control mechanisms by the database management systems and underlying file systems. Checkpointing and back-up of data.

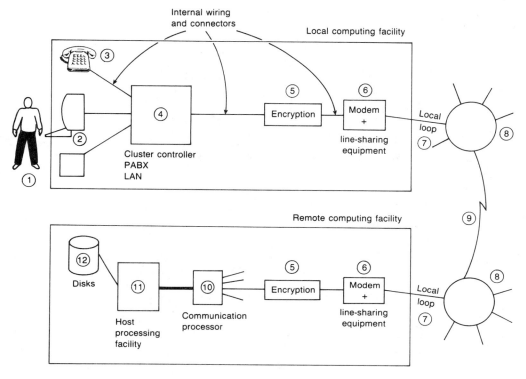

Figure 8.2(b)   Typical security control points.

The network management centre is a primary security control centre and should therefore be subject to stringent physical security and access control procedures.

In the analysis phase of SPIN, the existing network should be analysed to determine the extent to which security controls have been implemented at each control point. This data can be usefully summarised using a matrix, illustrated in Figure 8.2(c), that identifies for each control point likely threats and existing security controls relating to each threat. Any gaps in the matrix represent threats for which no security controls exist.

This is enhanced in the design phase of SPIN to include proposed security controls relating to the new network infrastructure.

8.5   Analysis of data networks

For the purposes of network design, the following analysis is required:

- Analysis of the current network configuration.
- Analysis of the current level of data traffic on the existing network.

Components	Threats	Data error/ transmission error	Service disruption	Theft or unauthorised access	...	...	...
Host processing facility	Host 01						
	Host 02						
	Host 03						
Communication processor	NCP01A					NA	
	NCP01B					NA	
						NA	
Modem/line-sharing equipment							
Local loop	All				NA		
Switching nodes							
Communication lines							
⋮							

Existing or proposed security controls

NA, not applicable

Figure 8.2(c) Matrix of existing or proposed security controls.

- Analysis of the extent to which current service-level agreements (formal or informal) are being honoured.
- Analysis of future network service requirements arising out of growth in existing workloads and proposed future applications.

8.5.1 Existing data communications networks and greenfield sites

Most organisations have evolved a data communications network over many years; some organisations will need to plan based on a 'greenfield' site. In most cases an existing network is being enhanced. Consequently an evaluation of the current network and workload will be required.

In a greenfield situation, it is likely that the initial network will be designed to meet a very specific application requirement. With very little data available an approach to network design is required based on the assumptions that the workload cannot be sufficiently well defined for detailed design purposes and that capacity requirements are difficult to determine.

Thus for greenfield sites, the ability to *enhance* that network easily and quickly becomes an important design factor. It is inevitable that, with so little data available, significant application tuning and system enhancements will be required before the system goes live. System testing and network flexibility are important design factors. Initially, the network topology is unlikely to be sophisticated and is focused to underpin the initial applications being developed. As more applications are developed the network infrastructure requirements become more complex.

In this section it is assumed that an existing network is being enhanced. However, the principles and techniques described apply equally to a greenfield site situation, except that the initial step which considers an existing network is not applicable, and the order in which individual tasks are carried out will differ. For example, some analysis will need to take place after the application is developed, the hardware is installed and performance-monitoring tools are available to provide sizing data.

For existing networks, it is important to adopt a quantitative approach towards the analysis of real traffic patterns and end-user profiles. The starting point is to build up a picture of the existing network configuration by gathering the following data for each site:

- Network equipment location, type, quantity, utilisation and cost.
- Equipment owners and user contacts.
- Applications accessed.
- Transaction volumes during a time consistent busy hour.
- Typical terminal-user profiles (including transaction mix).
- Service-level agreements (formal and/or informal agreements).
- Communication links used and data flows between processing centres.
- Reliability and capacity figures for network components.

Some of this information may be gained through existing inventory records and the network monitoring database. Unfortunately, these records will need to be

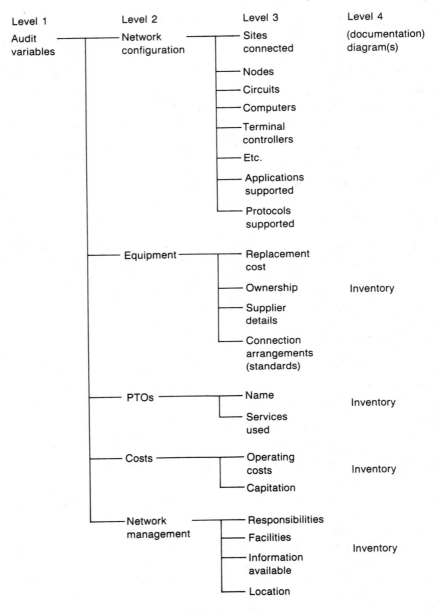

Figure 8.3(a) The audit template.

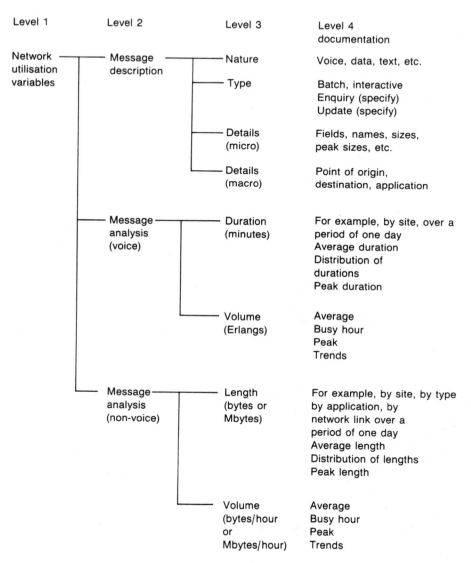

Figure 8.3(b)   The network utilisation template.

Terminal-user profile

Site name:
Location:
Contacts/telephone numbers:

Terminal cluster name	Terminal type	Number of terminals in cluster	Number of transactions per hour	Transaction mix identifier

Figure 8.3(c)   Terminal-user profiler.

supplemented by additional, up-to-date information solicited by the network planner. This is time consuming as it involves the use of interviewing, questionnaires and other data-gathering techniques to ensure that requirements are formulated based upon meaningful data about the existing network. Example forms illustrating the range of data required are given in Figure 8.3.

Ideally, the result of the data gathering is the formulation of a traffic matrix that identifies, in quantitative terms, the end-node to end-node data flow and routeing. Also, a thorough understanding of the capabilities and the current performance level of the network is gained and should be documented in the form of a detailed network configuration diagram with supporting documentation.

In circumstances where the backbone network connecting end-nodes is to be redesigned it is not strictly necessary to document existing routeing information. The design phase will simply use end-node to end-node traffic flows to design optimal switching node interconnections and routeing.

8.5.2   The adequacy of the present data communications network

The results of the data-gathering exercise should enable assessment of how well the network is delivering its services to end-users. A comparison of present network performance with end-user expectation (as identified in the service-level agreements) may reveal some network requirements as a result of deficiencies in the current network configuration and performance. These requirements should be documented as a list of general network requirements.

Site name:
Location:

Contacts/telephone numbers

Data
Network equipment inventory (use a separate sheet if necessary)

Network usage data

Peak hour occurrence:_____

Application name	Transaction name	Transactions per hour	Avg network response time		Avg terminal occupancy	Operational hours
			objective	measured		

Figure 8.3(d)   Documenting the existing network configuration.

161

Network link	Application name/ message type	Mbytes/hour									Mbytes/hour	
		8–9	9–10	10–11	11–12	12–1	1–2	2–3	3–4	4–5	Average	Peak
Totals												

Figure 8.3(e)   Current data traffic record table.

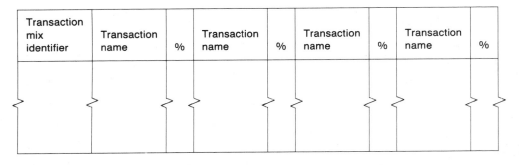

Figure 8.3(f)   Transaction mix definition.

8.5.3   Future requirements

The top-down requirements analysis carried in the strategic phase of SPIN delivered a high-level communications matrix. This matrix is expanded by estimating the site-to-site traffic levels for the applications portfolio identified. This is a difficult step and requires experiential knowledge and judgement.

   Bottom-up analysis of current traffic profiles provides a useful basis for the definition of requirements. But perhaps the most difficult task is to use the traffic matrix with additional information and combine these with projections for the future. Projections should address likely organisational changes regarding size and geographical location, growth in existing workloads that make use of network services, relocation of personnel, equipment and software, and finally new requirements as a

162

From	To	Traffic intensity (Erlangs)									Erlangs	
Node ID	Node ID	8–9	9–10	10–11	11–12	12–1	1–2	2–3	3–4	4–5	Average	Peak
Totals												

Figure 8.3(g) Current voice traffic record table.

result of new applications and deficiencies in the existing services.

Growth in existing workloads can usually be assessed by correlating business transactions to physical transactions and projecting into the future based upon changes in business transaction volumes. The characteristics of existing physical transactions are known (or can be obtained from performance data) regarding network usage and their impact on the network infrastructure. The projected growth estimates should be documented for later usage in the design phase. However, it is much more difficult to predict the effects of new systems upon existing service-level agreements and network infrastructures.

Predicting network requirements for new applications

When a new application is being developed, the application development team and users need to know how well an application is expected to function. Network capacity planning techniques have been used for some time to assess the performance capability of existing systems. These same techniques can be used to give application development practitioners opportunities to test service levels of a system during analysis and design and, more importantly to the network planner, to estimate the proposed system's impact on the existing network infrastructure.

There are many different types of application systems, each with differing network resource usage profiles. The following are examples of typical systems:

- Transaction-processing (TP) systems, which are either bespoke (developed using system development methods) or bought-in packages.
- Unstructured workloads associated with end-user, decision support and office systems. The development of these systems is increasing rapidly and characterised by resource profiles that are unstructured and *ad hoc*.

Security and control procedures (e.g. back-up and access control procedures)

Voice network configuration and usage
PBX type _____

Usage (peak hour) *Average Erlang per:*	*Extensions*		
Analogue extension _____	Extension type	Telephone type	Quantity
Digital extension _____			
Analogue private circuit _____			
Digital private circuit _____	Basic		
ISDN channel _____	Standard		
Grade-of-service	Standard + data		
Extension–extension _____			
Extension–private circuit _____	Mgr/secretary –secretary		
Private circuit–extension _____			
Private circuit–private circuit _____	Mgr/secretary –secretary + data		
	Mgr/secretary –mgr		
	Mgr/secretary –mgr + data		
	Executive		
	Executive + data		
	Data only		

Additional information

Figure 8.3(h) Security and control procedures and voice network configuration.

Analysis of the latter system type is carried out on a per-user basis, and consists of determining, for each class of user, the following:

- Whether the user is a light, medium or heavy user of the network (the classification is installation dependent based on frequency of usage and the nature of the work).
- The resource profile per class (determined by running benchmark tests).
- The concurrency of users in each class.

For TP systems, established network capacity planning techniques can be used that determine the data that need to be collected by application developers. A significant proportion of data required have already been collected by the developer as part of the development method used.

Established methods for the analysis and design of information systems, such as SSADM, concentrate on the functional definition of the information system. The linking of network capacity planning and systems development methods will give network planners earlier notice of new workloads that they will have to provide for.

Structured methods such as SSADM are very useful sources of data for the network planner, and in a form that can be readily converted into network workload requirements. Below is an example of the process involved in extracting network data from SSADM documentation for the case study example (see Appendix C for more details on application sizing and the SSADM method).

Network requirements for Scandania training

Scandania has established a mature management development and technical training division, and is planning to offer systems, programming, operations and management training services to customers in the United Kingdom and eventually in Europe. The Computer Services Division is currently developing a centralised computer system to deal with bookings and enquiries for the company's training courses. The company uses SSADM as its standard structured analysis and design method. This example covers the analysis phase of SSADM and demonstrates that this phase produces sufficient data to analyse the network requirements for the application.

A booking can be made either by letter or telephone call from the customer or via a salesman (in which case a sales enquiry form is completed). This is known as a provisional booking. The booking is confirmed when a completed booking form is received. The confirmation is acknowledged and joining instructions are sent. Details of accommodation arrangements are sent out with joining instructions. The accommodation is normally booked two months in advance of the course.

The customer can cancel a booking by letter only. A customer file is updated with copies of all correspondence.

Invoicing is handled by a local accounts system that is linked to head office. At the end of the month all invoicing details are sent to head office. Customer billing and queries are handled locally.

Management reports are produced every month for course management. Details of courses given, customer lists and course assessment summaries are included.

Course management are actively involved in promoting scheduled courses and on-site, special courses tailored to a particular customer's needs.

The main training centre will be established in Birmingham. Course sales and support teams will also be established in Leeds, Newcastle, Manchester and Oxford.

Message lengths

The first task is to establish the input and output message sizes associated with each screen that are sent either to or from the terminal. This information can be gained from the screen designs. The screen designs for the 'Scandania Training' system (Figure 8.4) show the 'static data' on the screen, i.e. the titles and headings. However, the contents and definitions of the data 'fields' are not shown clearly. To find out message lengths and the types of the data fields we must look at the SSADM I/O description forms. The I/O descriptions show the format and length of each field, and this allows the network analyst to determine exactly what data are transmitted each time the screen is updated. The I/O descriptions for Scandania Training are illustrated in Figure 8.5.

By summing the field lengths for each screen, we arrive at the figures shown in Table 8.1 (excluding the protocol overheads):

Table 8.1 The number of characters on each screen

Screen	No. of characters
Menu	234
Booking	557
Customer	501
Enquiry	113
Confirmation message	19
Rejection message	31

However, the type of communication protocols and terminal types in use (or proposed) will have an impact on actual message sizes as they determine the following:

- The total message length due to the addition of the protocol overhead bits.
- The unit of transmission. For example, if a maximum frame size of 256 bytes is in operation, with a protocol overhead of 6 bytes, then if the whole of an 80-column × 25-row screen is transmitted, eight data frames are actually transmitted together with additional control frames.

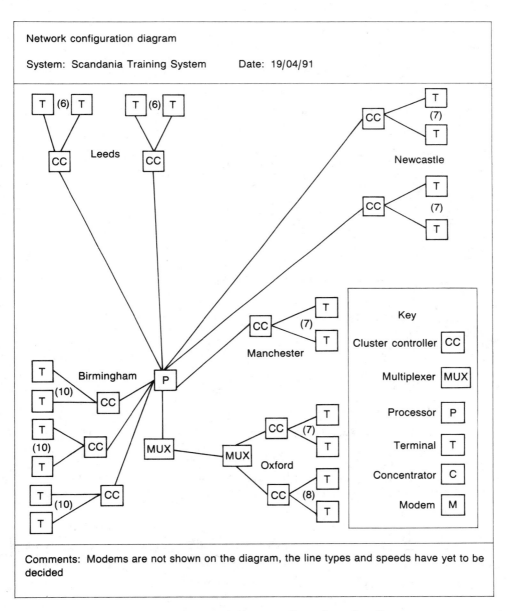

Figure 8.4 Scandania training network configuration diagram.

```
Scandania Training
Booking and Invoicing system


Enquiries ..........1
Customer details....2
Course details......3


Select a number (or Q to quit): ____
```

```
Date: 23/04/91
                    Scandania Training
                    Booking and Invoicing system


Course title:  An intro. to SSADM
Course code:   ISD06
Start date:    09/05/91    Places available: ___
 _  _  _  _  _  _  _  _  _  _  _  _  _  _  _  _  _

Booking      Booking     Delegate    Delegate    Customer    Status
no.          date        name        title       ID

DEL01        15/01/91    J. Davis    Analyst     M0051       CO
DEL03        16/03/91    S. Poole    Prog.       H0009       CO
DEL05
  :            :           :           :           :

ESC - exit    F1 - help
```

Figure 8.4 Scandania training network configuration diagram (continued).

- The error detection and correction technique employed.
- How much of the screen is refreshed by data transmission. Protocols such as IBM 3270 data-streams reduce the amount of data actually sent by sending field position and other attributes.

It is important when estimating message sizes to include non-displayed attribute bytes such as field position, colour, blinking and high/low intensity. It is also important to determine whether the terminal type and protocol supports the following:

- Transmission of only altered characters on a screen.
- Transmission of the entire screen refreshed by each message.
- Transmission using some other technique.

Additionally, the network analyst must understand the protocol overheads associated with terminal polls and responses, which generate extra traffic.

168

SSADM 7	Title		System	Document	Name	Sheet
	Bookings screen					

Screen	✓	**DFD process ID and name**				
Print		**Description of I/O**				
Flow		Customers send in a booking request form or via the telephone. Information is entered on-line to create the				
Document		booking.				

Data items	Format	Length	Comments
Current date	×	8	
Course title	×	30	
Course code	×	5	
Start date	×	8	
Places available	9	2	
			The next group of data items may be repeated
Booking number	×	5	
Booking date	×	8	
Delegate name	×	20	Up to 99 lines across
Delegate title	×	20	several screens
Customer ID	×	5	
Status	×	2	CO – confirmed CA – cancelled PR – provisional

Author	Issue		
ESS	Date	25/3/92	

Figure 8.5 I/O description.

All of the above data will be used at the design stage to model accurately the applications being developed. The use of existing network data and monitors provides a useful aid to determining the true profile of network traffic in terms of the above factors.

Message pairs

The network analyst must determine the order that the screens are presented for each dialogue at the terminal. This can be derived from the logical dialogue outline (LDO) SSADM forms. The LDOs for Scandania Training are illustrated in Figure 8.6. From the characters per screen and the logical sequence of screens on each of the dialogues, the network analyst can calculate the amount of data that is transmitted during each dialogue (Table 8.2). Note that the message pairs that have zero characters as input are those that follow directly from another dialogue.

Table 8.2 The number of characters transmitted per dialogue

Dialogue	Message pair number	No. of characters transmitted	
		Input	Output
Menu	1	234	234
Enquiry	1	113	501
Booking	1	0	557
	2	557	557
	3	557	31
Total		1114	1145
Customer	1	0	501
	2	501	501
	3	501	31
Total		1002	1032

Traffic level

The next step is to calculate transaction volumes. In SSADM, the event catalogue records the events (transactions) that cause an update to the data stores and the retrievals catalogue records all the transactions that access but do not update the data stores. It should be possible to match each event and retrieval with one or more LDOs; in so doing we will be able to identify the data flows for each event and retrieval. The event catalogue 'bookings' is illustrated in Figure 8.7.

SSADM does not require the analyst to record formally the cross-referencing of event, function, retrieval and dialogue outlines, and therefore has no official form for such a purpose. Figure 8.8 illustrates a suitable addition to the SSADM forms to aid cross-referencing. It simply identifies which LDOs are used, and therefore how many characters are transmitted per event.

The volumetric information, from which we derive transaction volumes, is contained in both the event and retrieval catalogues. However, the volumetric information available in SSADM is not sufficient for the needs of the network analyst. It is typical of information systems analysis and design methods that they focus on capturing data relating to the average, minimum and maximum values across all sites, without recording when busy periods occur. The network analyst needs to be aware of peak traffic levels per site, the variance in the traffic levels and any likely spurious busy periods. Ideally a transaction profile needs to be recorded that identifies, for each

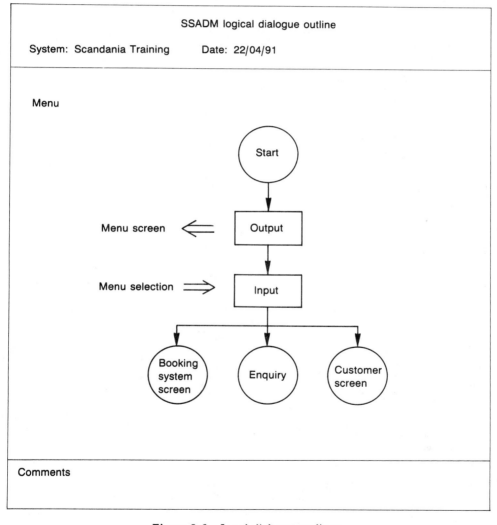

Figure 8.6 Local dialogue outlines.

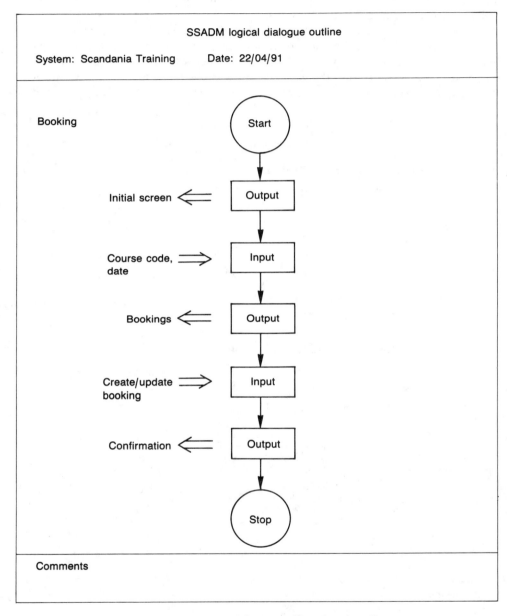

SSADM logical dialogue outline

System: Scandania Training   Date: 22/04/91

Booking

Start

Initial screen ⇐ Output

Course code, date ⇒ Input

Bookings ⇐ Output

Create/update booking ⇒ Input

Confirmation ⇐ Output

Stop

Comments

Figure 8.6   Local dialogue outlines (continued).

SSADM 11	Process/function title Process booking	System Bookings	Document	Name	Sheet

Event / Volumetrics table

ID	Name	Description	Entities affected	Effect	Per	Average	Max	Comments
ev1	Provisional booking	Provisional booking received for a timetabled course	Booking Timetabled course	I M				
ev2	Confirmed booking	Receipt of a firm or confirmed booking	Booking Timetabled course	I/M M				
ev3	Amended booking	Customer initiated amendment	Booking	M				
ev4	Cancelled booking	Customer initiated cancellation	Booking Timetabled course	D M				
ev5	Receipt of new customer details	Receipt of new customer details	Customer	I				
ev6	Receipt of customer amendment	Amendment(s) to comment customer details received	Customer	M				

| Author
ESS | Issue
date | |

Figure 8.7 Event catalogue.

Event/function/retrieval cross-reference					
No. of event	Function	Retrieval	LPO(s)	Characters	
				Input	Output
1			Menu + booking	1227	1378
2			Menu + booking	1227	1378
3			Menu + booking	1227	1378
4			Menu + booking	1277	1378
5			Menu + customer	1236	1266
6			Menu + customer	1236	1266
		1	Menu + enquiry	347	735

Figure 8.8 Event – LDO cross-reference form.

transaction, the hourly volume for the busy periods of the year. SSADM data often quote the volume of transactions per month and usually only give one figure indicating the transaction level for that time period.

A carefully plotted graph showing the hourly usage of the transaction per site on busy periods, and a comment on any spurious busy periods, would provide the analyst with all the required volumetric information. Figure 8.9 shows an example form on which to record this data.

Sufficient data can be extracted from the SSADM documentation to formulate the network requirements for this application. The data will be later used to illustrate its use in the design phase of SPIN.

8.6   Analysis of voice networks

The deregulation of the telecommunications market with consequent price competition has meant that designing cost-effective voice networks is becoming increasingly complex in many countries. The telecommunications sector is on the brink of a revolution in terms of choice and provision of services, and the relationship between price and performance. Understanding tariff structures has never been easy; however, great savings can be gained by making optimum use of the most appropriate services.

Traffic analysis is required to design circuit-switched voice networks. The grade-of-service (GOS) criteria in voice networks deal with the degradation in service caused by contention for critical resources when all resources are functioning.

For blocking switching exchanges, the GOS is determined by the probability that a call is blocked (blocking probability) due to the unavailability of a path through the network during the busy hour. The blocking probability is an important parameter in determining the number of links required to support a given throughput of call attempts.

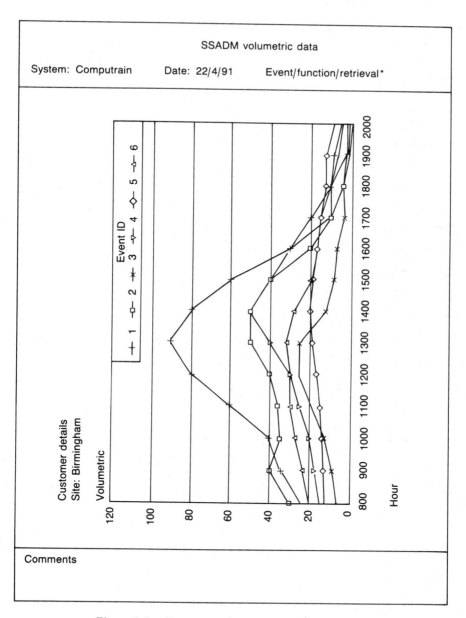

Figure 8.9 Site load graph of Scandania training.

8.6.1   Existing voice networks

Ideally, the existing network usage should be represented as a traffic matrix of routeing from site to site and call profiles. There are several proprietary packages available to help in the collection of this data. So-called 'call information logging equipment' (CILE) or 'call management systems' (CMS) vary in sophistication from simple call-logging systems to multi-PABX CMSs with the following functions:

- The capability to cost calls accurately to, from and through the network.
- A network-wide directory of equipment inventories and so on.
- The ability to measure PABX performance.
- Trunk-monitoring capability.
- A capacity for monitoring the response from incoming callers.
- The ability to monitor traffic flows.

Several software packages provide peak Erlangs by telephone extension or trunk line from a PABX. Few packages provide the ability to construct a traffic matrix of routeing from site to site in a multi-PABX configuration.

As with the existing data network, the starting point is to build up a picture of the network configuration by gathering the following data for each site:

- Network equipment location, type and quantity.
- Voice traffic in Erlangs during a time-consistent busy hour.
- Typical call profiles.
- Service-level agreement (formal and/or informal agreements).

Some of this information may be gained through existing inventory records and call management systems. These records will need to be verified and supplemented by additional, up-to-date information solicited by the network analyst.

8.6.2   The adequacy of the present voice network

A comparison of present voice network performance with end-user expectation (e.g. as measured by the grade of service required) may reveal requirements to improve the existing service. These requirements should be documented as a list of general network requirements.

8.6.3   Future requirements

The voice network design parameters are particularly sensitive to changes in organisational structure, size and geographical location. They will also be sensitive to the future demand for new services and technologies such as ISDN services.

One important design parameter for PABXs is the number of extensions required. The growth of extensions in use will depend on the number of staff employed, both present and future, and the density of telephones and other equipment per staff. The present level and projected changes in staffing levels are relatively straightforward to obtain; the difficulty is estimating the future density of telephones per staff. For example in an industry such as insurance the density is approximately 0.7, whereas in in some manufacturing environments the density is as low as 0.2. In estimating growth in telephone users, Table 8.3 is used. PABX equipment can be easily oversized or undersized by choosing an inappropriate value for the density per staff.

Table 8.3

	Present	1991	1992	1993	1994
Staffing	600	700	800	850	860
Density	0.7	0.7	0.8	0.8	0.8
Forecast	420	490	640	680	688

8.6.4   Data transmission over the voice network

Digital PABXs are now technically capable of providing switching of both voice and data traffic on either a local or wide area basis. The use of the PABX for data communications has the advantages of reduced cabling requirements and better utilisation of the PABX.

Traditionally the PABX has been designed based on the following assumptions:

● Even distribution of calls across telephone extensions.
● Short call duration (e.g. an expected call duration of 3 minutes)
● It is unlikely that everyone will want to call everyone else at the same time!

To reduce the costs of a PABX, the internal circuitry is concentrated to reduce the number of links between input/output elements. This imposes a limitation on the number of calls that can be in progress at any one time. A PABX with concentration is called a 'blocking' PABX, because though an extension may be free, the call is blocked as the links internal to the PABX are busy. A blocking PABX will therefore have a maximum traffic capacity (usually expressed in Erlangs) that is equivalent to the number of simultaneous calls per hour. With a blocking PABX, data calls could adversely affect the PABX because they have very different characteristics to voice calls, namely:

● Data calls are much longer in duration than voice calls.
● Call distribution tends to be concentrated between groups of extensions at different times during the day.

Thus, these characteristics are in direct contrast to the assumptions used to design blocking PABXs. Digital PABXs are now available that are 'non-blocking' and are therefore more suitable for carrying both voice and data traffic.

In summary, it is important to determine the potential for data transmission over the voice network. If this is a requirement, then this is an important design parameter that determines the type of PABX required.

8.7   Other network services

Traffic analysis must cover not just the traditional voice and data requirements but also areas such as voice messaging, facsimile, viewdata and videoconferencing. Organisations are rapidly expanding their communications infrastructure to integrate mainframe-based corporate information systems with desktop systems and office systems (including voice applications, facsimile and videoconferencing).

The integration of previously separate voice and data networks can lead to substantial benefits. To date, however, the approach to modelling and detailed design of integrated networks is in an embryonic phase of development. Currently, little experiential knowledge of analysis and design approaches exists for what is a highly complex network.

It would appear that separate voice and non-voice networks will coexist for some time to come. Therefore, in most cases organisations will regard voice applications, facsimile and videoconferencing requirements in isolation, but with a need to develop gateway services in order to provide access for users.

8.8   Summary

This chapter has described the approach used in the analysis phase of SPIN. Three deliverables have been identified and a straightforward case study has been used to illustrate the documentation that is required for each deliverable. The next chapter describes the design phase of SPIN.

CHAPTER 9

The design phase

9.1 Introduction

In this chapter we discuss various methods to design the topology of a communications network. Having completed the analysis phase of SPIN we have gathered data on the existing network, and have prioritised future requirements in terms of traffic demands (the traffic matrix) and service-level requirements. We use these data to design a network that will service these demands at the desired levels and at an affordable cost.

Aspects of the analysis and design phases of SPIN could be viewed as overlapping with network management. However, this chapter concentrates on the actual design task and is based primarily on the use of queuing network models to model the new network requirements. Of course this involves the utilisation of measurement data gathered during the analysis phase of SPIN.

The methodology described in this chapter can be used to design a network based in any country, or indeed spanning several countries. The main implication of network location in design is the range of carriers and carrier services available. We choose to illustrate the methodology by using the carrier services and tariffs found in the United Kingdom.

With large communication networks, the design process is potentially very complex and costly. It is not practical to consider, exhaustively, every possible topology even for relatively small networks. For example, suppose we wish to design a communications network consisting of ten minicomputers each supporting local and remote terminals. If we were to analyse a network design consisting of point-to-point links and wished to consider every possible configuration, then in a fully connected configuration $N(N-1)/2$ links (i.e. 45 when $N = 10$) are required. However, each link may be configured or absent; therefore there are 2^{45} possible configurations to consider! It is evident that some simplifying assumptions need to be made even when designing relatively small communication networks. The use of a computer-aided modelling package allows the designer to extend the range of configurations that can be analysed within the timescales of the development project, and to model larger networks than were previously possible.

The Scandania Training system will be used to illustrate the use of a computer-

179

aided modelling software package to design the required network. This example is chosen for illustrative purposes and is therefore simplified to avoid obscuring the design approach with unnecessarily large volumes of data such as would be required by a larger case study.

Many network-modelling software packages rely on queuing theory to arrive at performance estimates for a particular network topology. Other packages use simulation methods giving potentially more accurate results, but are more cumbersome and costly to execute (see Section 8.3 for a more detailed discussion). The use of queuing network models provides a close approximation to the actual performance experienced by the user – provided the input data and any underlying simplifying assumptions are appropriate to the environment to be modelled. It should also be recognised that the results are statistical approximations derived from general assumptions and, as such, provide the basis for prudent judgement and comparisons rather than a source for measuring actual network performance accurately.

Typically, an approximate solution to the problem is obtained by heuristic methods that combine queuing theory (and other techniques), trial and error, and common sense. A description of the queuing notation used in this chapter is found in

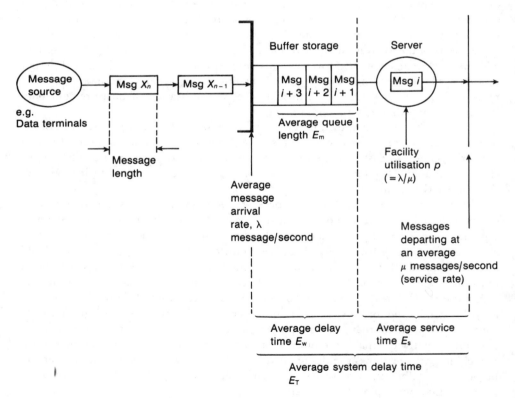

Figure 9.1(a)   Queuing notation: data networks.

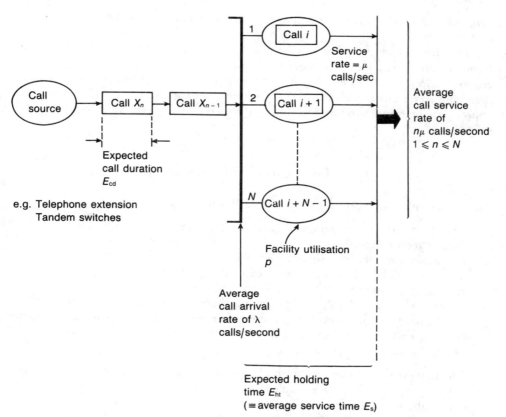

Figure 9.1(b)   Queuing notation: voice network with blocking switches.

p	Facility utilisation (λ/μ)
λ	Average arrival rate
μ	Average service rate
E_s	Average service time ($1/\mu$)
A	Traffic intensity (Erlangs)
N	Number of servers
P_B	Probability of blocking
P_D	Probability of delay
P_k	Probability of k messages in the queue (including the one in service)
E_{cd}	Expected call duration
E_{ht}	Expected holding time
E_m	Average number of messages waiting for service
E_n	Average number of messages in the system
E_T	Average system delay time
E_w	Average delay time

Figure 9.1(c)   Summary of queuing notation.

Figure 9.1. An introduction to the fundamental elements of queuing theory is found in Appendix D.

It is beyond the scope of this book to derive analytical expressions for all the formulae presented; it would require an entire book devoted to the subject. This chapter simply sketches the analytical formulae that may be useful to the analyst in designing communication networks; for a more in-depth study, references to more appropriate literature are provided in the Further Reading section at the end of this book.

9.2 The design phase in outline

The design phase of SPIN consists of the following steps:

1. Construct a model of the network incorporating existing and future workloads and growth requirements.
2. Evaluate the model for various combinations of communications subnets and local access technologies, using the documented service-level requirements as a statement of objectives.
3. Select the most desirable design among those considered, taking into account service-level requirements, migration requirements, training and management requirements, risk assessment and security and control requirements.
4. Obtain management and user approval.

The main design parameters for both voice and data networks are response time, throughput and cost. These are conflicting design requirements; the aim therefore is to achieve the desired balance between response time, throughput, cost and other service-level requirements. Other design parameters are reliability, availability, security and control.

9.3 Designing voice networks

For voice networks the major decisions to be made are the number of extensions required per site, the location and capacity of PABX and other switching equipment, and the type and number of exchange lines and private circuits required. The analysis phase of SPIN provides data on the number of telephone extensions per site, a traffic matrix and service-level (grade-of-service) requirements. The growth projection is an important parameter since any system should be sized to allow enough capacity for growth, but should avoid oversizing to meet the company's ultimate requirements. The planning horizon should therefore be chosen carefully as unnecessary expenditure is often tied up in equipment that will not be used for many years – if ever. A typical planning horizon is three to five years ahead. The longer the planning horizon the more difficult it is to project forward to the end of the planning horizon with a reasonable level of accuracy.

Traffic intensity is another important parameter in the design process. Although the traffic matrix of the existing voice network is a useful starting point, it is often the case that the network needs to be virtually redesigned from scratch or the new environment is significantly different from the present one. Constant restructuring is a feature of most organisations today. Thus simple extrapolation of the existing traffic matrix to take account of future growth projections is normally appropriate only for short-term projections.

One approach to estimating the busy hour traffic intensity for significantly new voice network requirements is to estimate the average busy hour traffic intensity (measured in Erlangs) per PABX extension, usually known as the calling rate. For blocking PABXs the calling rate is less than 1 Erlang (non-blocking systems are by definition capable of 1 Erlang/connection) and suppliers may specify a maximum calling rate (a PABX design factor).

Calling rates vary according to the type of organisation (e.g. a solicitor's office or a sheet-metal manufacturer) and the typical traffic type (e.g. voice, or PC-to-mainframe data flows). Studies of both public and private networks have shown that call rates for a typical business extension range between 0.20 and 0.30 Erlangs/connection. Thus, in the absence of more accurate data, the use of an average of 0.25 Erlangs/connection during the busy hour is reasonable.

EXAMPLE

A medium-sized manufacturer requires a total of 600 active extensions. At an estimated calling rate of 0.25 Erlangs per connection (e/conn.), an estimated 600×0.25 Erlangs of traffic, i.e. 150 Erlangs, is generated during the busy hour.

The company favours a telephone system capable of handling a maximum calling rate of 0.20 E/conn., therefore a 150/0.20 extension telephone equipment, i.e. a 750 extension system, would need to be installed.

9.3.1 The basic design model for voice networks

Typically, an organisation will use the public telephone network and, if it can be justified, a private voice network to carry the traffic levels identified in the analysis phase of SPIN. The main justifications for a private network are as follows:

- It avoids public telephone network charges for calls between sites within an organisation.
- It reduces the number of operators required due to the increased level of 'desk-to-desk' dialling.
- Desk-to-desk dialling reduces the time taken to make each call by approximately 30 seconds per call.
- Speech quality is improved (compared with a typical voice grade circuit on a public telephone network).

Typically, a private network consists of PABX equipment linked via a small number of tandem switching nodes. Figure 9.2 illustrates the typical components of

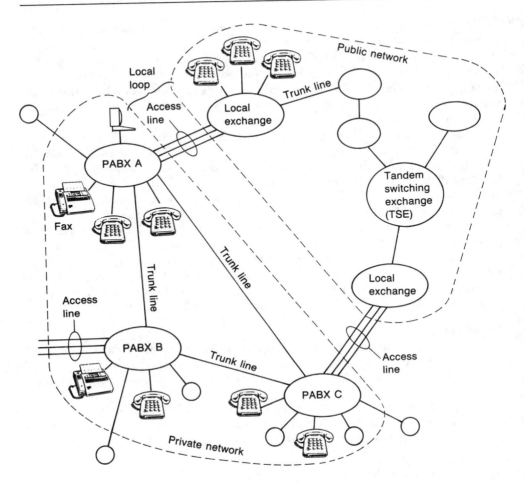

Figure 9.2 A typical circuit-switched network.

a circuit-switched voice network. A model of such a network would consist of various switching nodes interconnected via transmission links. Switches that handle mainly traffic generated by end-user equipment directly attached to it via access lines (e.g. telephone handsets, facsimile equipment and computers) are known as local exchanges (or local offices). Tandem switching exchanges (or tandem offices) receive traffic from one exchange and direct it to another. In this context, the PABX is a relatively small, privately owned switch whose input lines are connected to end-user equipment and whose output lines are connected to the public and/or private network. It therefore acts as a local switching exchange with a gateway device to allow inter-site (and inter-company) communication. A 'remote concentrator' is in effect a PABX that belongs to the public network operator.

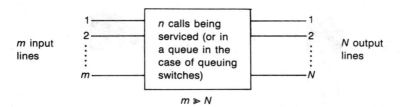

$m \geqslant N$

Blocking switches: no queuing occurs
Non-blocking switches: queuing of incoming calls

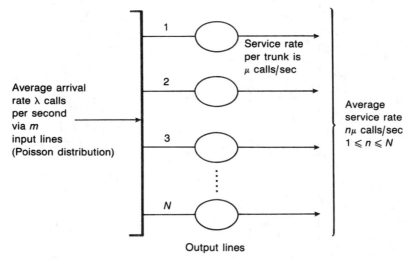

Average service time $\simeq$ expected call duration $= \mu$
Service time exponentially distributed

Figure 9.3 Modelling a switching exchange.

Modelling blocking switching exchanges

A simple model of any particular switching equipment is illustrated in Figure 9.3. The switch consists of M input lines, each exhibiting an arrival rate of calls per hour, and N output lines with average service time of E_{ht} hours. Obviously, blocking could be due to no available trunk lines, or due to concentration internal to the switching device. To simplify modelling complexity, all processing (and potential blocking conditions) internal to the switching device for connecting input lines to output lines are ignored. The typical call sequence for a circuit-switched network is illustrated in Figure 9.4.

The performance of a voice network is greatly determined by the following design parameters:

● call traffic intensity during the busy hour (arrival rate λ of calls).

185

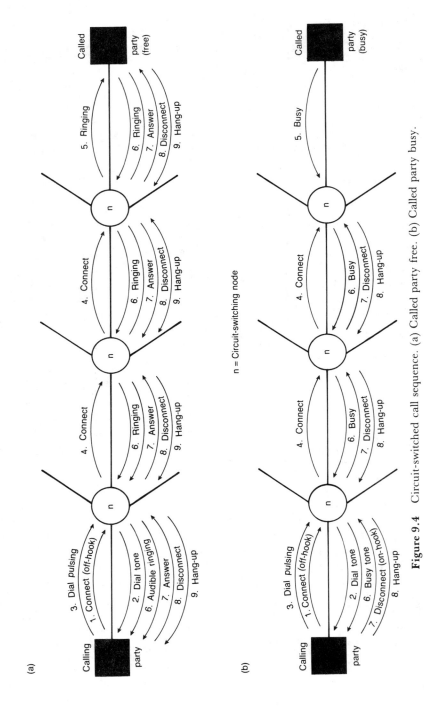

Figure 9.4 Circuit-switched call sequence. (a) Called party free. (b) Called party busy.

- Expected holding time (E_{ht}), which is defined as the time between transmission of the first connect message (see Figure 9.4) and receipt of the disconnection message at the destination exchange. (Obviously, this time includes the call duration time as it represents the total length of time that the link is held. A more precise definition would include the internal processing of the call request within the switching node.)
- The required grade-of-service as measured by the blocking probability P_B.
- The location and interlinking of PABX and tandem switching equipment.

Queuing theory plays a key role in the design of circuit-switched voice networks. Models of blocking switches use a special case of the $M/M/1$ queuing model, with a finite number of servers, and no waiting room – the $M/M/N/N$ queuing model. All arrivals are blocked if all servers (i.e. exchange lines) are occupied. Calls are assumed to exhibit an arrival rate (λ) obeying the Poisson probability distribution and with exponential service time (i.e. expected holding time E_{ht}) distribution.

If A represents the call traffic intensity (i.e. $\lambda \times E_{ht}$) on the system, measured in Erlangs, and N the total number of servers available to handle calls, the probability of blocking P_B is given by the so-called Erlang-B loss formula

$$P_B(N) = \frac{A^N/N!}{\sum\limits_{i=1}^{N} (A^i/i!)} \qquad A = \lambda \times E_{ht}$$

Thus, for a given blocking probability, the traffic intensity A determines the number of servers (i.e. links) that are occupied concurrently. This formula is applicable when the number of input lines M is very large, as is the case for most switching exchanges. A table of blocking probability for given values of A and N can easily be computed by observing that

$$P_B(0) = 1$$

$$P_B(1) = A/(1 + A)$$

$$P_B(N + 1) = A \times P_B(N)/[N + 1 + (A \times P_B(N))]$$

Figure 9.5 illustrates traffic intensity versus the number of servers for range of blocking probabilities. Hill (1979) derived an approximate linear relationship between A and N for given blocking probabilities when $5 < A < 50$ as

if $P_B(N) = 1$ per cent   then $N = 5.5 + 1.17A$
if $P_B(N) = 0.1$ per cent then $N = 7.8 + 1.28A$

For example, suppose a telephone exchange is required to handle 8 calls/minute and an expected call duration of 3 minutes. How many trunk lines are required to handle the load? The number of links required depends on the desired blocking probability. The call traffic intensity is $8 \times 3 = 24$ Erlangs; therefore, using the above approximations, the number of links required for P_B values of 1 and 0.1 per cent are approximately 34 and 39 respectively. The cost of an extra five links to improve the

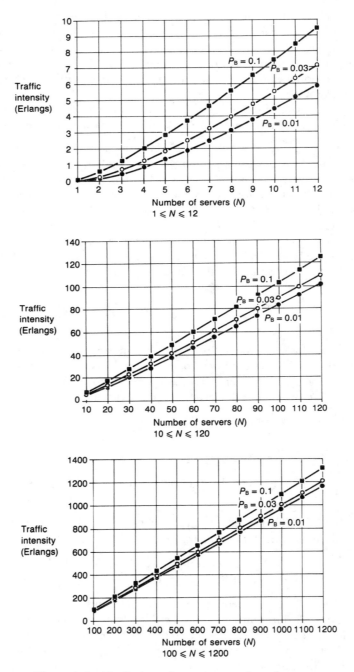

Figure 9.5 Traffic intensity versus number of servers.

blocking probability from 1 to 0.1 per cent is significant, illustrating the importance of choosing the most appropriate value for P_B. In general, the number of links should be at least equal to the traffic intensity in Erlangs in order to avoid a high blocking probability.

Modelling non-blocking (queuing) switches

Modern switching equipment is being designed such that calls are held in a queue rather than blocked or given a busy signal. A call request at the head of the queue is routed to any server (exchange link) that is available. Examples are non-blocking PABXs, some tandem-switching exchanges and automatic call distribution (ACD) systems. The main design parameters that replace the blocking probability for these systems is the probability of delay $P_D(N)$ and the average delay time E_w. In terms of analytical modelling, $P_D(N)$ is derived directly from an N-server queue where each link corresponds to a server. It is usually assumed that call requests arrive at a Poisson rate and call duration obey an exponential distribution. The assumption of a Poisson arrival is reasonable, but it is highly unlikely that the call duration obeys an exponential distribution. However, it would complicate the underlying mathematical model greatly if a more realistic distribution is assumed. In fact the assumption of an exponential distribution produces almost a worst-case scenario and is therefore a reasonable first-order approximation. Given the above assumptions, the model is simply an $M/M/N$ queuing model with P_D given by

$$P_D(N) = \frac{(A)^N P_0}{(1 - p)N!} \qquad\qquad p = A/N$$

$$P_0 = \left[\sum_{n=0}^{N-1} \left(\frac{A^n}{n!} \right) + \frac{A^n}{(1 - p)N!} \right]^{-1}$$

Where p is defined as the per trunk utilisation. This is known as the Erlang-C formula. It is often tabulated to provide a useful mechanism for determining the number of links required to obtain a specified probability of delay. Using Little's formulae, the following time delays can be derived

average wait time $E_w \times \dfrac{E_{ht} \times P_D(N)}{(N - A)}$

average system delay time $E_T = E_{ht} + E_w$

average number of messages waiting for service $E_m = [p/(1 - p)] \times P_D(N)$

average number of messages in the system $E_n = A + E_m$
$$= Np + E_m$$

Performance analysis of the total voice network

These basic models are extended to take account of such features as the following:

- Traffic routeing techniques.
- Processing and blocking internal to the switching exchange.

An open or closed queuing network model (see Section D.8 of Appendix D) is constructed to determine the performance of particular arrangements of switching nodes, access lines and trunk lines. The network analyst is interested in comparing end-to-end system throughput, call connect time, blocking probability and other design parameters for a range of network topologies. The cost of a particular topology is then computed for a range of tariffs offered by various carrier services. The objective is to choose the least cost network design that satisfies throughput, call connection, blocking probability and all other service-level objectives.

Computer-based voice network modelling software, such as Christie Telecom's Network Perception (see Section 9.6), provides essential support for the design of voice networks. It is important to ensure that the modelling tool used maintains a database of complete tariff data for all countries of interest and a complete and up-to-date directory of switching exchange locations.

9.4   Designing data networks

For data networks the following major decisions have to be made:

- The type, location and capacity of the switching nodes and transmission links that are used to construct the topology of the *data communications subnet.*
- The type, location and capacity of transmission links that will connect data terminal equipment to entry nodes of the subnet. This portion of the network is usually termed the *local access network.*

The analysis phase of SPIN provides data on the location of network equipment, in particular the data devices that need to communicate with each other. It also provides a description of each major workload, a traffic matrix and service-level requirements. The objective of the design phase is to design the topology of a network that meets at least the mandatory service-level requirements and with the minimum capital investment and operating costs.

It is likely that parts of the local access network are already established and the subnet needs to be designed within the constraint of an existing network. In many cases this simplifies the design exercise by reducing the number of alternatives to be considered.

9.4.1   The basic design model for the data communications subnet

In the case of a data network a typical subnet topology consists of either data transmission over essentially a circuit-switched voice network, or a packet-switching network. We have already dealt with models of circuit-switched networks, and the same modelling approach applies to data carried over the PSTN or private voice network.

EXAMPLE

A non-blocking PABX connects many terminal connections to a mainframe computer via the public telephone network (PTN). The average data message takes 10 seconds to transmit, and messages are generated at the average rate of 1.2 messages/second. How many PABX outgoing lines are needed to accommodate this traffic?

SOLUTION

The number of lines required depends on the blocking probability required. The traffic intensity A is $10 \times 1.2 = 12$ Erlangs. Using the approximations to the Erlang-B formulae for the number of lines (N), for P_B values of 1 and 0.1 per cent, the number of PABX outgoing lines required are approximately 20 and 24 respectively.

A typical data application, however, exhibits very different characteristics to voice calls in terms of call duration and call distribution (see Section 8.6.4). This means that sizing the PABX may not be as straightforward as is implied by the above calculation. The effect of data transmission through a PABX will depend on the PABX's internal design. Consequently, PABX supplier guidelines will need to be referenced.

In this section we shall concentrate on modelling a data communications subnet link in order to contrast voice and data queuing models.

The $M/M/1$ queuing system is the simplest model of a data communications link. As the Kendall notation suggests (see Section D.2 of Appendix D), it assumes that messages arrive at a single queuing server (i.e. a single transmission line) according to a Poisson process with mean rate (λ), and with service times (i.e. transmission times) that have an exponential distribution with a mean service time of ($1/\mu$) seconds. In this case, if $p = \lambda/\mu$, then the stability condition is that p must be less than 1, and it can be shown that:

the probability of k messages in the system $P_k = (1 - p)p^k$

the probability of k or more messages in the system $= p_k$

the mean number of jobs in the system $E_n = p/(1 - p)$

the mean response time $E_T = 1/[\mu(1 - p)]$

the variance of the response time $\text{var}[E_T] = 1/[\mu(1 - p)]^2$

q-percentile of the response time $= E_T \times \ln[100/(100 - q)]$

the cumulative distribution function of the response time conforms to the exponential function $G(t) = 1 - e^{-\mu t(1 - p)}$, $t \geqslant 0$.

the cumulative distribution function of the wait time conforms to the exponential function $G(t) = 1 - pe^{-\mu t(1 - p)}$

EXAMPLE: An application of $M/M/1$

A transmission link between a personal computer and mainframe computer operates at a speed of 9600 b.p.s. Messages arrive in the form of a Poisson stream with an average arrival rate of 5 messages/second, and message lengths are exponentially distributed with an average length of 1000 bits. Determine the average response time and percentage of messages delivered within half a second.

SOLUTION

The average transmission time is $1000/9600 = 0.1$ second. The transmission rate is 9.6 messages/second, giving a value of $p = 0.52$. Therefore, the average response time is $1/[\mu(1-p)] = 1/[9.6(1-0.52)] = 0.22$ second. The percentage of messages delivered within half a second is

$$G(0.5) = 1 - \exp(-9.6 \times 0.5 \times 0.48) = 90 \text{ per cent.}$$

The value of E_n and E_T rise rapidly as p exceeds 0.7 and hence serve as a useful rule of thumb for network components that approximate to the $M/M/1$ model.

The above model assumes an infinite queue, but the model can be modified to consider the case where there is a limited buffer for storing messages.

The assumptions underlying the $M/M/1$ model afford simple analysis and easily computed values for response times and other relevant values. However, many data communication systems have a more complex behaviour that is better approximated by use of the $M/G/1$ queuing model with extensions. The essential difference is the relaxation of the assumption that service times are exponentially distributed. In packet-switching systems, real analysis of the packet length distribution has shown that, typically, it is either of constant length (in which case an $M/D/1$ queuing model is appropriate) or of a random length with the protocol imposing a minimum and maximum value. Furthermore, most distributions are bimodal due to the fact that data networks usually support both interactive traffic (producing short packets) and batch or file transfer workloads (producing long messages).

The $M/G/1$ model assumes that messages arrive at a single server according to the Poisson stream, but service times have a general distribution. In this case, the following formulae can be verified:

$$\text{average waiting time } E_w = \frac{pE_s}{2(1-p)} [1 + C(E_s)^2]$$

where $C(E_s)$ is the coefficient of variation of the service time, calculated as the ratio of the standard deviation to the mean of the service time distribution.

$$\text{average response time } E_T = E_s + E_w$$

$$\text{average number of jobs in the system } E_n = p + \frac{p^2}{2(1-p)} [1 + C(E_s)^2]$$

These are called the Pollaczek–Khintchine formulae and are used extensively in modelling data networks. These formulae illustrate that if the server is lightly loaded

192

(i.e. p is nearly zero), wait times are very low. The more irregular the service times [(i.e. $C(E_s)^2$ is high], the higher the wait times. If $C(E_s)^2 = 1$ – the worst case (exponential service) – you would wait twice as long as if it were equal to zero (constant service time). At $p = 75$ per cent, the wait time is 1.5 times the service time, whereas at $p = 90$ per cent, the wait time is 4.5 times the service time.

EXAMPLE: An application of the $M/G/1$ model

A subnet transmission link receives input packets that which follow a Poisson stream with an average arrival rate of 2 packets/minute. Suppose messages are transmitted in order of arrival and that the mean and standard deviation of the packet transmission time are 20 and 5 seconds respectively. Determine the average response time and average number of messages in the queue.

SOLUTION

The situation can be represented by an $M/G/1$ queue using the Pollaczek–Khintchine formulae. Link utilisation $p = 2/3$, service time $E_s = 1/3$, and the coefficient of variation of the packet transmission time $C(E_s) = 5/20 = 1/4$. Therefore

average waiting time $E_T = E_s + \dfrac{pE_s}{2(1-p)}\,[1 + C(E_s)^2]$

$$= (1/3) + (2/3) \times (1/3)(1 + 1/16)/[2 \times (1/3)]$$

$$= 0.69 \text{ minutes or } 41.3 \text{ seconds}$$

average number of jobs in the system $E_n = p + \dfrac{p^2}{2(1-p)}\,[1 + C(E_s)^2]$

$$= 1.38$$

The above models allow optimisation of the average delay per packet or message. However, there are other service-level requirements, such as reliability and cost, which need to be modelled and the most desirable balance between these conflicting requirements found. An exact solution to the problem is at best computationally expensive, at worst virtually impossible; as a result, the use of heuristic schemes is popular. These schemes typically start with some network topology, and progressively 'search' around the existing topology, reducing the search space until given constraints are satisfied. The base topology from which a search is initiated is usually one that satisfies the performance and reliability constraint. The search is thus seeking an improvement in costs. Heuristic methods do not guarantee an optimal solution, but provide solutions that are close to the best possible. One such heuristic method is a constrained minimum-weight spanning tree algorithm. Each link is given a weight representing the communication cost of a message along the path in either direction, forming a cost matrix. The minimum-weight spanning tree (MST) is a series of links joining nodes, resulting in a minimum total sum of the link weights. This achieves a given throughput at minimum total cost. A constrained MST imposes an upper bound on the amount of traffic that can be carried by any one link. The upper bound can be used to impose a base level of performance.

Another approach is illustrated by the Esau–Williams algorithm, which applies to the special case of a central node (e.g. a host processor, branch exchange or concentrator) to which N other 'terminal' nodes are directly attached, and where reliability is not a serious issue (or simply not considered). It is assumed that all traffic must go through the central node so that there is input traffic only from the N terminal nodes and vice versa.

The Esau–Williams algorithm initially connects all terminal nodes to the central node. It then attempts to remove connections iteratively from the central node and insert those links between terminal nodes (avoiding cycles) so as to maximise the cost reduction while not exceeding capacity constraints. The algorithm terminates when there are no nodes for which exchanging links will improve cost reduction while satisfying constraints. Note that once a link has been reconfigured the algorithm does not allow for subsequent readjustment (i.e. it is not re-examined based on subsequent choices).

Other examples of heuristic algorithms for topology design are the Kruskal and Prim–Dijkstra algorithms and their derivatives. These algorithms can be run with only a cost constraint or with additional constraints such as link capacity, total number of drops on a multipoint line, total number of terminals on a line and so on.

9.4.2 The basic design model for the local access network

The local access network connects a number of terminals to the data communications subnet. Terminals are typically connected via a number of technologies:

- Point-to-point or multi-point links.
- Concentrator (cluster controller) equipment.
- LANs with communications servers.

We have already dealt with point-to-point links in the context of the data communications subnet. Here a terminal is simply connected to a subnet node via a point-to-point link, which is modelled using an $M/M/1$ or $M/G/1$ scheme.

Concentrator-connected terminals
For concentrator networks the design parameters are the location of concentrators, the assignment of terminals to concentrators, and the capacity of links and concentrator equipment. The optimal design is one that minimises cost while maximising concentrator and link utilisation and maintaining service-level requirements. Heuristic methods are used to arrive at an approximate, but near-optimal solution.

Terminals connected via a LAN
The LAN demands a more complex model. The difference, in modelling terms, is that each node maintains its own queue and is unaware of the existence of other queues of packets competing to use the server (i.e. the shared transmission media). Thus

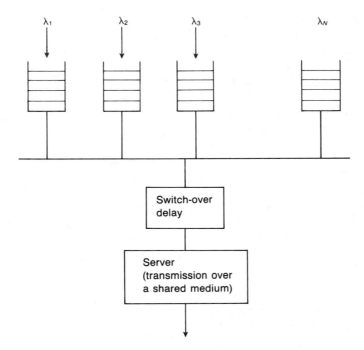

Characteristics

1. *N* stations each generating frames with average arrival rate of λ_i frames per second ($1 \leqslant i \leqslant N$).
2. Switch-over delay is the maximum end-to-end propagation delay (bus topology using CSMA/CD) or the round-trip delay (token-ring).

3. Average service rate = $\left(\dfrac{\text{length of frame header} + \text{average frame data length}}{\text{transmission rate}} \right)$

Figure 9.6   A generalised model of an *N*-station LAN.

LANs operate a distributed queuing scheme. A general model is illustrated in Figure 9.6. The model is modified to reflect the differing access control mechanisms (i.e. token passing or CSMA/CD) in use in the more popular LAN products. The queuing formulae are necessarily more complex than those previously discussed. The reader is referred to Bertsekas and Gallager (1987) and Stallings (1990) for a detailed treatment of LAN performance issues. The chief factors that affect performance across a LAN are as follows:

- Capacity of the network (measured in frames per second).
- Propagation delay.
- Number of bits per frame.
- Local area protocol in use (typically token-ring or CSMA/CD).
- Traffic intensity.
- The number of stations attached to the shared medium.

195

The first four parameters are normally given for a particular LAN product. The latter two parameters are generally a function of the application workload presented to the LAN. Consequently, the number of design alternatives to be considered is considerably less than for WANs.

An analytical model of a LAN will need to be combined with a model of the communications server used to provide a link to the data communications subnet. The communication server can be modelled as an $M/G/1$ or an $M/M/n$ scheme depending on the number of transmission links attached.

9.5   Data network modelling software

There are a number of network modelling packages on the market which aim to model the network and provide the network analyst with information on network performance and cost. In this section we will examine one such package: the NDS series of software from Logica plc. It is typical of a queueing network model based modelling package and provides the network analyst with the following capability:

1.   Predictive performance analysis of point-to-point, multipoint and packet switched and other mesh-type networks.
2.   Topological optimisation and alternative price comparisons for data communication.

NDS has two major components: Multipoint Network Design Software (MNDS) and Distributed Network Design System (DNDS). MNDS performs point-to-point and multipoint modelling, whereas DNDS performs packet-switched and mesh-type network modelling. We concentrate on the use of MNDS and illustrate its use by modelling the Scandania Training application.

MNDS uses a modified version of the Esau–Williams algorithm to provide topological designs from traffic details and service-level requirements.

MNDS has two components that can be used to find the most suitable topology: the Response Model program (which determines the required response times), and the Link Model program (which determines the required throughput levels within a given cost or performance constraint).

The software architecture of MNDS is illustrated in Figure 9.7. The file-building portion of the software consists of five major modules, each designed to assist the network analyst in defining the existing network configuration and to define the network workload to be modelled. Before any design can take place, the analyst must build a network database by use of the following five modules:

● The *message file*, which contains details of each of the applications which operate on the network.
● The *protocol file*, which describes the communication protocols in use on the network. The file is already prepared with four default protocols. The analyst can modify any existing protocol or create customised protocols.

- The *network file*, which is used to enter default values for network characteristics such as propagation delay and modem CTS delay. It is needed for performance analysis.
- The *site file*, which contains the specifics of each physical site in the network.
- The *traffic file*, which contains the number of times each application occurs at each site defined in the site file during the busy hour.

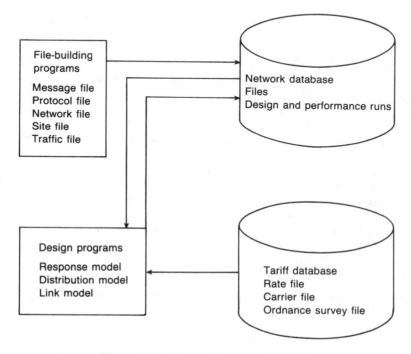

Figure 9.7 The architecture of MNDS

The tariff database stores predefined (and user-defined) tariffs for use with subsequent design activities. The product comes equipped with, for example, the UK British Telecom Keyline, Analogue Multipoint, Kilostream, Megastream and Mercury tariffs. The modelling component of the software allows the user to act on the database and to perform a series of comparative analyses for both performance and network cost and design. The Response Time Model component allows the analyst to calculate the estimated response time and line utilisation for each of the application types defined. MNDS calculates the expected time it will take to process each transaction type through the network, plus the variance of each value. The Pollaczek–Khintchine formulae are then used to calculate the queuing delay, based on the $M/G/1$ queuing model.

The Link Model component provides topological optimisation and pricing portions by use of a modified version of the Esau–Williams algorithm. The Link

197

Model allows the analyst to create a new network design in which the software seeks to provide the absolute least-distance theoretical network that matches user-defined design constraints.

The following sections outline the steps required to model an existing network based upon data gathered in the analysis phase of SPIN. The Scandania Training case study is used to illustrate how NDS is used to model the network; tariffs for leased lines refer to the PTOs in the United Kingdom in the example. However, the model could use any tariff file corresponding to the carrier services available to a particular country.

9.5.1 Site information

The first task is to enter site details. This data is readily obtained from the analysis phase of SPIN. Firstly, the analyst must enter site 'class' details into NDS. This is made up of five components:

1. *Local end pricing treatment.* This defines whether the local site is connected to the exchange using London cable or a microwave link (this field affects Mercury tariffs only; however, a value must be entered regardless of carrier).
2. *Destination or natural domain.* This defines the site relationships that must be adhered to in the subsequent network design (i.e. which host or concentrator/ multiplexor site that a site must be connected to).
3. *Role.* This specifies the role of the site. A site can have three basic roles:
   - *Node site* – a site where a number of terminals are located.
   - *Host site* – a site where the host computer is located (terminating site).
   - *Mux/conc* – a site at which a multiplexor or concentrator is located. These multiplexors and concentrators are used to provide access to the host sites from the node sites.

Other site data to be input are as follows:

- *Cluster controllers* – a site at which a number of cluster controllers are located. If the throughput at each cluster controller must be assessed, then it needs to be defined.
- *Number of terminals* at each site.
- *Physical location of the site* – this is entered in one of two ways: manually (i.e. entering site coordinates) or automatically by specifying the STD code (MNDS converts from STD code to site coordinates).
- *Distance from local exchange* – the distance from the local exchange is required to calculate local connection costs.

If a site has multiple roles, then a separate definition should be provided for each of them. For example, in the case of the Scandania Training system the host computer resides in Birmingham, but this site also has a number of terminals and cluster controllers. Therefore, it is the node site 'Birmingham', with cluster controllers CC1, CC2 and CC3, and host site 'Birmingham HOST'.

```
14:20:12                          ********************                    12-04-1991
                                  *                  *
Network name: SCANTRA             *   SITE FILE      *
                                  *                  *
                                  *     Page 1       *
                                  ********************

                                                              Site     Office
                               Cluster              Dialling  Ordnance Ordnance                  Local
     Town/Country      Class   Control  Terminals   Code      Survey   Survey   Zone  Digital    End KM
  1: BIRMINGHAM HOST   1  0 1    0          0        021  452                    SP0586      Y      0.00
  2: OXFORD MUX        1  0 3    0          0          0  865                    SP4409      Y      0.00
  3: LEEDS             1  0 2    2         12          0  532                    SE2139      Y      0.00
  4: MANCHESTER        1  0 2    1          7        061  431                    SJ8892      Y      0.00
  5: NEWCASTLE         1  0 2    2         14        091    0                    NZ4341      N      0.00
  6: BIRMINGHAM MUX    1  1 3    0          0        021  452                    SP0586      Y      0.00
  7: BIRMINGHAM        1  1 2    3         30        021  452                    SP0586      Y      0.00
  8: OXFORD            1  3 2    2         15          0  865                    SP4409      Y      0.00
```

Figure 9.8 Example data from Scandania training.

Figure 9.8 shows example data entered into MNDS for the Scandania Training case study.

9.5.2 Protocol information

The analyst must specify the protocols in use (or to be used) when modelling the network. Popular protocols are already predefined in the MNDS database; however, there are a number of dialects of these protocols, and the analyst can vary the features of the basic protocols to meet the system requirements. The analyst can also ignore any predefined protocols and create completely new definitions.

The manufacturer and model of existing equipment will largely determine the type of protocols to be used.

9.5.3 Physical network information

Default information about the network characteristics must be entered into the network file. Modification of these defaults is subsequently done in the Response Model when the network is being modelled. The default information is as follows:

- Line speed.
- Half-duplex or full-duplex connection.
- Input and output modem CTS delay.
- Input and output propagation delay.
- Input (terminal) and output (host) processing time.
- Multiplexor average delay.
- Multiplexor throughput capacity.
- Number of bits per character.

Inevitably, a network consists of transmission lines with a variety of values for the above attributes. The default values should be set to known common values.

Figure 9.9 shows example default network data entered for Scandania Training.

9.5.4 Application workload information

For each application, details of each transaction type must be entered into MNDS and stored in the message file. The following information is entered:

- *Transaction name* (MNDS refers to this as the 'Application' name)
- *Input and output message lengths*. A range of input and output message lengths can be entered together with the percentage of time each message length occurs. This enables a detailed specification of the distribution of message lengths to be entered.
- *Variance*. Alternatively, a single input or output message length can be entered and the nature of the variance (exponential, constant or other) can be indicated. A variance calculated from sample data can be entered.

200

```
14:19:52                    ***********************
                            *    NETWORK FILE     *
Network name: SCANTRA       *                     *
                            *       Page 1        *
                            ***********************

                            Line speed: 9.6  KBPS
                            Transmission mode: Half Duplex

                            Input modem CTS delay:       0.020 secs
                            Output modem CTS delay:      0.020 secs

                            Input propagation delay:     0.002 secs
                            Output propagation delay:    0.002 secs

                            Input processing time:       0.050 secs
                            Output processing time:      0.050 secs

                            Multiplexor Average delay:      0.050 secs
                            Multiplexor Transfer Capacity:  500.0 Kbps

                            No. of bits per character:   8.0
```

                                                            12-04-91

Figure 9.9 Default network data for Scandania.

```
14:19:07                                    *********************
                                            *   MESSAGE FILE    *
Network name: SCANTRA                       *                   *
                                            *       Page    1   *
                                            *********************

Method of describing message lengths: WEIGHTED AVERAGES
Method of describing message volumes: NUMBER OF WHOLE TRANSACTIONS
Period described: BUSY HOUR

                         *** WEIGHTED AVERAGES ***

                         Application name: PRO-BOOK

                              Message lengths

           Average number                    Average number
          of input characters              of output characters

           1227,      100.0%                1378,      100.0%

        Variance= 0 CHAR                  Variance= 0 CHAR

Average number of transaction units:  4
Host response time:  2
Selected method of calculation: CONSTANT
Variance in host response time:  0
```

Figure 9.10 (a)

Transaction	Application	Input	Output
Event 1	Prov Book	1227	1378
Event 2	Conf Book	1227	1378
Event 3	Amend Book	1227	1378
Event 4	Can Book	1227	1378
Event 5	Rec Cust	1236	1236
Event 6	Amend Cust	1236	1236
Retrieval 1	Cust Enq	347	735

Figure 9.10 Input and output message lengths for the Scandania training system. (a) MNDS message file definition for PRO-BOOK. (b) Message length data for all transactions.

● *Average number of transaction units.* A transaction unit is an MNDS term synonymous with the term message pair. MNDS is interested in the average number of message pairs and does not model response times and throughput at the message pair level.

Transaction	Application	No. of transaction units (average)
Event 1	Prov Booking	3
Event 2	Conf Booking	3
Event 3	Amend Booking	3
Event 4	Cancel Booking	3
Event 5	Rec Cust	3
Event 6	Amend Cust	3
Retrieval 1	Cust Enquiry	4

Figure 9.11 Average transaction units per transaction for Scandania training.

For the Scandania Training application, Figure 9.10 illustrates the input and output message lengths associated with each transaction type. Figure 9.11 illustrates the average number of transaction units associated with each transaction. This data is easily derived from the data collected during the analysis phase of SPIN.

9.5.5 Traffic distribution

The number of transactions that occur at each site during the busy hour is entered into the traffic file. Again, this information should be evident from the traffic matrix and load graphs output from the analysis phase of SPIN. Figure 9.12 shows the traffic matrix for the Scandania Training case study.

9.5.6 Modelling and reporting

The modelling process

The previous steps outlined create the network database of existing and proposed

203

```
14:20:30                                                                    12-04-91

Network name: SCANTRA                    ***********************
                                         *   TRAFFIC FILE      *
                                         *                     *
                                         *     Page 1          *
                                         ***********************

Time period: Busy Hour       Message volumes are in: Units


Site   Town / County    PRO-BOOK CON-BOOK AMM-BOOK BOOK-CAN REC-CUST AMM-CUST CUST-ENQ
1: BIRMINGHAM HOST
2: OXFORD MUX
3: LEEDS                  30       23       25       40       33       45       73
4: MANCHESTER             82       50       40       70       40       40       40
5: NEWCASTLE              33       50       40       55       40       40       27
6: BIRMINGHAM MUX
7: BIRMINGHAM             90       50       25       50       35       20       90
8: OXFORD                 80       40       25       40       32       20       45
```

Figure 9.12 Traffic matrix for Scandania training.

message types, sites and protocols. When the network database is complete, network modelling is used to design the network to meet service-level objectives identified. The network model provides the ability to analyse a variety of assumptions about changing workload characteristics, and pinpoints potential bottlenecks and other problem areas.

MNDS provides three basic modelling programs which automatically use the network database that stores model data:

1. All performance analysis is accomplished in the *Response Model* program. Response time and line utilisation are calculated for a selected set of network characteristics.
2. The *Link Model* program is used to create least-distance network configurations and conduct alternative pricing comparisons.
3. The *Distribution Model* is a companion to the Response Model (RM) and allows the user to display RM results as a series of curves that illustrate the performance characteristics of RM runs.

Normally, performance analysis is conducted in order to design an initial network that meets performance design goals. A subsequent Link Model design is generated using the performance values as design constraints. The general design steps are as follows:

1. Set clear design goals. These should be translated from the service-level requirements identified in the analysis phase of SPIN.
2. Build a validated baseline model of the existing network. This involves defining in the network database the existing network characteristics. The RM is then used to evaluate the characteristics of the existing network, and a comparison is made between benchmarked data and the RM reports. The workload characteristics and/or network configuration is amended until a good match is found.

    The process of establishing a baseline model is a key step in the modelling process as it determines the accuracy of the whole exercise. The complexity of many networks is such that the results of changes in workloads and network configuration are not intuitively obvious. Therefore, any network model must be calibrated based upon comparisons with real benchmark data (a representative sample of current network performance).
3. Evaluate the effect on performance of traffic growth through increased volumes, new applications, new sites, new equipment or any other change over the planning horizon identified.

    The predicted performance of all or part of the changed network may not meet service-level requirements. MNDS allows the network planner to examine a variety of possibilities to improve predicted performance by experimenting with the following factors:
    - Reducing the number of sites on the line(s).
    - Increasing line speed on specific lines.
    - Changing network characteristics.

    The network is improved iteratively until the desired solution is found.

4. Use the Link Model to reconfigure the network, using the network design identified in step 3 as a baseline and a variety of tariff information until the desired balance between response time, throughput and cost is arrived at.

It is important to reiterate that the results of an MNDS exercise may not be the best possible design. Network design is both an art and a skill, and it is the artist that creates a great design, not the instrument!

Response Model reports
There are two basic report formats generated from the Response Model of MNDS. The first reports on the performance levels of all the sites in the network, the second reports on specific sites, specific lines and theoretical (hypothetical) lines.

All-site runs
An example of this report is given in Figure 9.13. It is structured so that it first shows the line parameters, growth rates for each application, host response time and variance in host response time values. The report then shows the average and standard deviation response time values and the 95th percentile. The system utilisation (i.e. the time that it takes to process a message multiplied by the average arrival rate) and average queue length are also shown.

Non-all-site runs
A report can be generated for specific lines, specific sites or theoretical lines. The report includes all information contained in the all-site report. Additionally, growth rates, response time and throughput information are given for each application using a particular line, or generated from a particular site. Figure 9.14 shows an example of the output for a Scandania Training model.

Distribution Model graphs
The Distribution Model program illustrates graphically the variance in response time across specific lines. Two types of graphical reports are generated:

1. *Response time versus percentage of occurrence curve*, depicting the distribution of response time occurrences for the specific line utilisation calculated. A very wide variation is unacceptable and is easily detected by a sloping curve, whereas a more acceptable variance is indicated by a near vertical or steeply sloping curve. This is illustrated in Figure 9.15.
2. *Response time versus traffic growth curve*, depicting the traditional response time versus throughput curve. It illustrates the degradation in the average response time that will occur as traffic growth (throughput) increases. Traffic level is measured by the line utilisation observed. The graph is used by the network planner to select the threshold utilisation which is used by the Link Model as the design constraint. This is illustrated in Figure 9.16.

```
Time: 09:30:11              ************************           Date: 12-04-91
                            *   RESPONSE MODEL    *
Network name: SCANTRA       *   PCOM1    RUN      *            Run name: PCOM1
                            *      Page   1       *
Time created: 09:26:30      ************************           Date created: 12-04-91

Desired Performance: All sites on pt. to pt. lines

                                          Line Parameters
Protocol: HDLC       Input CTS delay:  0.020  Input prop. delay: 0.002  Bits per char: 8.0  Channel run names:
Line KBPS:   9.6     Output CTS delay: 0.020  Output prop. delay: 0.002
Line tran. mode: H   Input proc. time: 0.050  Output proc. time: 0.050

                            *** Traffic Parameters ***
```

Application	Growth(%)	Host R.T.	Host Var.
1 PRO-BOOK	5	2.000	0.000
2 CON-BOOK	5	0.200	0.000
3 AMM-BOOK	5	2.000	0.000
4 BOOK-CAN	5	2.000	0.000
5 REC-CUST	5	1.000	0.000
6 AMM-CUST	5	3.000	0.000
7 CUST-ENG	5	2.000	0.000

```
                      *** Line Performance Results ***
```

Line No. (Site)	Avg.R.T. (Secs)	Std Dev (Secs)	95% (Secs)	In.Queue (Secs)	Out.Queue (Secs)	In.Util %	Out.Util. %	Tot.Util. %
1	0.000	0.000	0.000	0.000	0.000	0.00	0.00	0.00
2	0.000	0.000	0.000	0.000	0.000	0.00	0.00	0.00
3	6.178	2.345	10.488	1.416	0.542	29.33	32.38	61.71
4	36.989	33.689	%103.975	31.615	1.189	46.00	50.24	96.24
5	8.259	4.580	16.895	3.323	0.780	36.72	39.80	76.52
6	0.000	0.000	0.000	0.000	0.000	0.00	0.00	0.00
7	11.119	7.658	25.990	6.113	0.926	40.01	44.84	84.85
8	7.349	3.675	14.249	2.520	0.707	34.21	37.75	71.96

Figure 9.13 MNDS 'all sites' run for Scandania training.

```
Time: 13:27:31                          *********************      Date: 12-04-91
                                        * RESPONSE MODEL *
Network name: SCANTRA                   * MSCOM3    RUN  *         Run name: MSCOM3
                                        *   Page   1     *
Time created: 13:26:54                  *********************      Date created: 12-04-91

Desired Performance: One line with specific sites

                              Line Parameters
Protocol: HDLC        Input CTS delay:  0.020  Input prop. delay:  0.002  Bits per char: 8.0  Channel run names:
Line KBPS:  9.6  Output CTS delay:  0.020  Output prop. delay:  0.002
Line tran. mode: H  Input proc. times: 0.050  Output proc. time:  0.050
```

			*** Line Number: 1 ***					
Avg.R.T. (Secs)	Std Dev (Secs)	95% (Secs)	In.Queue (Secs)	Out.Queue (Secs)		In.Util. %	Out.Util. %	Tot.Util. %
6.178	2.345	10.488	1.416	0.542		29.33	32.38	61.71

Application	Resp Time	Std Dev	95%	Trans (Units)	Growth(%)	Host R.T.	Host Var.
1 PRO-BOOK	6.542	2.321	10.785	32	5	2.000	0.000
2 CON-BOOK	4.742	2.321	9.085	24	5	0.200	0.000
3 AMM-BOOK	6.542	2.321	10.785	26	5	2.000	0.000
4 BOOK-CAN	6.542	2.321	10.785	42	5	2.000	0.000
5 REC-CUST	5.450	2.321	9.755	35	5	1.000	0.000
6 AMM-CUST	7.417	2.321	11.626	47	5	3.000	0.000
7 CUST-ENQ	5.233	2.321	9.543	77	5	2.000	0.000

Size nos.: 3

Figure 9.14   MNDS non-all site run for Scandania training.

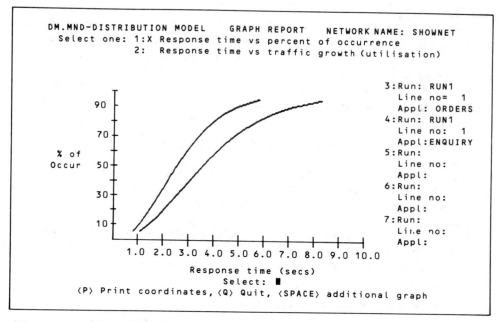

Figure 9.15   Response time versus percentage of occurrence.

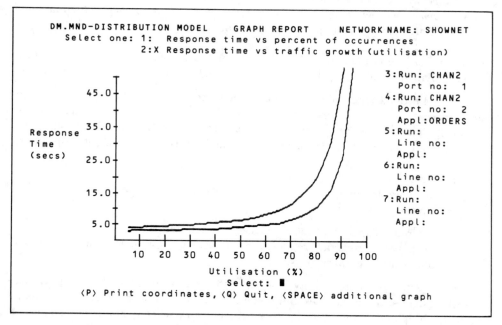

Figure 9.16   Response time versus traffic growth.

Link Model reports

The Link Model (LM) program uses information derived from the Response Model to create a network topological design using a modified version of the Esau – Williams heuristic algorithm. It derives a least-distance design using the rate file for cost comparisons to a direct, point-to-point line from the site to the host.

The LM can be used to create a network design using an existing network as a baseline, or as a 'greenfield' exercise. LM can be totally unconstrained, or constrained by such design factors as the following:

- Maximum line utilisation (response time constraint).
- Average response time limit.
- Number of transaction units per hour limit (throughput constraint).
- Branching limit (multipoint circuits). This constraint is normally imposed by the common carrier (e.g. British Telecom imposes a limit of twelve sites per branching panel).
- Nesting limit (multipoint circuits). This is a limit on the total number of branching panels that can be configured between a site and its host. This is normally imposed by the common carrier (e.g. British Telecom imposes a limit of two branching panels).

For all designs, the LM produces the following reports:

1. A *design summary* (Figure 9.17) showing a summary of design for the whole network with design statistics, link costs, ancillary costs and equipment costs.
2. A *line summary* showing detailed design statistics and costs for each individual line. The report includes some performance statistics. An example report is shown in Figure 9.18.
3. A *link details* report (Figure 9.19) showing the costs of each link associated with a particular line. Costs are shown as local end, service access and main link costs.

The LM provides the ability to perform pricing comparisons of the network design using different carriers and carrier services. MNDS is supplied with a complete set of rate (tariff) files for a variety of carriers and carrier services. This facility provides the basis for financial analyses of various scenarios, and return on investment projections.

Sensitivity analysis

Before the network design is finalised, a sensitivity analysis must be performed in order to determine the following:

1. The maximum capacity of the proposed network design.
2. The design weaknesses that renders the proposed network design unstable under particular workload characteristics.

The objective of the sensitivity analysis is to assess how vulnerable the proposed network design is to inaccuracies and invalid assumptions that may have been made during analysis and design. Ideally, the final network design should be capable of absorbing the inaccuracies that are inherent in the assumptions made thus far in the

```
10:02:52                                                          12-04-91

Network name: SCANTRA                            Design name: RMLM

Time created: 15:02:18                           Date created:12-04-91
Rate file name: KLN390                           Based on: ORIGINAL

        **********************
        *    LINK  MODEL     *
        *   RMLM    DESIGN   *
        *      Page  1       *
        **********************

-------------------- INPUT SUMMARY --------------------------------------

                        Design Parameters
                        -----------------

Design type: Multipoint
Site selection: All sites

-------------------------------------------------------------------------

                         Design weights
                         --------------

        RM performance was selected.      Avg. response time: 5.000 sec

RM ALLSITES run name: PCOM1            Utilisation 40.00 %

-------------------------------------------------------------------------

                          Design pricing
                          --------------

  Site to Site Links      Concentrator to Host Links      Host to Host Links

Line speed:  9.6 KBPS     Line speed:  9.6 KBPS

        Annual   Connection        Annual   Connection       Annual   Connection

DCE costs                 DCE costs                     DCE costs
  Modem   £ 171.00  £ 290.00  Modem   £ 171.00  £ 290.00   Modem   £ 0.00  £ 0.00
DTE costs: £ 0.00  £ 0.00   DTE costs: £ 0.00  £ 0.00   DTE costs: £ 0.00  £ 0.00
```

Figure 9.17 An example design summary.

211

```
5:02:52                                                                          12-04-91

Network name: SCANTRA                                                 Design name: RMLM

Time created: 15:02:18                                                Date created:12-04-91
Rate file name: KLN390                                                Based on: ORIGINAL

                              *********************
                              *  LINK  MODEL      *
                              *  RMLM    DESIGN   *
                              *    Page  2        *
                              *********************

----------------------------- DESIGN SUMMARY ----------------------------------

                                  Statistics
                                  ----------

Number of lines = 7    Number of terminals = 78           Average response time = 15.30 secs
Number of sites = 8    Number of transaction units/hour = 5966.0   Utilisation = 79.86 %

                              Channel costs

                                          Annual              Connection
Distance               607.00   £       13687.00      £        6812.00
Ancillary charge 1                          0.00                   0.00
Ancillary charge 2                          0.00                   0.00
Ancillary charge 3                          0.00                   0.00
Ancillary charge 4                          0.00                   0.00
Branching                                   0.00                   0.00

            TOTAL CHANNEL   :  £         13687.00      £        6812.000

                             Equipment costs

                    QTY         Annual              Connection
Modems               14   £      2394.00      £       4060.00
DTE                   7              0.00                  0.00

            TOTAL EQUIPMENT :  £      2394.00      £       4060.00

                                 Annual              Connection
            TOTAL DESIGN COST: £ 16081       £       10872.00
```

Figure 9.18 An example line summary report.

```
15:02:53                        *******************              12-04-91
                                *   LINK MODEL    *
Network name: SCANTRA           * RMLM   DESIGN   *     Design name: RMLM
                                *     Page  4     *
Time created: 15:02:18          *******************     Date created:12-04-91
Rate file name: KLN390                                  Based on: ORIGINAL

                                    ** LINE  1 **

-------------------------- LINK DETAILS --------------------------

                                    Channel costs
                                    -------------

                                    Local End
            N
         D  O
         I  N
From  Town/County    G E To  Town         Distance  Annual  Connection
 3 LEEDS             Y  1 BIRMINGHAM         0.00 £  390.00 £  670.00
H 1 BIRMINGHAM HOST  Y  1 BIRMINGHAM         0.00 £    0.00 £    0.00

TOTAL FOR RATE FILE KLN390 :                 0.00 £  390.00 £  670.00


                                    Service Access                Main Link
            N
         D  O
         I  N
From  Town/County    G E To  Town         Distance  Annual  Connection Distance  Annual  Connection
 3 LEEDS             Y  1 BIRMINGHAM         0.00 £    0.00 £    0.00    154.00 £ 2764.00 £  548.00
H 1 BIRMINGHAM HOST  Y  1 BIRMINGHAM         0.00 £    0.00 £    0.00      0.00 £    0.00 £    0.00

TOTAL FOR RATE FILE KLN390 :                 0.00 £    0.00 £    0.00    154.00 £ 2764.00 £  548.00
```

Figure 9.19 An example link details report.

213

analysis and design phases of SPIN. The level of accuracy that can be achieved depends on a variety of factors including the inherent stability of the applications being modelled, and the level of changes to the network configuration required. It is not unreasonable to expect 10–20 per cent error levels for models that have been carefully constructed according to the principles outlined in this chapter.

9.6   Voice network modelling software

There are fewer modelling software on the market that provide the network analyst with support for designing complex voice (and data) networks using the full range of carrier services available in major countries. In this section we will examine one package: Network Perception from Christie Telecom for designing voice and data networks. It provides the network analyst with the following functions:

1. The ability to catalogue details of networks with respect to sites, nodes, links and pipes within links.
2. The ability to detail the types of services available over specified links, and valid paths within the network for specific types of traffic
3. The ability to break down the network and model into manageable segments while maintaining overall connectivity.
4. The accommodation of cable or microwave, voice and data links irrespective of whether they are on fixed channel allocation, drop and insert, bandwidth multiplexing or Erlang-based traffic. This gives the ability to model voice and non-voice integrated networks.

Network Perception has the following module components:

- *Network Information Manager* is the primary module and provides facilities for cataloguing the details of networks to be modelled.
- The *Network Modeller* module provides network capacity planning and route allocation facilities.
- The *Quality Manager* module checks the conformance of network design to given quality standards (e.g. in the United Kingdom, NCOP – the Network Code of Practice) for private networks connecting to the public network.
- The *Topology Optimiser* module provides high-level topology design tools to ensure cost-effective solutions while still meeting service-level requirements.
- The *Network Price* module, which details carrier services and tariffs.
- The *Resilience Manager* module, which provides the ability to assess the resilience of a network design and to improve resilience by adding in components.

The network analyst inputs node details, a profile of the type of equipment that may be used in the network, possible link types and a traffic matrix of end-to-end traffic flows. The traffic matrix can be imported from a Lotus 1-2-3 spreadsheet, allowing direct input of the traffic figures.

A *site* (also referred to as a node) is defined as any location that is either the source and/or destination of a link in the network. A site can be as all embracing as a geographical location, e.g. Birmingham, as specific as a piece of equipment, e.g. a terminal concentrator or PABX, or as detailed as a telephone junction unit.

A *link* is defined as any connection between two sites (nodes). The *type* of link, number of circuits, channels and bandwidth is not defined at the link level but at the pipe level. A *pipe* is defined as a specific type of connection, line or circuit within a link. It can consist of a number of similar lines, e.g. parts of a wideband circuit such as 1 mbps of a 2 mbps link. Network Perception allows up to 255 pipes per link.

A *channel* is defined as a specific circuit allocation in a pipe, and is sometimes referred to as a 'traffic slot' when bandwidth pipes are being manipulated. Each pipe can accommodate up to 128 channels.

A *path* is defined as the route taken through the network by a circuit. A *circuit* is the name given to a specific end-to-end connection through the network. Each circuit has a unique reference number.

The above definitions provide the potential for modelling complex voice, data and integrated voice and data networks. By predefining pipes in terms of their usage (telemetry, speech, data, video, etc.) and also by type (microwave, fibre optic, analogue, etc.) circuits can be selected according to the type of traffic flowing over the network. The modelling of integrated voice and data networks is possible when voice is defined in terms of bandwidth rather than Erlangs.

Data on individual nodes and link pipes are recorded on special forms called *preforms*. A preform is unique to each node or link pipe. The recorded information is user defined and can be in almost any form, within the rules of preform layout. A preform in its basic form consists of 10 pages each with a 16×18 matrix of user data entry fields. Each type of preform (node and pipe) have different rules for construction that reflect the way each is used by other parts of the program and other modules. Predefined *keywords* are used to enable calculation of metrics such as delay, traffic loading, set-up time, grade of service, distortion and loss. The data associated with each preform is used for example by the network modeller to total and present a set of values for a circuit.

Topology optimisation is performed using both a multiple star network design algorithm (e.g. for speech tandem or star data network design) and a mesh network design algorithm (e.g. for pure data networks).

The common approach in the multiple star network is to use a multilevel hierarchical star network design. This concentrates the sites into a number of star networks, each centred on a hub site within a geographical area. These stars are then further divided into stars at the second level or more until all sites communicate with each other. An important factor affecting design is the amount of traffic passing to or through the sites. A heavily loaded site will naturally serve as hub sites to reduce the cost of links. A triangulated or point-to-point backbone link results, which can be modified by the routeing and resilience module to minimise the number of hops associated with routeing traffic, and by the network analyst to add resilience and so on. The mesh network design algorithm uses a complex, proprietary heuristic algorithm.

Typical reports on node equipment details, link details, circuit details, link loadings, system costs and delays may be stored or printed from the system. For each route through the network, Network Perception will accumulate various factors such as link delay, loss (dB), cost, distortion, multiplexor delay, length (km), resistance and echo loss. The network analyst chooses the best routes based on these values.

9.7 Obtaining management and user approval

The final network design must be seen by management as the solution to a stated set of requirements. Some of these requirements (i.e. strategic requirements) relate to tangible cost savings, while others often relate to less tangible savings (e.g. growth in certain existing workloads).

The case for upgrading the existing network should therefore be presented as a network capacity plan, with an associated cost/benefit analysis. The goal is to get senior management to approve the plan and to authorise the required expenditure.

The network capacity plan, which is a tactical planning document, should include the following:

1. A section outlining *where* the organisation intends to get to in terms of how the communications infrastructure supports its business strategy. Indeed, the communications infrastructure may well be a key determinant of the organisation's future strategy. This section should be a summary of the strategic phase of SPIN. Some infrastructure requirements will be the result of 'bottom-up' analysis of the existing portfolio of applications. Growth of existing workloads, and other factors will also be documented in this section.

2. A section outlining the timescales for milestones to be achieved.

3. A section summarising the benefits of achieving the stated milestones, and the costs of not achieving them. The risks of overrunning timescales should also be outlined.

4. A section detailing the resource implications (i.e. technological, human and financial) of meeting each milestone. The risks of exceeding the stated costs should also be outlined.

5. A section detailing final recommendations and financial commitments required.

The delivery of a well-structured report encompassing the above information, followed by a verbal presentation, is found to be the best approach for seeking management approval.

9.8 Summary

This chapter has described the approach used in the design phase of SPIN to design a flexible, cost-effective communications infrastructure to meet the present and future needs of an organisation.

The deliverable from this phase is a network capacity plan detailing the precise network components and design proposed to meet a stated set of requirements. The financial and human resource implications are also included.

The next chapter describes the implementation phase of SPIN.

216

CHAPTER 10

The implementation phase

10.1 Introduction

The use of the term 'implementation' in this context refers to the acquisition, installation and satisfactory operation of the new network infrastructure which was designed in the design phase of SPIN. It includes ensuring support of the implementation by the appropriate user(s).

In essence, this is a change management exercise. The change required involves both technological change and 'people' changes (e.g. a realignment of skills). Despite growing awareness of 'people' problems when information technology is introduced, network planners still focus on the technical aspects of implementing a particular network design without due regard to the eventual users of the service. Factors such as ease of use, reliability, responsiveness, availability and adherence to budget and project timescales tend to engender either positive or negative feelings about the system being implemented.

There is also a wealth of other factors that determine whether the implementation phase will be smooth or problematic. At this stage, being aware of these factors is instructive and serves to reinforce the importance of proper project management, taking into account user perceptions, training requirements and the interface through which the user accesses network services.

In this chapter we discuss the range of activities required to convert the network design delivered by the design phase of SPIN into an operational system. The process is illustrated in Figure 10.1. The deliverables from this phase are as follows:

- An implementation plan, identifying what tasks are to be carried out, and timescales.
- A management plan, identifying the organisational structure, skills and resources required to implement and subsequently manage the network.
- A contingency plan, identifying potential sources of failure and action plans for service restoration.
- A financial plan, identifying the capital costs, recurring costs and cash flows associated with the above plans.

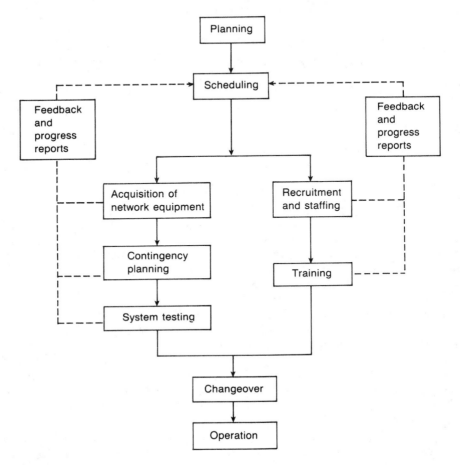

Figure 10.1   The implementation phase of SPIN.

The implementation phase of SPIN can account for as much as half of the total resources allocated to the development of the communications network. Effective project management that takes into account all aspects of implementation planning will lead to successful implementation of the network design.

10.2   The planning and scheduling phase

A project plan must be developed that identifies in advance what is to be achieved, how it will be done and a forecast of timescales. It consists not only of a detailed implementation plan, but must incorporate training plans and identify tasks requiring user involvement.

218

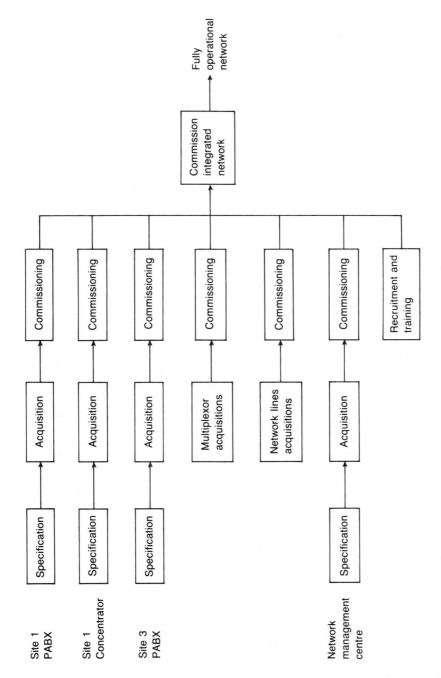

Figure 10.2 The implementation plan: logical view.

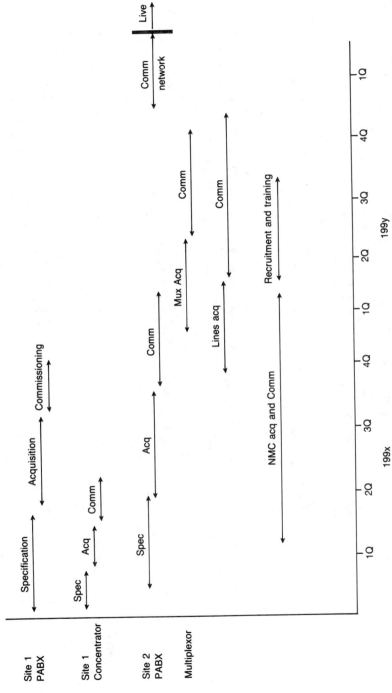

Figure 10.3   The implementation plan: physical view.

The tasks involved in acquiring network equipment and implementing the new design can be difficult and very complex. The implementation plan will necessarily be complex and detailed. The use of project management aids such as Gantt charts, critical path analysis (CPA) or program evaluation and review technique (PERT) should be used in order to take full account of lead times for equipment, staffing levels and other factors.

The network capacity plan should provide timescales and risk analyses that need to be taken into account. In particular, the implementation approach (e.g. a phased, pilot or a 'big-bang' approach) needs to be determined.

Another key factor is the network management centre (NMC). The NMC for the new network must be in place before user acceptance in order to ensure a smooth transition. Implementation planning must include the following features:

- Controlling all necessary resources.
- Motivation of users.
- Production of training material and operating manuals.
- Organisation of the changeover.

The first step is to identify the main tasks necessary to implement the network. The task specification should be detailed enough to identify which individuals or departments should be assigned to the task. The relationship between tasks (i.e. the precedences) should also be identified in order to construct a logical view of the implementation plan. This is illustrated in Figure 10.2. The logical view is then converted into a detailed implementation plan by identifying the duration of each task. A Gantt chart (Figure 10.3) or PERT network is used to illustrate the implementation plan graphically.

The use of project planning aids enables the 'critical path' in the implementation and the key tasks to be identified.

10.3   Acquisition of network equipment

When purchasing electrical equipment such as a video-recorder, the technology used and the vast array of features available may be attractive, but the final selection is usually based on a set of mandatory and desirable features, performance levels and cost. The same single-minded approach must be used when procuring network equipment. In many cases there is considerable choice of equipment ranging from the basic level to a full-featured product. The most cost-effective solution should be chosen.

When procuring network equipment, there will be a requirement to purchase both standard, routine equipment, and more complex equipment where it is less certain which product most suits a particular requirement. A simple request for a quotation is sufficient for standard equipment, but an invitation to tender (ITT) (or request for

```
┌─────────────────────────────────────────────┐
│             Invitation to tender             │
│                     for                      │
│                Scandania Ltd                 │
│                                              │
│   1.  Introduction                           │
│       1.1  Purpose of ITT                    │
│       1.2  Confidentiality                   │
│       1.3  Summary of requirements           │
│                                              │
│   2.  General information                    │
│       2.1  The selection process             │
│       2.2  Timescales                        │
│       2.3  Workload to be supported          │
│       2.4  Outline of alternative proposals  │
│                                              │
│   3.  Specification                          │
│       3.1  Hardware requirements             │
│       3.2  Software requirements             │
│       3.3  Support requirements              │
│       3.4  Cost requirements                 │
│                                              │
│   4.  Reply formats                          │
│       4.1  Configuration details             │
│       4.2  Cost schedule                     │
│       4.3  Underlying assumptions            │
│                                              │
└─────────────────────────────────────────────┘
```

Figure 10.4 Example invitation to tender (ITT).

proposal) is required for complex equipment. A typical ITT is illustrated in Figure 10.4.

The responses to the request for quotations and ITT provide the base information required to conduct an evaluation and selection exercise. The outcome is the selection of the most cost-effective solution to a given requirement. A systematic means of evaluating alternatives should be devised. The following are important factors to be considered in the evaluation process:

● Analysis of financing options (rent, lease or buy).
● Post-purchase maintenance and support service. Both prime-shift and overtime charges should be examined. The terms of the maintenance agreements and the quality of maintenance should be assessed.
● Assessment of whether the equipment will indeed handle the proposed workload. Benchmark analysis is useful here, but requires time and effort.

A template of evaluation criteria is illustrated in Figure 10.5. A matrix of evaluation criteria versus ITT submissions can be created. A weighting can be attached to each criteria, thus generating an overall rating for each ITT. The most cost-effective proposal is finally selected.

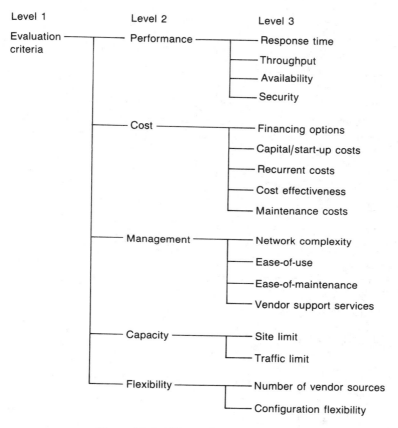

Level 1	Level 2	Level 3

Evaluation criteria

Performance — Response time — Throughput — Availability — Security

Cost — Financing options — Capital/start-up costs — Recurrent costs — Cost effectiveness — Maintenance costs

Management — Network complexity — Ease-of-use — Ease-of-maintenance — Vendor support services

Capacity — Site limit — Traffic limit

Flexibility — Number of vendor sources — Configuration flexibility

Figure 10.5 The evaluation template.

10.4 The contingency plan

A contingency plan should identify action plans for back-up and recovery of the entire environment. This includes buildings, hardware, software, data and communication lines. The plan should identify the sources of failure for which it supplies a recovery plan. Departments and individuals responsible for carrying out aspects of the action plan should be clearly documented.

The first step in developing a contingency plan is to assess existing recovery and back-up controls within the network. This may be achieved by starting at one end of an existing link and checking each component of the link to establish whether a fallback procedure exists (or whether it is cost effective to provide fallback for that component). The matrix in Figure 10.6 can be used during this review to document

223

all components considered. Components that should be considered include the following:

- Communication lines.
- Concentrators, multiplexors and switching equipment.
- Terminal equipment.
- Power and other non-commmunications support facilities.

Of course, the contingency plan itself should be stored in a safe place where it cannot be destroyed in the event of a major disaster (but must also be accessible to those personnel who need to use it!)

Back-up and recovery controls/threats and omissions

Components						
Host computer						
Applications software						
Operating software						
Front-end processor						
Multiplexor/concentrator						
Communication line(s)						
Modems/termination units						
Terminals/workstations						
People						

Figure 10.6 Contingency review matrix.

10.5 Recruitment, staffing and training

The management plan can be developed in parallel with the implementation and contingency plans (though they will have a bearing on personnel in terms of skills and training requirements). The plan identifies three aspects:

- The proposed organisational structure of communications management in relation to other structures.
- Skills and resource requirements.
- Recruitment and training requirements.

224

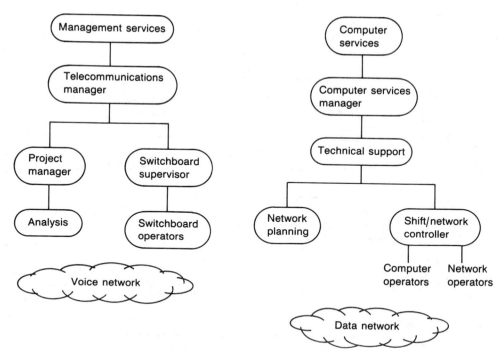

Figure 10.7   Separate management structures.

Organisations have traditionally developed separate structures for managing voice and data networks. This is illustrated in Figure 10.7. With the move towards the integration of voice and data networks it is problematic to maintain separate structures. These problems are greatest at the level of network management where it is difficult to implement a coherent and efficient network management centre.

A more integrated organisational structure is illustrated in Figure 10.8. In particular it illustrates that the user interface (the help desk) services both voice and non-voice problems and maintains a single point of contact for problem resolution.

10.6   The changeover

Changeover from the old system to the new should be considered only when the new system is fully tested. It is often not possible, however, to test fully the configuration until it is operational because of the complexity of the network configuration.

A large steel manufacturer decided that an essential prerequisite to changeover was formal factory acceptance testing procedures. An entire network was assembled, tested and quality assured on the factory floor prior to delivery of equipment to the sites. In the case of this company, it was impossible to plan a phased approach to the

225

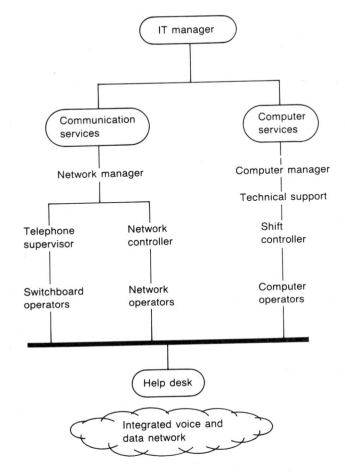

Figure 10.8   An integrated management structure.

new network. A direct changeover or 'big-bang' was required over a single weekend involving the commissioning of 11 tandem switches, reconnection of over 30 2 mbps links, transfer of 700 analogue private wires and other lines!

It is essential, if a direct changeover is adopted for implementation, for the network planner to have previously established complete confidence in the new network configuration. Meticulous co-ordination procedures and communication are required throughout the changeover if the outcome is to be successful.

10.7   Summary

This chapter has described the approach used in the implementation phase of SPIN to ensure a successful transition from the final network design (delivered by the design phase of SPIN) to a fully operational network approved both by management and users. The deliverables from this phase are as follows:

- An implementation plan, identifying what tasks are to be carried out, and timescales.
- A management plan, identifying the organisational structure, skills and resources required to implement and subsequently manage the network.
- A contingency plan, identifying potential sources of failure and action plans for service restoration.
- A financial plan, identifying the capital costs, recurring costs and cash flows associated with the above plans.

CHAPTER 11

Network management

11.1 Introduction

Network management (NM) is the corner-stone of the successful operation of network facilities. The objective of the NM phase of SPIN is to bring all these facilities under complete control. This chapter will describe a number of functions that are associated with NM and will examine how this functionality can be achieved in practice. Finally, the role of NM standards will be considered in the light of today's approaches to NM solutions.

11.2 What is network management?

Network management has, in the recent past, been largely associated with those tasks involved with the day-to-day operation and control of networks. However, some current perceptions and definitions have widened the scope of NM to include other activities and tasks that go beyond routine operational functions. For example, a data-processing manager who spoke at a recent NM conference in the United Kingdom, identified his main requirements as planning and implementation of voice and data networks, as well as real-time control. A similar, broader scope can be seen from the following categories, used to judge the Network Manager of the Year, awarded in 1989 by a consortium in the United Kingdom.

- Use of appropriate technology.
- Cost management.
- Support of the business objectives.
- Service to users.
- Measurement of NM objectives.
- Future directions.

This broadening of the scope of NM reflects the increasing importance of information networks in organisations that use networks to deliver services both internally and externally. As we have shown in this book, networks are critical to the operation of the business enterprise and are of fundamental importance in product or service delivery systems in many organisations. Consequently, the strategic importance of networks has raised the profile of NM in the overall IT management sphere.

The scope of NM also reflects the nature of today's enterprise networks. Information networks are often multivendor and may include interconnected LANs and public and private WANs. Information networks tend to grow in size and complexity; they are rarely static, but are subject to change. Consequently NM is, in its broadest sense, concerned with ensuring that all the network facilities used by an organisation meet the day-to-day requirements of the organisation and are responsive to change. In other words, NM covers the day-to-day, routine control of the network *and* the management process associated with the continued operation of the network in the future. In short, NM ensures the provision of networking services throughout the whole enterprise and the planning of future services.

A useful definition which encapsulates the broad scope of NM has been put forward by the Butler Cox Foundation (London, UK) in their Research Report No. 65 (August 1988). The report defines NM as:

> The set of activities required to plan, install, monitor and maintain all network components in order to achieve specified service levels reliably, at an acceptable and an agreed cost.   (Butler Cox, 1988)

The process of network planning has been described in earlier phases of SPIN and SLAs have been referred to in Section 8.4. The reminder of this chapter will focus on the broad set of functions that fall within the scope of NM as described in this section.

11.3   Network management requirements

The conference speaker referred to at the beginning of Section 11.2 also made the point that one of his principal requirements was a personal computer with each part of his organisation's network plugged into it; i.e. a single NM device which monitors each component of the network in an integrated manner. Research by Butler Cox (1988) confirms this clear need for an integrated network management (INM) system and identifies a number of functional requirements of an INM system, based on responses from network managers. According to the research, most managers believed that an NM system should carry out the following functions:

- Perform as an integrated whole.
- Collect information from any network component.
- Control any network component.
- Support the majority, and preferably all, NM activities (see Section 11.4).
- Minimise, or eliminate, duplication of information.
- Automate routine tasks.
- Provide a consistent and easy-to-interpret user interface.
- Display graphically, in real-time, the current configuration and status of the network.
- Reduce the expertise or time required to perform an activity.

In essence, network managers express a clear need for INM systems which combine NM tools that monitor a wide range of multivendor products and network environments. However, such INM systems are not yet available; NM 'islands' or separate 'element' managers exist in most organisations. In general, separate NM tools cover the routine management of the element parts of the information network. Tools are often proprietary and do not interface with one another, which leads to a complex NM environment. Furthermore, today's NM tools cover only routine NM functions rather than the broader range of NM activities referred to in Section 11.2.

Despite the inadequacies of today's NM tools and their level of integration, it is nevertheless helpful to describe NM as a set of activities, even though some of these activities are not yet supported by tools.

11.4 Network management functions

The need for INM systems indicates the scope of management requirements of voice and data networks in many organisations. Consequently, it will be helpful to describe NM in terms of a set of functions that cover the real-time control of network services and the on-going provision of network services. There are two groups of functions:

1. Day-to-day functions.
2. Planning functions.

11.4.1 Day-to-day functions

Day-to-day functions cover the routine, real-time control of the information network and the associated administration of network operations. These functions include the following:

- Monitoring and maintaining SLAs.
- Fault management.
- Change management.
- Performance monitoring.
- User support.
- Security.
- Accounting.

Monitoring and maintaining SLAs
Service-level agreements (SLAs) were discussed in Section 8.4. They are the basis for the development of network services and provide a base from which to monitor and review the performance of network facilities.

Fault management
This activity covers the identification, diagnosis and repair of faults in network components and the provision of an alternative service where possible and, if necessary, in line with SLAs. NM tools are available for this activity.

Change management

This activity covers inventory management of all network components and control of the configuration of the network, including principal and alternative network routes. Change management also covers controlling additions, moves and other changes in end systems, circuits and other network hardware and software. Change management should be supported by an inventory and configuration database, which also supports the graphical representation of parts of or the whole of the network configuration. If possible, this database should interface with network-modelling tools. Some NM products provide an inventory and configuration database.

Performance monitoring

This activity monitors the utilisation of the network in order to deliver network capacity to meet current requirements and plan for additional capacity. This involves monitoring and analysis of network utilisation in terms of traffic throughput and trends. NM tools are available that perform the monitoring function of network components and circuits. Monitoring of performance is closely linked to the maintenance of SLAs.

User support

This activity covers user training, advice, consultancy and support in all matters associated with access to and use of network facilities and services. A help desk is usually established as a point of contact which is staffed by personnel who can give immediate support and assist in solving problems quickly.

Security

Security concerns access to applications and information that are located in network components such as centralised or distributed computers. Access to these resources is usually implemented in the operating system of multi-user, centralised computers. In the case of LANs, network operating systems provide varying degrees of security. Security is necessary to ensure that access to these services is controlled and authorised. Security procedures should be subject to regular audit and review.

Accounting

This activity involves converting the costs of operating the network facilities and services into acceptable costs to end users. Users can be charged for using the network on a budget or profit centre basis, or some other appropriate basis. Information concerning who is logged on to what processor or what service must be collected and processed in order to produce invoices or bills to users. In WANs, mainframe computer and minicomputer operating systems usually provide statistics that can be used as the basis for accounting purposes. In LANs, some network operating systems gather similar statistics on the use of network services. In both cases, these facilities are separate from today's NM tools.

231

11.4.2 Planning functions

Planning functions cover the longer-term activities, and associated management and administration, that are linked with the continued operation of network facilities in the light of future requirements. These activities include the following:

- Tactical planning and design.
- Cost control.
- Supplier relations and policies.

Tactical planning and design
This activity involves planning to ensure that the network will be able to respond to growth in traffic volumes and will accommodate new applications and services. Detailed analysis and design of new applications is achieved by carrying out the appropriate phases of SPIN.

Cost control
This activity involves monitoring the long-term costs of operating the network and the adherence to agreed budgets.

Supplier relations and policies
The objective of this function is to monitor the policy of suppliers and vendors on issues such as the following:

- Purchase charges.
- Tariff structures (PTTs/PTOs).
- Maintenance charges and contracts.
- Standards supported.
- Standards developments.
- Technical developments.

Supplier relations refer to those activities surrounding the negotiating of purchase and maintenance contracts associated with the acquisition of equipment and services.

11.5 An integrated network management architecture

The previous section discussed the set of activities that fall within the scope of NM. Figure 11.1 presents a model architecture of an integrated network management (INM) system that would support most of these activities. The model shown in Figure 11.1 comprises a number of modules, each of which supports a different NM activity. Integration of activities is perceived by using a common database for inventory, configuration and utilisation statistics. This database provides data to the other modules. All the diagnostic tools for monitoring and control are connected to the network components and gather and present diagnostic information. As shown in the model, NM tools interwork and present consistent information to the main database.

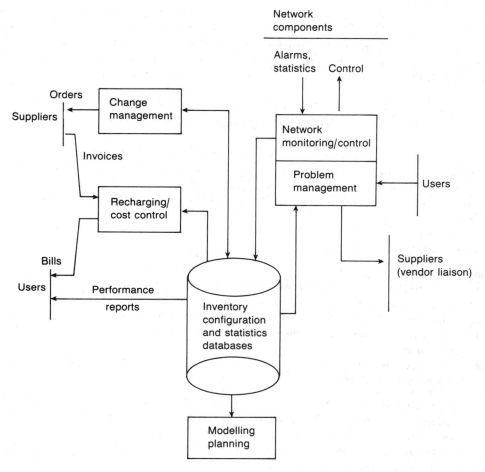

Figure 11.1 A model architecture for an INM system. (Source: Butler Cox, 1988.)

However, a fully integrated NM system of the type shown in Figure 11.1 does not exist today. The network monitoring and control module would be the most difficult to construct because of the wide variety of network components to which it must interface and the proprietary nature of the messages used by separate diagnostic tools. The other modules depend on the construction of the common database, which would be specified and constructed using established database design techniques. We have already seen (in Chapter 9) that network-modelling packages are available, though these have not yet been integrated with NM tools.

Although individual modules of the ideal INM system are available, it would be costly and complex to integrate them at present. Integration of diagnostic tools depends on standard NM protocols to pass messages between the tool (the manager) and its agent located in a network component. Although standards are under development (see Section 11.9), most existing tools will not inter-operate in the way implied in the ideal model. Nevertheless, the model shown in Figure 11.1 can be used by the network manager as a framework within which to place NM activities and upon which to build an architecture based on diagnostic tools that are currently available.

11.6   Network management solutions

As has been mentioned earlier, today's NM products are mainly of the diagnostic type, i.e. they monitor network components and collect and display diagnostic information in a way that allows skilled staff to respond to events reported in the network. In other words, today's NM tools focus on routine, day-to-day NM functions.

There are, however, limitations associated with many of today's NM tools. These are summarised as follows:

- They are often proprietary.
- They are often narrow in focus, e.g. WAN only or LAN only.
- They lack integration with other tools and operate in isolation.
- They often provide data rather than information upon which to act.
- They control rather than manage, i.e. tools are reactive rather than proactive and preventive.
- They are limited to real-time control; they do not offer historical or trend-reporting capabilities.

Consequently several NM tools are required for multivendor WAN/LAN environments, which results in a complex NM facility that requires several terminals, interfaces and protocols. For example, an audit conducted in 1988 by one of the world's largest automobile manufacturers revealed that the company had information contained in 18 different NM systems!

Despite these limitations and complexities, a number of NM architectures are evolving in suppliers' products. The main architectures are as follows:

- The single, centralised solution.
- The manager of managers or 'umbrella' management solution.
- Multiple, co-operative managers.

Single centralised management
In this type of system, all information from network components is collected and stored at a single point. A schematic view of this approach is shown in Figure 11.2.

This type of system is generally provided by a supplier in order to manage its network equipment. The system is based on a highly centralised management organisation and usually requires a powerful computer to run it. This approach to NM is typified by IBM's NetView, a host-based system designed for the management of

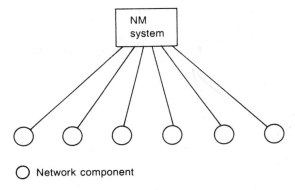

◯ Network component

Figure 11.2   Centralised management.
(Source: Butler Cox, 1988.)

SNA networks. Several other major computer suppliers are developing NM systems that conform to the architecture shown in Figure 11.2. In some cases, the supplier is constructing the core of the system and is encouraging other suppliers to develop interface modules. These systems provide a platform for the development of off-the-shelf and customised NM systems.

Umbrella management
Some suppliers have recognised that it is too costly and complex to provide a solution that will manage all network elements or components. Instead, these suppliers are building NM systems that will manage other element management systems. This 'overlay' or 'umbrella' approach is depicted in Figure 11.3.

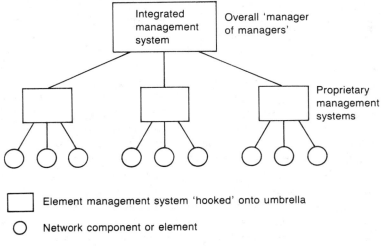

⬜ Element management system 'hooked' onto umbrella

◯ Network component or element

Figure 11.3   Umbrella management.
(Source: Butler Cox, 1988.)

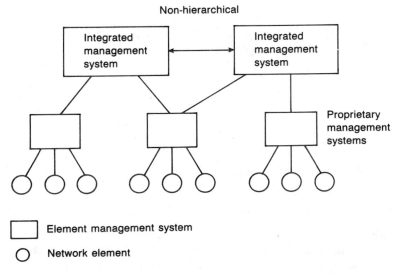

Non-hierarchical

Figure 11.4   Multiple, co-operative management (MCM).
(Source: Butler Cox, 1988.)

The umbrella or manager of managers (MoM) type of system relies on co-operation between suppliers of NM systems to achieve a degree of integration so that the overall manager of managers can be constructed. This is achieved by means of a common NM protocol to pass messages between the element management systems and the manager of managers. As NM protocols become standardised, this type of NM approach will emerge as a practical solution in multivendor, multiple-element management environments. Several of the PTTs, PTOs and larger computer suppliers appear to be moving towards MoM solutions; AT&T's Integrator product, for example, is designed to be an MoM.

Multiple co-operative management

This approach moves away from the single point of collection of diagnostic information, as seen in the previous architectures, towards a non-hierarchical co-operative management system. The architecture is depicted in Figure 11.4.

As can be seen from Figure 11.4, the architecture is an extension of the umbrella management approach. Element managers can report to more than one overall manager, and overall managers co-operate and exchange diagnostic information. The diagnostic database is, consequently, distributed, which makes the whole system more complex to construct than an MoM system. The distributed nature of the multiple co-operative management (MCM) system depends on the use of standard NM protocols to define the nature and meaning of event and control messages which pass between elements and their managers and between co-operating managers.

The MCM architecture provides an opportunity to divide NM functionality between several co-operating management systems and may prove to be the most appropriate long-term solution for complex network environments. Given the complexity of the MCM architecture, however, it will be some time before products appear.

11.7 LAN management

In the recent past, the focus of most NM activity has tended to be associated with the management of WANs. LAN installations were often straightforward and easy to manage. However, organisations today are interconnecting LANs and connecting them to corporate WANs. Consequently, LANs are becoming subject to the same NM requirements as wide area data networks. Furthermore, our experience has indicated that, due to the increase in the installed base of LANs, users are becoming increasingly aware of the need and the importance of managing their LANs. Unfortunately, our experience also tells us that managers of user departments often seriously underestimate the time and skills required to manage LANs effectively. Many LAN installations are now becoming too complex for user departments to manage themselves and they are seeking support from the NM function in the organisation. Consequently, it is important to recognise the need to integrate the management of LANs and WANs into a single management function. While integration of LAN management tools with WAN tool is desirable, most LAN NM tools are not integrated. However, several tools for monitoring the performance and utilisation of LANs are available today.

11.8 Voice network management

The cost of voice communications in most organisations can be several times as much as that of data communications. Customer service departments in organisations rely on PABXs and telephones to provide an efficient service, and the internal telephone network is vital in everyday business activities. Despite the importance of voice communications, many organisations devote relatively little effort to the management of voice networks and the control of costs. This is partly due to the perception that voice networks are essentially straightforward, trouble-free and are such a vital necessity that nothing much can be done about their cost.

The most common type of voice NM tool is known as a call logger. This determines usage of PSTN connections and forms the basis of billing users for external calls. Other tools, known as automatic call distributors, show real-time displays of calls waiting in a queue. This type of tool has been employed in organisations that rely on an efficient telephone answering service to handle customer calls and monitor the level of service being offered.

Today, voice NM tools are limited to those that can contribute to controlling the cost of voice communications and to automatic call distributors; some tools provide limited performance statistics. There is little sign that voice NM tools will be integrated with data NM tools in the near future. This means that the business function responsible for NM in an organisation must ensure that it possesses the tools and skills to manage WANs, LANs and voice networks. In most cases, this situation results in separate NM systems.

11.9   Network management standards

The emergence of the MoM and MCM architectures depends upon the presence of common management information that is passed between separate element managers. The major difficulty in integrating NM tools is the proprietary nature of the protocols used by separate tools. Consequently, the only way to overcome this problem is to use tools that conform to a common protocol for the exchange of NM information. Clearly, the development of standards is the most appropriate way to develop common protocols.

Work is progressing on the ISO standards for NM and a number of *de facto* standards are also emerging in advance of the completion of the work within the ISO. The emergence of *de facto* standards offers the best hope for network managers to develop INM systems and adopt a migration strategy towards the eventual implementation of *de jure* standards. The subsections that follow examine the main features of the *de jure* and *de facto* NM standards that are currently under development.

11.9.1   The work of the International Organization for Standardization

Open NM standards are based on the ISO's Common Management Information Protocol (CMIP). CMIP is a protocol that enables management requests and responses to be exchanged by means of a set of services known as Common Management Information Services (CMIS). Work is still in progress within the ISO to define CMIP/CMIS.

Another major task to be completed is the definition of the Management Information Base (MIB). The MIB will outline what network elements and classes of elements can be managed and will define these elements as managed objects. Given that there are thousands of network components in use, this gives an indication of the scale of the task. The MIB corresponds to the inventory, configuration and statistics database shown in Figure 11.1.

Although the work on the ISO's NM standards is unlikely to be completed much before 1993, an influential industry pressure group has been formed to accelerate the inter-operability of NM systems. The group, known as the OSI/NM Forum (based in New Jersey in the United States), has based their specification on CMIP. Other Forum specifications define managed object classes within the MIB. The Forum's long-term objective is to develop a global library of managed object definitions, which will include the Forum's agreed, core-managed object classes as well as proprietary definitions. The objective of this global library is to encourage the integration of NM tools.

The work of the OSI/NM Forum is important in the promotion of OSI NM standards, particularly given the complexity and scope of NM as a discipline and given the time it takes to develop and implement *de jure* standards. It is through industry groups such as the OSI/NM Forum that suppliers will be encouraged to implement OSI NM standards in their NM products. It is likely that there will be a great deal of activity in developing and promoting OSI NM standards throughout the 1990s.

11.9.2 The work of the Internet Engineering Task Force

The Internet Engineering Task Force (IETF), in the United States, has been charged with the development of a NM protocol for the popular TCP/IP networking protocol. The work of the IETF resulted in a *de facto*, industry standard known as the Simple Network Management Protocol (SNMP). SNMP is supported by several manufacturers for the purpose of managing TCP/IP WANs and LANs.

SNMP is less complex and less sophisticated than the ISO's CMIP. The MIB is simpler than that associated with CMIP, as might be expected from an industry standard protocol. Consequently, SNMP is becoming well established in the TCP/IP community and is likely to enjoy a relatively long life, due to its simplicity and ease of implementation.

Essentially, CMIP and SNMP have the same purpose: they both specify how NM information is exchanged between NM tools. Consequently, some network managers and users regard SNMP as a migration step towards CMIP, just as they regard TCP/IP as a migratory step towards OSI. However, due to the relatively faster development of SNMP and TCP/IP than that of CMIP and OSI, it is likely that SNMP will coexist with CMIP for some considerable time. Convergence of SNMP and CMIP is, clearly, desirable, but is likely to take some time. In the meantime, it is probable that INM systems that support both OSI and TCP/IP NM protocols will emerge during the 1990s.

11.9.3 Heterogeneous LAN management

A second *de facto* industry standard should be mentioned at this point. Heterogeneous LAN management (HLM) is an important standard since its aim is to address the problem of managing mixed LANs such as interconnected Token Ring and Ethernet environments.

HLM is a specification that has been developed jointly by two companies: IBM and 3Com. The specification comprises a management protocol and an MIB, in common with CMIP and SNMP. The protocol is based on the CMOL: CMIP over LLC, i.e. CMIP running over the LLC LAN layer 2 protocol (see Figure 4.4). HLM, therefore, uses the lowest two layers of the OSIRM to transfer NM information and is suitable for managing LANs and mixed, bridged LANs. The most obvious limitation with HLM is that management messages cannot be routed, since the protocol does not use the OSI Network Layer protocol. Routers require a layer 3 protocol and CMIP will have to be used to manage LANs that are interconnected by routers.

The approach of the HLM protocol is similar to the IEEE's 802.1 committee's approach to LAN management, in that the 802.1b protocol is also based on a layer 2 protocol. At the time of writing, HLM is undergoing balloting within the IEEE and could soon be endorsed by that body.

11.9.4   Progress towards network management standards

Industry standards will develop faster than OSI standards, but will not cater for all of the NM functions outlined in Section 11.4. Consequently, progress towards a fully integrated NM architecture will be slow and will probably extend beyond the timeframe of the next five years. Even when standard protocols exist for exchanging management information between NM tools, the development of INM systems that cater for WANs, LANs and voice networks will necessitate a major undertaking on behalf of suppliers. Because of the scope and complexity of INM systems, it is unlikely that the network managers will be able to purchase a comprehensive INM product much before the end of the 1990s.

Despite the slow progress towards INM systems, network managers should adopt a policy of purchasing the best and most appropriate tools available and should aim to migrate the overall NM environment in the organisation towards the model shown in Figure 11.1. This will mean a piecemeal approach initially with, for example, several WAN tools and separate LAN tools. However, by replacing NM tools with those that support international standards, network managers will be in a better position to build integrated NM systems that meet the requirements of their organisations.

In summary, we can say that NM is a relatively new discipline and NM architectures and standards are at an early stage of development. While work on OSI standards is progressing, suppliers are introducing new products. These products are, however, currently still some way short of delivering a substantial degree of integration except where there is demonstrable inter-operability and conformance to standards such as SNMP or the ISO/NM Forum's CMIP specification. There seems little doubt that the 1990s will witness new developments in NM systems and an increasing recognition of the importance of the need for effective and comprehensive INM systems to support the requirements expressed by today's network managers.

11.10   Summary

This chapter has described the management issues that are addressed by phase 6 of SPIN: the management phase. The scope of network management has been interpreted broadly, in order to reflect the requirements expressed by network managers. A set of NM functions has been described, some of which can be supported by NM tools and some of which are supported by management procedures.

In the light of the broad scope of NM and the need to integrate NM tools, an ideal integrated network management (INM) architecture has been presented. The objective of this is to provide an architecture towards which network managers should migrate. Emerging architectures adopted by suppliers have been considered and compared. The problem of managing multiple networks of LANs, WANs and voice networks has been highlighted.

The chapter has also made the point that the solution to many of the problems of managing multiple networks lies in the development of standard protocols for the exchange of NM information between NM tools. The progress towards the establishment of *de facto* and *de jure* NM standards has been discussed and their importance in the development of INM systems has been highlighted.

(Before reading the Postscript, the reader is reminded to return to Chapter 7, which covers the feasibility phase, if that was passed over on the first read through.)

Postscript

In this book we have described a methodology for planning and designing information networks. For a large organisation, network planning and management can be a lengthy and complex process. The methodology breaks down this complex process into a number of manageable phases. The application of the methodology realises the following benefits:

- Evolution of a network infrastructure that underpins strategic and other applications, thus ensuring the explicit link between the IT strategy and the business strategy.
- Better control of network planning and management.
- Better co-ordination of human resources through well-defined tasks and links between tasks.

In any organisation there will be new applications being developed, and changes in the organisation's strategic position giving rise to new corporate strategies and supporting information systems. Therefore, SPIN is an iterative process triggered by these changes. However, SPIN will often be an updating process that will not require the use of the full methodology. For example, a full strategic analysis involving the strategic phase of SPIN is not required when an existing application is being significantly enhanced.

In situations that trigger a major change – for example changes in the market; a major acquisition; the availability of technology that provides new strategic opportunities – the use of the full methodology is required.

It requires experience and judgement on the part of the network analyst to decide which phases and tasks within phases are appropriate to a particular project.

For small and medium-sized organisations (SME) it is still necessary to use the methodology, though the scale and the scope is reduced. This is because the number of locations, applications, personnel and computing resources are significantly less than in a large organisation. In order to realise the benefits outlined above, the judicious use of SPIN is recommended in an SME. However, it is often the case that SMEs do not have the in-house skills to carry out SPIN. In these circumstances, SPIN provides the framework that helps to decide where to employ existing skills, build appropriate in-house skills, and where to use consultants and vendors. This will ensure that the organisation controls the process even though parts of it may be contracted out to consultants and vendors. Consequently, SPIN is as important to SMEs as it is to large organisations.

APPENDIX A

The capacity of an information channel

Prior to the advent of the digital computer in the 1950s a number of key developments refined knowledge of the limitations of transmission paths to communicate information. In 1928, a rigorous analysis of the fundamental theory of digital transmission was given by H. Nyquist (Nyquist, 1928a) and, in the same year, he published his classic paper, which presented an understanding of the significance of channel noise (Nyquist, 1928b). It was soon realised that there was a trade-off between noise and the bandwidth of a channel, and this was put on a formal theoretical basis by Claude E. Shannon working at Bell Laboratories. Shannon had read a paper by Ralph Hartley (Hartley, 1928) that presented a theory of communication in terms of the quantitative information capacity of a channel. This was much refined by Shannon who suggested that all forms of information could be encoded and transmitted as bits converted into electrical pulses along a channel. He added probability, entropy and noise to Hartley's picture and published his information theory in 1948 (Shannon, 1948). The key equation of the theory refers to the information capacity of a communication channel, and will be reproduced here because of its importance in quantifying this capacity in terms of the physical properties of the transmission medium. Applied to a noisy channel, the information carrying capacity (C) of a channel is given by:

$$C = w \, \log(1 + s/n) \text{ bps}$$

where w is the bandwidth and s/n is the signal-to-noise ratio.

It should be noted that C is a maximum value for a given channel; in practice it is difficult to approach this limit. For example, using typical signal to noise parameters of the PSTN, a telephone channel of bandwidth 3000 Hz can never transmit more than 30,000 bps. Current modem technology can deliver rates of the order of 19,000 bps. Higher bandwidth channels can transmit information at higher rates. For example, typical leased lines transmit data at rates up to 64,000 bps per channel.

APPENDIX B

Application sizing using the SSADM structured method

B.1 Introduction

Network capacity planning, part of the activity of network management, is used to predict the network capacity needed to support existing applications as they grow and new applications as they are implemented. Network capacity planning techniques are used to influence the design of applications to optimise the performance of applications sharing the same network infrastructure.

In the mid-1960s a number of large, costly and embarrassing failures in large data-processing applications occurred. It was evident at that time that the major contributor to failure was poor or non-existent use of system development techniques and project management. An understanding of the significance of information systems development methods emerged.

Methodology proposals were introduced by various sources, each consisting of the execution of several major phases of activity, from investigation to system implementation. A common set of processes emerged and the term *system development life-cycle* was used to describe the following phases of development:

1. Planning.
2. Analysis.
3. Design.
4. Implementation (construction).
5. Maintenance.

Early methodologies consisted simply of following steps similar to those given in Figure B.1. It was found, however, that this practice was not sufficient to yield successful information systems. It was realised that additional tools and techniques, and project management procedures were also required. *Structured* methods attempt to provide tools and techniques, in addition to the basic steps involved in the traditional development life-cycle concept, to increase the probability of developing a successful information system.

Examples of industry standard structured system development methods are Structured Design (by Yourdon), Jackson Systems Development (JSD), Information

245

```
I.   Planning
          1.1.  Request for a system study
          1.2.  Initial investigation
          1.3.  Feasibility study

II.  Analysis
          2.1.  Redefine the problem
          2.2.  Understand the existing system
          2.3.  Determine user requirements and constraints on a new system
          2.4.  Logical model of the recommended solution

III. Design
          3.1.  System design (or system specification)
          3.2.  Detailed design

IV.  Implementation
          4.1.  System building
          4.2.  Testing
          4.3.  Installation/conversion
          4.4.  Operations (refinement/tuning)
          4.5.  Post-implementation review

V.   Maintenance
          5.1.  Maintenance and enhancements
```

Figure B.1   The information system development life cycle.

Engineering (by Martin and Finkelstein) and SSADM. All of these methods concentrate on the information system's *functional* definition; few incorporate techniques for assessment of the level of that functionality – how well the system is expected to work (i.e. service level assessment). For illustrative purposes we will concentrate on the SSADM method.

The linking of network (and host) capacity planning and structured methods such as SSADM provides opportunities for systems analysts/designers to test the levels of service that the new information system is designed to provide against the results of a modelling exercise.

At the same time, the interface between structured methods and network capacity planning techniques allows modelling results to be fed back to analysts/designers at key points within the development life-cycle. It gives network (and host) designers earlier notice of new workloads that they will have to provide for.

B.2   Structured Systems Analysis and Design Method (SSADM)

SSADM was developed by the UK Government advisory body, the Central Computer and Telecommunications Agency (CCTA), in conjunction with Learmonth and

Burchett Management Systems (LBMS), a consultancy organisation. The CCTA specified that the methodology should have the following properties:

- It should be self-checking.
- It should use tried and tested analysis and design techniques.
- It should be tailorable.
- It should be teachable.

The method was fully accepted by the CCTA in January 1981, and became the recommended method for UK government projects from 1983. Today, SSADM is regarded as the *de facto* standard in the United Kingdom and is growing in significance on a European and international level. The CCTA is currently working with the British Standards Institute to define SSADM as a British Standard.

Currently, Version 3 is the most widely used release of SSADM, though the CCTA has recently (1990) launched Version 4. Version 4 is significant for network designers for it incorporates explicit links with capacity planning techniques and modelling. This is a much needed enhancement to the method. However, due to the lack of experience and availability of material on Version 4 at the time of writing and the widespread use of Version 3, it was decided to concentrate on Version 3 for the purposes of illustration.

SSADM (Version 3) is a six-stage method. The stages, illustrated in Figure B.2, broadly correspond to the typical development life-cycle. There is an optional feasibility phase, which is an abbreviated version of stages 1 – 3. Each stage of SSADM is further divided into steps where each step has a list of tasks, inputs and outputs. The purpose of each stage is as follows:

Stage 1 – Analysis of the current system

This involves the analysis of the current system and ensuring that it is correctly documented using *data flow diagrams* (DFD) and *logical data structure* (LDS) *diagrams*. A Problem/Requirements list (PRL) and a Base Constraints list are used to record functional and service-level requirements.

Stage 2 – Specification of requirements

This involves building on the user requirements specified in the PRL, adding audit, security and control requirements, and arriving at a required system specification. The specification includes, in addition to DFD and LDS techniques, the more dynamic view of the system data using the Entity Life History (ELH) technique, and the definition of Logical Dialogue Outlines (LDO) for those events which require an on-line interaction with a user.

Stage 3 – Selection of technical options

At this stage users are invited and assisted to choose a technical option from usually around six options which provide a solution to the system specification. The chosen

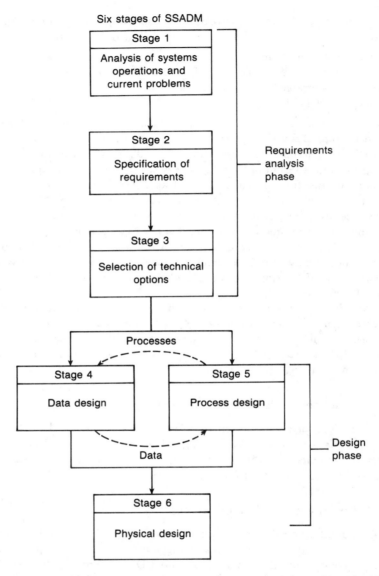

Figure B.2 SSADM (Version 3): a six-stage method. (Source: Simon, 1989.)

technical option forms the basis for implementation (i.e. the specification of the physical system). This is an important stage at which the capacity planner (network designer) interfaces with the user and analyst/designer to construct practical technical options, and to assist the user in choosing an option. The essential tasks for this stage are as follows:

1. If not produced during the feasibility phase, create up to six high-level technical options.
2. Create a list of base constraints (service-level objectives) which the options must satisfy.
3. Reduce the technical options to two or three based on technical feasibility.
4. Expand each remaining option into a more detailed specification which should contain:
   - a technical environment description;
   - a functional description;
   - an impact analysis;
   - an outline development plan;
   - a cost/benefit analysis.

Stage 4 – Data design

The data structures produced in stage 2 for the required system are designed at this stage. The principal technique used here is relational data analysis (RDA), which carries out data normalisation to third normal form. This provides a bottom-up view of the data, in contrast to the top-down view of the LDS produced in stage 2. These views are then merged to form the composite logical data design (CLDD).

Stage 5 – Process design

This stage is normally carried out in conjunction with stage 4. Here the logical processes are divided into enquiry processes and update processes and validated against the data design produced by stage 4. The detailed logical enquiry process outlines (LEPO) and logical update process outlines (LUPO) are completed at this point.

Stage 6 – Physical design

The required system is physically designed by creating the following:

- Physical data designs based on the specified DBMS product.
- Program specifications.
- System test plans.
- Operating instructions.
- Implementation plans.
- Manual procedures.

B.3 Interfacing network capacity planning and SSADM

At key points within SSADM, network (and host) capacity planners can use their expertise to offer assistance in assessing how well the new application will work. It can

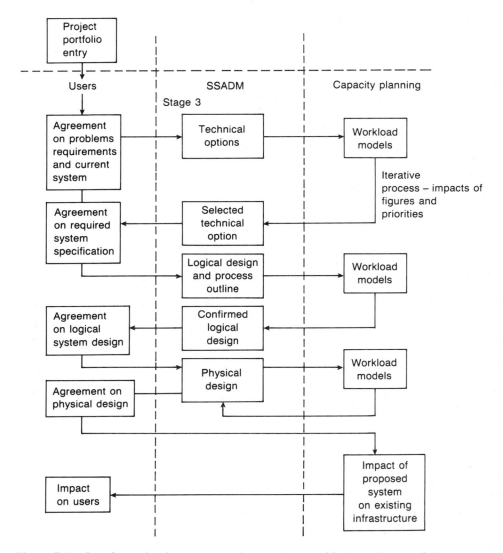

Figure B.3   Interface points between capacity planning and SSADM. (Source: CCTA, 1990.) (Reproduced with the permission of the Controller of HMSO)

be seen from Section B.2 that, for example, stage 3 of SSADM is a key stage for assessing service-level requirements.

Figure B.3 illustrates the key points at which information is passed to the users, the SSADM developers and capacity planners (CCTA, 1990). These interface points are described more fully in (CCTA, 1990) and rely on the following information being available at each point:

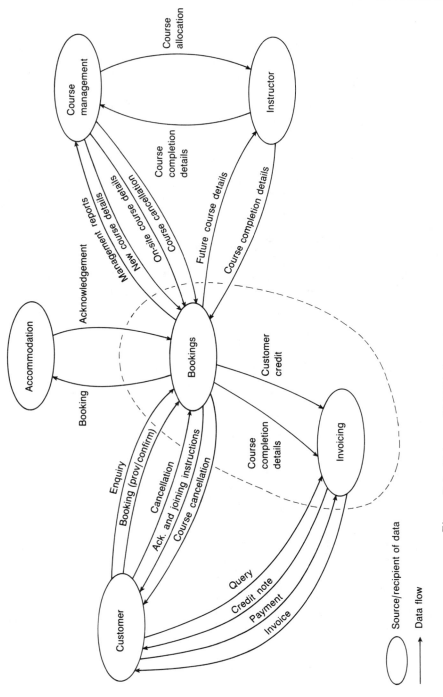

Figure B.4   Relevant SSADM forms for the Scandania training case study.

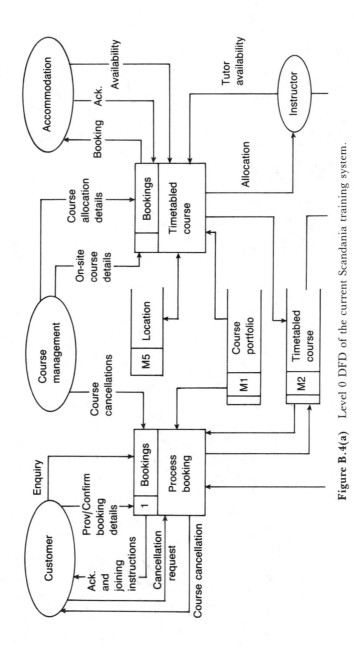

Figure B.4(a) Level 0 DFD of the current Scandania training system.

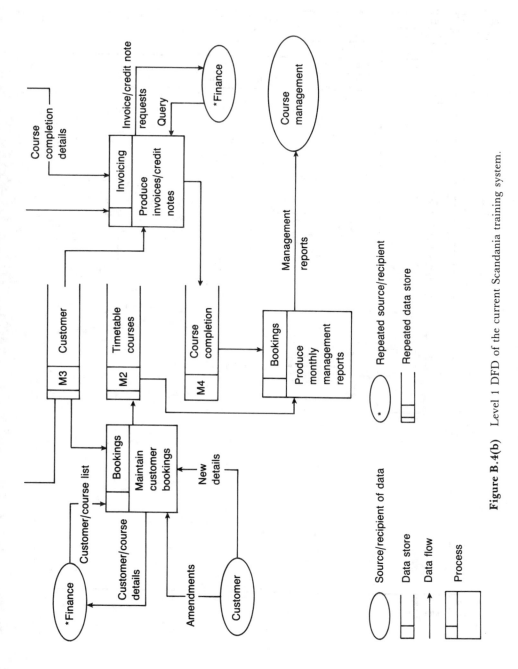

Figure B.4(b) Level 1 DFD of the current Scandania training system.

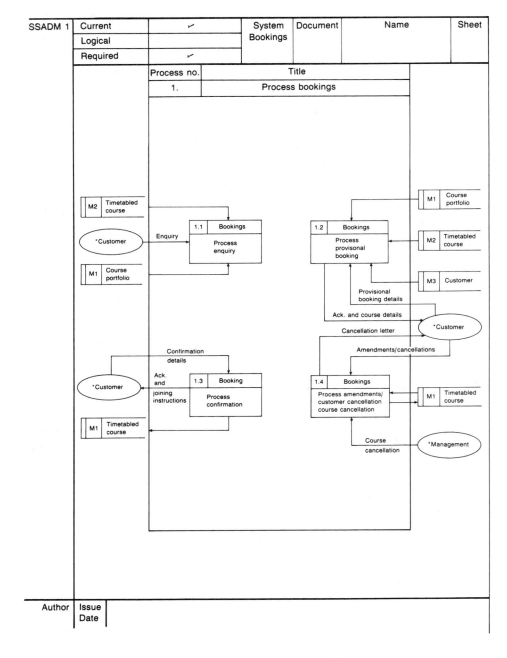

Figure B.4(c) Lower level DFD.

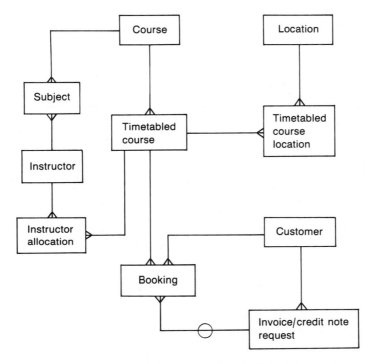

Figure B.4(d)   LDS of the current Scandania training system.

- Data sufficient to build workload models and hardware configurations.
- Service-level requirements attached to each workload.
- Modelling results describing throughput, response times, hardware utilisations and other data of interest, and a comparison against service-level requirements for each workload to assess whether the requirements are achievable, reasonable, and if so at what cost. These results must be presented in a form that is meaningful to the SSADM analyst/designer and user.

Intimate involvement in the development project will enable the capacity planner to use the information about workloads and hardware utilisations to optimise the design of the IT infrastructure and to carry out meaningful sensitivity and impact analyses. The greatest benefit will be advanced warning of the impact of new applications on the existing infrastructure.

B.4   Support for application sizing

The wealth of information produced by system development project teams that is of direct use to capacity planners has been underutilised. There are possibly four main reasons for this:

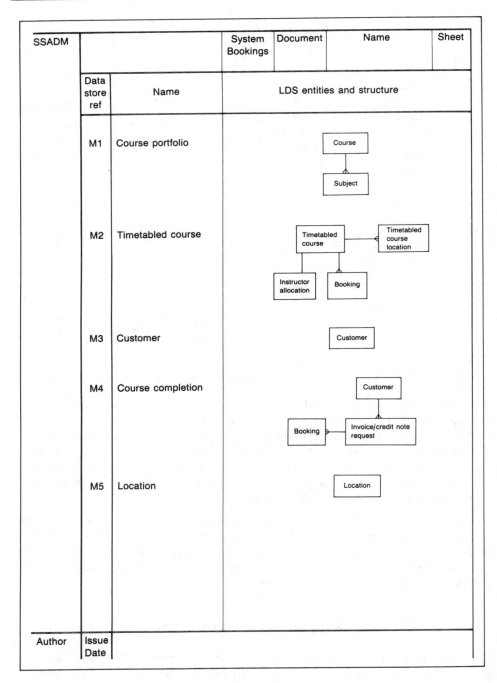

Figure B.4(e) Data store/entity cross-reference.

SSADM 2			System Bookings	Document	Name	Sheet

PRL ref. no.	User/ name ref.	Priority	Problems/requirements — Brief description	External document ref.	DFD/ LDS ref.	Solutions — Brief description	External document ref.	DFD/ LDS ref.
P001		1	Potential increase in volume due to support of external customers. Will not be able to offer a quality service unless all aspects of booking and invoicing are automated.					
P002			Timetabling of rooms, computers and other equipment is not handled well. Double booking of resources a frequent occurrence.					

Author	Issue Date	

Figure B.4(f) Problems/requirements list.

257

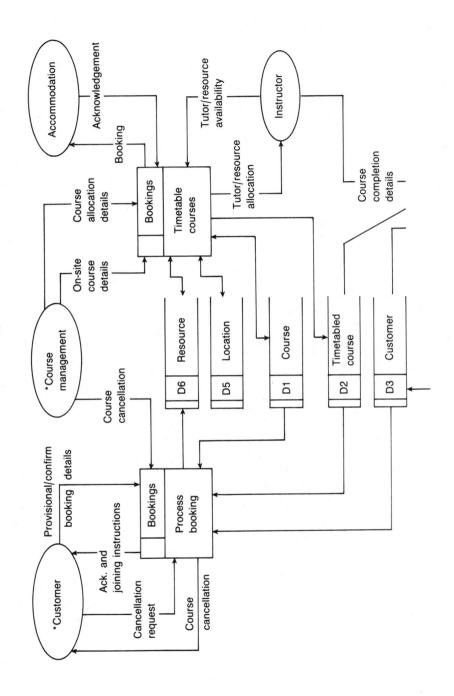

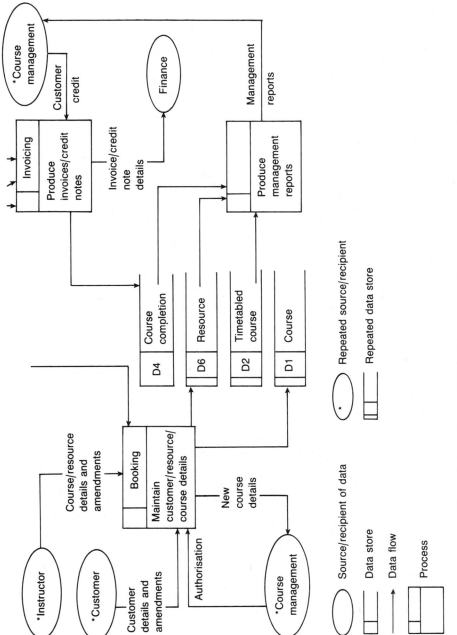

Figure B.4(g) Level 1 DFD of the required Scandania training system.

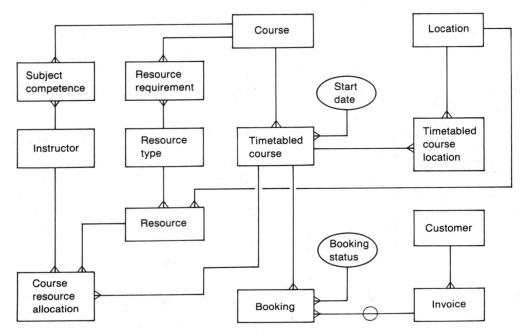

Figure B.4(h)   LDS of the required Scandania training system.

1. Structured development methods have not encouraged the involvement of capacity planners early in the development life-cycle. The result is a lack of well-defined interface points in established methods.
2. The application modelling and sizing is not a well understood subject by analyst/designers.
3. Capacity planners are often not well trained in structured system development methods and therefore find it difficult to be involved in the development process.
4. The application sizing process itself can be a long and arduous exercise without the use of computer-aided sizing tools. Application sizing tools are most useful if they can be used to model easily the proposed hardware/software platform, if they allow both crude and detailed sizings of workloads to be performed with a minimum of effort, and if they allow easy access to application data (for example by direct connection to the CASE tool being used by the developers).

Therefore there are four main actions required for successful application sizing:

1. Choosing a systems development method that incorporates interface points, or amendments to the current methods in use by the organisation.
2. Mounting an awareness campaign for application developers on the importance of application sizing early in the development life-cycle and the various approaches used. Also the role of capacity planners and the beneficial information that can be fed back on the proposed design should be emphasised.

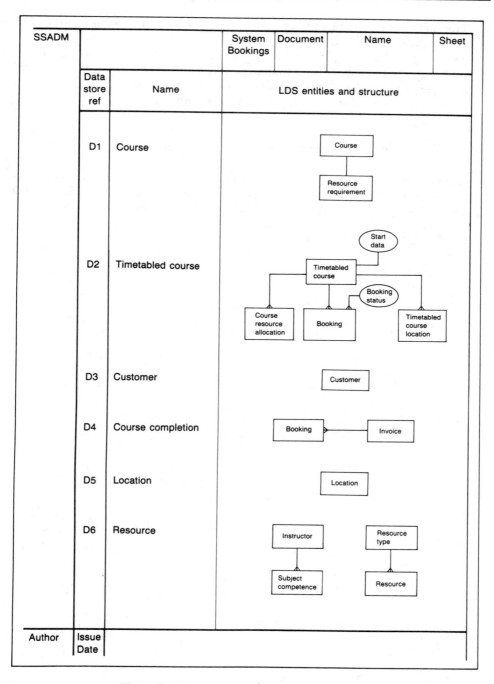

SSADM			System Bookings	Document	Name	Sheet
	Data store ref	Name	LDS entities and structure			
	D1	Course				
	D2	Timetabled course				
	D3	Customer				
	D4	Course completion				
	D5	Location				
	D6	Resource				
Author	Issue Date					

Figure B.4(i) Data store/Entity cross-reference.

3. Training for capacity planners on the system development method currently in use by the organisation.

4. Reviewing and selecting an application sizing tool that is most appropriate to your environment in terms of existing performance monitoring and capacity management tools, existing hardware/software vendor products, CASE tools installed, and maturity of the application sizing and capacity planning functions.

B.5 An example SSADM application

To illustrate the typical data that are available on applications developed using a structured development method, Figure B.4 contains a sample of SSADM data relevant to the sizing of the Scandania Training booking system.

APPENDIX C

An introduction to queuing theory

C.1 Introduction

Queuing theory has been used very successfully to estimate the performance of a number of facilities. In particular, components of computer and communication systems such as computer processors, disks, terminals, data-access mechanisms, communication links, concentrators and memory can be modelled as queuing systems.

Queuing theory is simply a mathematical tool for describing, in mathematical terms, the behaviour of queues in a system so that realistic estimates of response times and other values of interest can be computed.

In this appendix we examine the fundamental elements making a quantitative analysis of a communications network. A detailed mathematical description with supporting proofs is beyond the scope of this book. The reader is referred to several excellent texts in the Further Reading section of this book.

C.2 Overview of queuing systems

In computer and communication networks the contention for resources is an ever-present characteristic. Contention results from the inability of a resource to service immediately all requests demanding service from it. The result is usually a build up of queues and a delay in obtaining service. In some cases (e.g. the telephone system) contention for resources may result in the rejection or 'blocking' of requests for service (i.e. the request leaves the system without receiving any service).

It is obviously desirable to design a system that is capable of providing the service demanded – for example in terms of response time and maximum delay service-level objectives – under varying levels of demand. To achieve this, the behaviour of all the resources in the system must be understood in terms of likely service levels and delays under the range of predicted demand. Queuing theory is used to model as a queue any resource that is subject to contention. A queue is simply a service facility with a waiting room able to accommodate a line of requests (initiated by customers) waiting for service. A queue can therefore be characterised by six parameters that fully describe the behaviour of the queueing system:

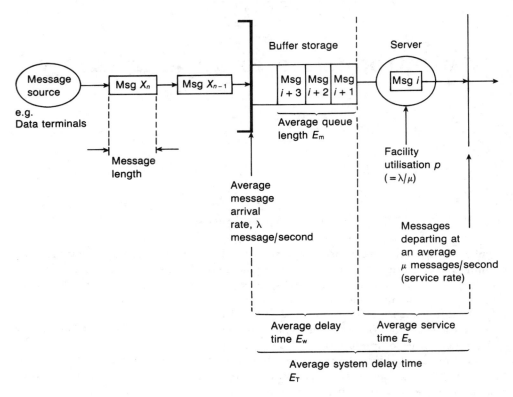

Figure C.1(a)   Queuing notation: data networks.

A   *The distribution of request arrivals.* For communication networks it is the message or packet arrival rate.

B   *The distribution of service times.* For communication networks the server is simply the communication link and the service time is the link transmission time. Consequently, for data networks *B* relates to the message or packet length distribution, and for voice networks the call duration distribution.

c   *The number of servers.* For communication networks it is the number of communication links servicing the queue.

K   *The maximum capacity of the queue.* For communication networks this relates to the maximum queue length or buffer size.

m   *The population of potential customers in the given source population.* If the customer population is very large (practically infinite) the arrival of a customer at a queue will not affect the rate of subsequent arrivals. If the customer population is relatively small, i.e. less than about 30, a single arrival will deplete the population and affect subsequent arrivals.

Z   *The queuing discipline.*

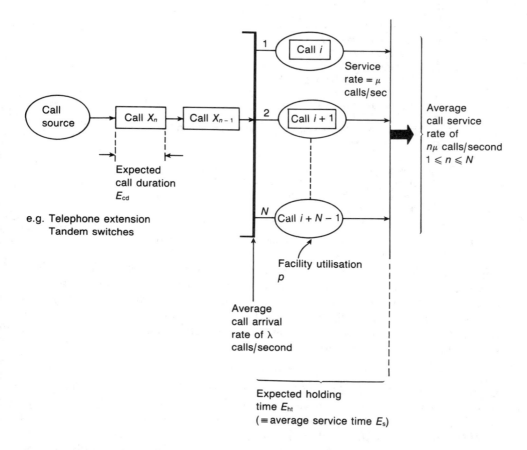

Figure C.1(b) Queuing notation: voice network with blocking switches.

Figure C.1 illustrates the important elements of a queuing model for data and voice networks.

The letters A and B in the Kendall notation refer to the characteristics of the input and output processes and are commonly described using the following symbols:

D Deterministic (constant) request arrival or service distributions.

M Exponential (Markov) inter-arrival or service time distribution (i.e. Poisson arrival or service rate distribution).

G General service time distribution (i.e. few assumptions are made about the service time distribution).

The queue discipline (or more accurately described as the 'service' discipline) specifies the order in which arriving requests are placed in the queue for service (which

p	Facility utilisation (λ/μ)
λ	Average arrival rate
μ	Average service rate
E_s	Average service time ($1/\mu$)
A	Traffic intensity (Erlangs)
N	Number of servers
P_B	Probability of blocking
P_D	Probability of delay
P_k	Probability of k messages in the queue (including the one in service)
E_{cd}	Expected call duration
E_{ht}	Expected holding time
E_m	Average number of messages waiting for service
E_n	Average number of messages in the system
E_T	Average system delay time
E_w	Average delay time

Figure C.1(c)   Summary of queuing notation.

implies the order in which they are serviced). Commonly used disciplines are FIFO (first-in, first-out) also known as FCFS (first-come, first-served), LIFO (last-in, first-out), FIRO (first-in, random-out) or some form of priority discipline. A notation defined by D. G. Kendall, known as Kendall's notation, is used to describe conveniently the value of the six parameters associated with a particular queuing system. In its most general form it is given by:

$$A/B/c/K/m/Z$$

Using this notation, each of the above letters is replaced by the corresponding value or symbol which corresponds to the queue of concern. In practice, K, m and Z are commonly assumed to be equal to infinity (i.e. no limit) and the notation shortened to $A/B/c$. For example the simplest model, the $M/M/1$ model, describes a queue with a Poisson request arrival rate distribution, an exponential service time distribution and a single server.

C.3   The Poisson distribution

The Poisson distribution is widely used in queuing theory since for many real-world systems (including communication systems) it approximates well to the actual behaviour of these systems.

In communication networks (like other systems) a message arriving is an event that is randomly occurring in time; their duration is relatively short and the main characteristic of the event is the time of arrival. Message arrivals may also be described by the length of time between arrivals (the inter-arrival time) and the number of arrivals in a given time interval. Furthermore, it is a common characteristic that a series of message arrivals in a time interval has no influence on arrivals in other non-overlapping time intervals.

Three basic assumptions are used to derive a message arrival rate based on the Poisson distribution:

1. Within a very short interval, the probability of only one message arriving in that interval is high.
2. Arrivals are memoryless, i.e. arrivals of messages are independent of each other. This is likely to be the case when the messages are generated from a large number of independent sources.
3. The characteristics of the message arrival distribution do not vary depending on the observation period.

It can be shown that the above characteristics of the message arrival events lead to the Poisson probability density function which is given by:

$$P_k(t) = \frac{(\lambda t)^k \, e^{-\lambda t}}{k!}$$

The parameter λ is the mean rate of Poisson arrivals. It turns out that the variance of the Poisson arrivals is also equal to λ.

The time between arrivals in a Poisson-distributed arrival rate turns out to be *exponentially distributed* where the probability between two successive arrivals decreases exponentially with the time between them. The probability density function of the inter-arrival time distribution is given by:

$$F(t) = \lambda e^{-\lambda t}$$

Again, λ represents the average arrival rate. The average time between arrivals is as expected $1/\lambda$. It turns out that the standard deviation of interarrival times is equal to the average, i.e. $1/\lambda$.

In the case where in a service facility the next customer is served as soon as the one in service leaves the system, it is apparent that the time between service completions must be equal to the service time. Therefore if the time between completions is exponentially distributed, then the service time itself is exponentially distributed in time. Hence the service time distribution in this case is a Poisson process.

The Poisson process is a special case of a more general process known as the Markov process (for a detailed discussion see King, 1990). A Markov process is a stochastic process that exhibits a particular characteristic, namely that the distribution at any time in the future depends only on the current state of the process and not on how that state was reached. This is known as the memoryless property and, as stated previously, is one of the basic assumptions of the Poisson process.

Other useful properties of the Poisson process are that, firstly, a distribution resulting from the sum of Poisson distributions retains the Poisson distribution. Secondly, if a Poisson stream is split into multiple substreams, each with a probability P_i of a job going to the ith substream, each substream is also Poisson with a mean rate of P_i. Finally, if the arrivals to a multiserver facility are Poisson with each server having exponential service times, the departures also constitute a Poisson stream. This is useful, for example, when modelling concentrators where several terminals are connected to a concentrator that is modelled by a single server.

C.4   Little's theorem

If there are a large number of requests in the system, then one would expect that the wait time for these requests will be long. This implies, as one would expect, a relationship between the number of requests in the system and response time. Little proved the following simple relationship:

$$E_n = \lambda E_T$$

The constant of proportionality is simply the average arrival rate (λ). A corresponding relationship also holds between the average queue length E_m and the average wait time E_w:

$$E_m = \lambda E_w$$

The above relationships are commonly known as Little's formulae and are extremely general in that they apply to general conditions met by most queuing systems. Using the fact that:

$$E_T = E_s + E_w$$

and multiplying by the average arrival rate, we derive the following:

$$E_n = \lambda E_s + E_m$$

This means that given the average arrival rate λ and average service time E_s, knowledge of any one of E_T, E_w, E_n, E_m allows the three others to be determined using the simple relationships above.

C.5 $M/M/1$ queue

In the context of communication networks, the simplest queuing system is the case where a single communication link of capacity C bit/sec services an infinite Poisson stream of messages according to the FIFO discipline and with no limit on the size of buffer memory. The Poisson stream has an average arrival rate of λ messages/second and that the length of messages is exponentially distributed with mean $(1/\mu)$ bits/message.

Since the link has a fixed capacity, it follows that the assumption of an exponential distribution of message length also implies an exponential distribution of service time with mean $1/(\mu C)$ – hence the notation $M/M/1$. The product μC is the service rate in messages per second. These assumptions help to simplify the calculations required to obtain response times, throughput, etc.

When a queuing system such as an $M/M/1$ queue is in equilibrium, the

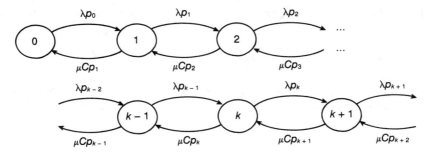

Figure C.2   State transition diagram for an *M/M/1* queue.

probability P_k that there are exactly k requests in the system does not change with time. In the equilibrium state messages are arriving and queued messages are being serviced at the same rate. This can be represented by a state transition diagram known as a birth–death process or Markov chain and is illustrated in Figure C.2. Thus in the steady (equilibrium) state the following relationships apply:

$$\lambda P_0 = \mu C P_1$$
$$P_1 = \mu C P_2$$

and in general

$$P_k = \mu C P_{k+1}$$

Defining $p = \lambda/\mu C$ (known as the facility utilisation or traffic intensity) and solving the above leads to the following relationship:

$$P_k = (1 - p)p^k$$

The mean number of messages in the system is given by:

$$E_n = p/(1 - p)$$

Little's formulae allows the simple derivation of the average system delay time:

$$E_T = E_n/\lambda$$

$$= \frac{p}{p\mu C(1 - p)}$$

$$= \frac{1}{\mu C - \lambda}$$

C.6   *M/M/1* queue with finite buffer memory

The above *M/M/1* analysis can be extended to consider the case where buffer memory is not infinite but has a maximum capacity of N messages. The probability P_N that the queue is full (i.e. the blocking probability) is of main interest and can be shown to obey the following relationship:

$$P_N = \frac{(1-p)p^n}{1-p^{N+1}}$$

This relationship is useful for calculating the buffer memory size required to achieve a given blocking probability.

C.7 $M/G/1$ queue

The assumption of an exponential distributed service time is convenient but in practice not very realistic when modelling communication networks. Fortunately, this assumption can be relaxed and yet a relatively straightforward mathematical model can be used to calculate queuing characteristics. These formulae are known as the Pollaczek–Khinchine formulae and are valid for any service time distribution. If there is a Poisson stream of arrivals with mean rate λ messages/second, and message lengths are distributed with a mean of $(1/\mu)$ bits/message, then, defining $p = \lambda/\mu Z$ (where Z is the line speed in bps):

$$\text{average waiting time } E_w = \frac{pE_s}{2(1-p)} \ [1 + C(E_s)^2]$$

where $C(E_s)$ is the coefficient of variation of the service time, calculated as the ratio of the standard deviation to the mean of the service time distribution.

$$\text{average response time } E_T = E_s + E_w$$

average number of jobs in the queue (including those in service)

$$E_m = p + \frac{p^2}{2(1-p)} \ [1 + C(E_s)^2]$$

The above calculations depend only on the facility utilisation (p), the mean and variance of the message length.

C.8 Networks of queues

A communication network consists of nodes that are interconnected by communication links. A communication network (in particular the backbone network) can thus be modelled as a network of queues. Figure C.3 illustrates two types of queuing network. An *open* queuing network is one in which there are exchanges (arrivals and departures) of messages with the outside world. A *closed* queuing network involves no exchanges with the outside world; a fixed number of messages are internally circulating among the interconnected nodes. Thus a closed queuing network is an open network with all source and destination rates set to zero.

270

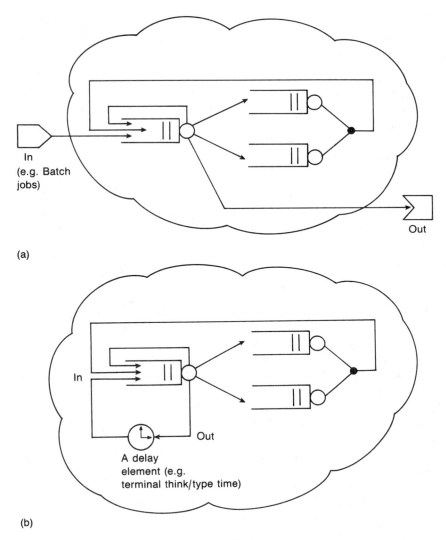

(a)

(b)

Figure C.3 Example (a) open and (b) closed queuing network models.

The open queuing network model is appropriate for modelling on-line transaction processing environments where the arrival rate does not depend on the response time perceived by the user. This is not the case for workloads such as batch and interactive systems in which a user continually interacts with the system over a long period of time, submitting a new request each time a reply is received. In this case a closed queuing network model is appropriate.

For an open queuing network, if we assume an interconnection of $M/M/1$ queues and the route from one queue to another is selected randomly (with fixed routeing probabilities) then Jackson's theorem allows each node to be analysed as if it was an isolated $M/M/c$ queue. The network designer calculates the overall system delay time by performing the following:

1. Construct a traffic matrix which details average arrival rates, and average message lengths in each direction for each line which interconnect the network nodes. To do this the routeing policy of the network must also be known.
2. The total traffic entering each node is calculated.
3. The total system delay time is calculated by summing the system delay time at each node (using the appropriate $M/M/c$ formulae) on route between source and destination.

The use of the above techniques has been shown to be capable of modelling device utilisations to within 10 per cent and response times to within about 30 per cent of actual measured values. This is within acceptable limits given the typical accuracy of input data.

The $M/M/1$ approximation for open queuing network models does not hold for some typical networks. For example, datagram packet-switching networks allow each packet to be routed independently through the network between a source and destination. Typically packets will be routed dynamically according to the least busy route. This is modelled by each arriving packet being assigned to the queue containing the least number of bits awaiting transmission (assuming each line has a transmission rate of C bits/second). In this case an $M/M/1$-based model would not be appropriate. However, in a virtual-circuit-based packet-switching network, where all packets associated with a virtual circuit connection follow the same predefined route, an $M/M/1$-based model *may* be appropriate.

The above model obviously assumes infinite buffer memory at each node. In reality buffer memory is limited and leads to discarded messages or graceful 'slowdown' where the arrival of messages into the system is restricted depending on the utilisation level of buffer memory. These and other situations (e.g. interactive systems) are modelled as closed queuing networks and require more difficult mathematical analysis using techniques such as *mean value analysis* (*MVA*) algorithms derived from Little's law (see Reiser, 1982, or Jain, 1991). Procedures for solutions based on MVA are beyond the scope of this discussion.

Glossary

ACU Automatic calling unit. A device that permits a computing facility to dial calls automatically (usually in response to a user attempting to dial in and having identified the user). It is also known as a callback modem or automatic dial-up unit.

Address A location of, for example, an end system in a network. Each end system is assigned a unique address.

ARPA Advanced Research Projects Agency: an agency of the US Department of Defense that sponsors research.

ARPANET The ARPA network.

Asynchronous transmission A technique used to transmit data between end systems as individual characters. Each character is preceded by a start signal and terminated by one or more stop signals which are used for synchronisation purposes.

ATM Automatic teller machine.

AT&T The American Telephone and Telegraph Company.

Availability The percentage of planned available time that is to be (or has been) available for users to use a service. It does not include scheduled time for maintenance and service facility upgrades.

Bandwidth The difference between the highest and lowest frequencies that can be transmitted by a communications channel (expressed in Hertz); determines the capacity (in bits/second) of the channel to carry information.

BER Bit error rate: the number of bits received in a transmission that are in error, relative to a specific number of bits transmitted; usually quoted as a proportion of a power of 10, e.g. a BER of 1 bit in 10^9.

BERT Bit-error rate testing. Testing a communication link with a pattern of bits that are compared before and after the transmission to detect errors.

B-ISDN Broadband ISDN: a high bandwidth network that will provide bit rates of the order of hundreds of mbps.

bits/sec bits per second.

Blocking The inability of a PABX to grant service to a requesting user, resulting in the request leaving the system unserviced.

BOC Bell Operating Company; a PTO, of which there are seven in the United States.

bps bits per second: 1 kbps is 10^3 bps and 1 mbps is 10^6 bps.

BRI Basic Rate Interface to the ISDN: provides two 64 kbps user channels known as B channels and a 16 kbps D channel used for signalling purposes; known as 2B + D.

273

Bridge An interworking device that operates up to layer 2 of the OSI Reference Model (OSIRM).

BT British Telecom, the largest PTO in the United Kingdom.

Buffer Temporary storage of data.

BW See bandwidth.

CAD Computer-aided-design.

CAM Computer-aided-manufacturing.

CCITT Comité Consultatif International Téléphonique et Télégraphique: a committee of the International Telecommunications Union (ITU), which is an agency of the United Nations. The CCITT are concerned with devising recommendations for communications standards.

CCS Common channel signalling: a signalling system developed for use between voice-switching nodes in which all the signalling information associated with call supervision and requests for services is transmitted using a dedicated channel.

CDM Corporate data model.

Channel A path over which information flows between communicating devices. In some wide area networks, a primary circuit may comprise a number of logical, multiplexed channels. In some local area networks, all communicating devices share the same channel.

CILE Call information logging equipment. Call-logging equipment that records details of voice calls, which can be used for monitoring and capacity planning purposes.

CIM Computer-integrated manufacturing.

Circuit A communications path between communicating devices; may comprise a number of logical, multiplexed channels.

Circuit switching A technique of switching whereby a fixed path is dedicated to two end systems for the duration of the connection.

CL mode Connectionless mode of service: a service that has a single phase of data transfer; each packet of data that is transmitted is treated independently of previous and subsequent packets.

CLNS Connectionless mode network service.

CMIP Common Management Information Protocol: the OSI protocol for network management.

CMIS Common Management Information Service: the application service element that is responsible for carrying CMIP network management information.

CMOL CMIP over LLC.

CMS Call management system. A more sophisticated call-logging system with accounting, performance monitoring, inventory management and other facilities.

CO mode Connection-oriented mode of service. A service that has three distinct phases: establishment, in which two end systems are connected; transfer, in which information is transferred; and release, in which the connection is released.

CONS Connection-oriented network service.

Connection A logical binding between two end systems.

CPA Critical path analysis. A technique used in project planning.

CSF Critical success factor.

CSMA/CD Carrier Sense Multiple Access with Collision Detection: an access algorithm used in the Ethernet local area network in which contention for the use of the channel is resolved.

DARPA Defense Advanced Research Projects Agency: DARPA was previously known as ARPA, the Advanced Research Projects Agency, when the ARPANET was built.

DARPANET The DARPA network.

Datagram The name given to the independent packets of the connectionless-mode network service in, for example, packet-switching networks.

DCE Data circuit-terminating equipment: the term given to the equipment for the attachment of user devices (end systems) to a network. For example, a modem is used to attach an end system to an analogue circuit in a WAN; a network access device such as a network terminating unit (NTU) in the United Kingdom or a digital service unit (DSU) in the United States is used to attach to a digital circuit.

DFD Data flow diagram: a technique used in systems analysis to represent the flow of data in an information system.

Digital PABX A PABX designed to switch digital signals.

DOVE Data over voice equipment: a system that carries data at a frequency higher than that used for voice communications in, for example, internal telephone wiring.

DP Data processing.

DPNSS Digital Private Network Signalling System: signalling standard for digital private PABX networks, formulated by British Telecom and PABX manufacturers.

DSS1 Digital Signalling System No. 1; based on the CCITT's Q.931 signalling standard.

DTE Data terminal equipment: an alternative term for an end system.

EC European Commission.

ECU European Currency Unit.

EDI Electronic data interchange.

EFT Electronic funds transfer.

EM See Email.

Email Electronic mail.

Encryption A security technique of modifying a known bit stream on a communications link so it appears to an unauthorised user to be a random sequence of bits.

Erlang A unit used to measure the utilisation of a communications system such as a PABX. The unit is named after a Danish engineer (Agner Erlang) who was a leader in the development of traffic theory. An Erlang is a measure of traffic intensity, e.g. traffic of 10 Erlangs means that 10 voice calls are in progress in a specified unit of time (usually 1 hour).

ES End system: a communicating system or device that is connected to a network. An end system is capable of transmitting information to another end system.

ETSI European Telecommunications Standards Institute.

FD Functional decomposition: a technique that is used to identify business functions and processes within functions.

FDM Frequency division multiplexing: see multiplexing.

FDDI Fibre-distributed data interface: a LAN technology that permits 100 mbps data transfer rates.

FEP Front-end processor: a special computer that relieves a host computer of communications tasks.

FTAM File transfer, access and management: the OSI file service.

FTP File transfer protocol: the Internet file service.

Gateway A device that interconnects networks with different communications protocols; a gateway operates up to layer 7 of the OSI Reference Model.

GOS Grade of service. For voice networks this is a measure of the quality of service, usually measured in terms of system response time, call connection time and call set-up time.

GOSIP Government Open Systems Interconnection Profile: a version of the OSI protocols that is supported by government, e.g. the US GOSIP. GOSIP compliance is a requirement in government networking purchases.

GW   See gateway.

HDLC   High-level data link control: A layer 2, ISO protocol for point-to-point and multipoint links in wide area networks.

HLM   Heterogeneous LAN Management: a specification for the management of mixed Token Ring and Ethernet local area networks, jointly developed between IBM and 3Com.

IAB   The Internet Activities Board: the technical body charged with overseeing the development of the Internet suite of protocols. The IAB comprises several task forces, each of which is responsible for a particular area of protocol development.

IBM   International Business Machines.

IEEE   Institute of Electrical and Electronic Engineers (USA): a professional organisation that, among other things, develops networking standards.

IETF   The Internet Engineering Task Force: a task force of the IAB that is responsible for developing standards for the Internet suite of protocols.

IN   Information network, or intelligent network.

INM   Integrated network management.

internet   An interconnection of two or more networks forms an internet.

Internet   A large collection of interconnected networks, mainly in the United States, that runs the Internet suite of communications protocols. The Internet suite of protocols was originally developed under the DARPA project; the Internet suite of protocols is currently the *de facto* open networking architecture.

IP   Information processing.

IP   Internet protocol: the connectionless-mode network protocol in the Internet suite of protocols.

IPA   Information processing architecture.

IS   Information system.

IS   Intermediate system: an intermediate system performs the functions of the lowest three layers of the OSI reference model; an IS is commonly thought of as performing routeing or switching functions in a wide area network.

ISDN   The Integrated Services Digital Network will eventually replace the PSTN; it will provide switched, digital, end-to-end connectivity for voice and non-voice services via a set of user interfaces.

ISO   See ISO/IEC.

ISO/IEC   An abbreviation for the International Organization for Standardization and International Electrochemical Committee: the members of the ISO/IEC are national standards bodies. The ISO/IEC liaises with other standards bodies such as the IEEE and the CCITT. There are subcommittees of the ISO/IEC that are responsible for producing standards. The documents produced by the ISO/IEC are termed International Standards.

ISPBX   Integrated Services Private Automatic Branch Exchange.

IT   Information technology.

IWU   Interworking unit: the ISO term for a device that interconnects subnets in an internet. An IWU is commonly referred to as a relay, of which bridges, routers and gateways (protocol converters) are examples.

JIT   Just in time manufacturing.

LAN   Local area network.

LDO   Logical dialogue outline. An SSADM diagramming technique to describe dialogues. A useful source of information for application sizing of applications designed using SSADM.

LLC   Logical link control: a protocol that forms part of layer 2 in a LAN architecture.

MAC   Media access control: a set of protocols that form layer 1 and part of layer 2 in a LAN architecture.

MAN   Metropolitan area network.

MAP   Manufacturing Automation Protocol: MAP defines a set of OSI functional standards to support manufacturing applications. It is being developed by a large user group led by General Motors.

MAU   Multistation Access Unit: a multiport hub or concentrator for Token Ring LANs that provides a physical star topology implementation. An MAU provides a built-in bypass to prevent a break in network service should a connection or an end system fail.

MCM   Multiple co-operative management: an architecture for network management (NM).

Message switching   The switching of messages whereby the entire message being transmitted is transmitted from node to node in a store and forward fashion.

MHS   Message handling system: a store-and-forward service for delivering electronic messages.

MIB   Management information base: a collection of objects that can be accessed by means of a network management protocol.

MNDS   Managed data network service.

Modem   A concatenation of *mo*dulation-*dem*odulation: a modem is a device that converts digital signals from/to assigned frequencies for transmission over voice-grade circuits in WANs or radio frequencies in broadband LANs.

MoM   Manager of managers: an architecture for network management.

MST   Minimum spanning tree. Algorithm used in configuring paths in multiple-path, bridged networks.

MTBF   Mean time between failure. A measure of reliability.

MTTR   Mean time to repair. A determinant of availability. It measures the time it takes to fix a fault in equipment once notified that a fault has occurred.

Multiplexing   A technique for dividing a circuit into a number of logical channels; a multiplexed channel is a single channel that occupies a particular frequency band (in frequency division multiplexing) or a time slot (in time division multiplexing).

NET3   ETSI's Normes Européenes de Télécommunications No. 3; used for ISDN 2B + D access.

Network   A general term used to describe a population of end systems and the means to interconnect them, e.g. a local area network of computers; a wide area network of computers.

NM   Network management.

OA   Office automation.

Non-blocking PABX   A PABX in which a path always exists between an output line and each attached station. Thus there is no possibility of blocking due to the volume of calls.

OSI   Open systems interconnection: an architecture that facilitates communications between computers of different manufacturers; OSI is sponsored by the ISO.

OSIRM   The Open Systems Interconnection Reference Model: the OSIRM is used to describe computer communications in an abstract way. The model divides the task of computer communications into seven layers so that standards can be developed within a structured framework. OSI standards are divided into two parts: one part defines the service offered by a communications entity and the other specifies the protocol used by that entity to offer that service.

PABX   Private Automatic Branch Exchange: a private exchange that provides automatic circuit switching within a private domain such as a building or site. Most PABX traffic is telephone speech, though data communications is possible.

Packet   A block of data and control information associated with layer 3 of the OSIRM.

Packet switching   A technique of switching whereby individual packets of data are routed to their destination by the network.

PAD A concatenation of packet assembler/disassembler: a PAD is a device that permits end systems that do not have an interface that is suitable for direct connection to a packet-switched network to access such a network.

PDN Public data network.

PERT Project evaluation and review technique. A technique used for project planning.

PRI Primary Rate Interface to the ISDN: 30B + D in Europe and 23B + D in the United States. (See BRI for the meaning of B and D.)

Private network A network established and operated by an organisation primarily for the users within that organisation.

Protocol A commonly agreed set of rules which makes meaningful communication possible between different computer systems.

PSE Packet switching exchange: a device that performs packet switching in a packet-switched network.

PSTN The public switched telephone network.

PTO Public telecommunications operator; commonly known as a common carrier in the United States.

PTT A post, telephone and telegraph authority: a PTO often associated with European countries where the PTT is the monopoly supplier of telecommunications services.

Public network A network established and operated by a PTO/PTT/common carrier for the provision of packet-switched and circuit-switched network services primarily to business organizations.

QA Quality assurance.

QOS Quality of service.

Q-SIG Developed by ETSI (European Telecommunications Standards Institute); based on the CCITT's Q.931 signalling standard.

Relay The generic term for a device that interconnects subnets in an internet.

Reliability The probability that a system will continue to function within a given timescale.

Response time The total time a system takes to react to a given request.

Session A connection between two end systems that allows communication between application programs to take place.

SISP Strategic information systems planning.

SLA Service-level agreement.

SMTP Simple Mail Transfer Protocol: the application protocol that offers message handling services in the Internet suite of protocols.

SNA Systems Network Architecture: IBM's proprietary networking architecture.

SNMP Simple Network Management Protocol: the network management protocol associated with the Internet suite of protocols.

SPIN Strategic planning for information networks.

SSADM Structured Systems Analysis and Design Method.

STA Spanning tree algorithm: STP uses an algorithm that facilitates routeing in interconnected LANs. The algorithm is based on an IEEE standard (802.1D).

STD Subscriber trunk dialling.

STP Shielded twisted pair: twisted pair wire that is wrapped inside a metallic sheath that provides protection from electromagnetic and radio frequency interference (EMI/RFI).

Subnet End systems are interconnected by a communications subnetwork or subnet. The function of the subnet is to carry information from end system to end system.

Switching Identifying and connecting independent communication links to form a continuous pathway between source(s) and destination(s).

Switched network Any network consisting of switching nodes and communication links to support message transmission between a number of sources and destinations.

SWOT Strengths, weaknesses, opportunities and threats.

Synchronous transmission A technique used to transmit data between end systems; data are transmitted in the form of blocks, each comprising a string of binary digits. The transmitter and receiver clocks are in synchronism.

Tandem office A high-level switching and control facility set up by the local telephone company to which subcribers are attached.

TC Telecommunications.

TCP The Transmission Control Protocol: the connection-oriented transport protocol in the Internet suite of protocols.

TCP/IP Transmission Control Protocol/Internet Protocol: an alternative term for the Internet suite of protocols.

TDM Time division multiplexing: see multiplexing.

TELENET The applications protocol that offers the virtual terminal service in the Internet suite of protocols.

TIA Technology impact analysis.

TOP Technical office protocol. TOP defines a set of OSI functional standards to support office applications. It is being developed by a large user group led by Boeing.

TPN Third-party network.

Twisted pair wire A cable comprising two 18–24 AWG (American Wire Gauge) copper conductors twisted around each other. The twisting provides a measure of protection from interference from other nearby conductors. When used in telephone networks, the twisting minimises cross-talk interference from nearby pairs.

UTP Unshielded twisted pair: twisted pair wire is wrapped in a plastic sheath; the covering does not provide protection from EMI/RFI.

VADS Value-added data service.

VANS Value-added network service.

VC See virtual circuit.

Virtual call A type of service offered on a packet-switched data network where a virtual circuit is established between end systems that wish to communicate.

Virtual circuit A virtual circuit is established between end systems in some packet-switched networks. The virtual circuit is a logical association between end systems and resembles an end-to-end connection.

VPN Virtual private network.

V-Series CCITT recommendations for data transmission over analogue networks.

VT Virtual terminal: An application layer protocol that enables an application process to have a dialogue with a terminal in a standardised way, without regard to the type of terminal.

WAN Wide area network.

X-Series CCITT recommendations for data transmission over digital networks.

X.21 A standard for the interface between end systems and data circuit-terminating equipment (DCE) for synchronous operation on public data networks.

X.21bis Standard interface between end systems that are designed for interfacing to synchronous V-series modems and DCE for public data networks.

X.25 The set of network access protocols defined for interfacing data terminal equipment (DTE) to a public packet-switched data network.

X.400 The CCITT recommendations for message handling systems.

279

X.500 The CCITT recommendations for directory services.

8802/x The ISO standards for LANs; equivalent to the IEEE 802.x standards for LANs. 8802/3 Ethernet, 8802/4 Token Bus, 8802/5 Token Ring.

Further reading and references

Further reading

Suggested reading, by chapter(s), is as follows:

Chapters 1 – 3

For a good, general introduction to local and wide area networks and OSI, we recommend:

Fred Halsal, *Data Communications, Computer Networks and Open Systems*, 3rd edn, Addison-Wesley, 1992.
Andrew S. Tanenbaum, *Computer Networks*, 2nd edn, Prentice Hall, 1988.

For a more detailed treatment of the technical aspects of local area networks:

William Stallings, *Local Networks*, 3rd edn, Macmillan, 1990.
Brendan Tangney and Donal O'Mahony, *Local Networks and their Applications*, Prentice Hall, 1988.

Chapter 4

For a detailed exposition of OSI standards:

William Stallings, *Handbook of Computer Communications Standards*, vol. 1: *OSI Standards*, 2nd edn, Macmillan, 1990.
William Stallings, *Handbook of Computer Communications Standards*, vol. 2: *LAN Standards*, 2nd edn, Macmillan, 1990.

The following book concentrates on the upper layers of the OSI reference model:

John Henshall and Sandy Shaw, *OSI Explained*, Ellis Horwood, 1988.

For a good introduction to the practical issues surrounding OSI:

Marshall T. Rose, *The Open Book: A practical perspective on OSI*, Prentice Hall, 1990.

For a detailed exposition of TCP/IP standards:

William Stallings, *Handbook of Computer Communications Standards*, vol. 2: *Department of Defense (DOD) Protocol Standards*, Macmillan, 1990.

Douglas E. Comer, *Internetworking with TCP/ IP*, vol. 1: *Principles, Protocols and Architecture*, 2nd edn, Prentice Hall, 1991.

Publications from the Department of Trade and Industry (DTI) in the UK:

Open Systems: Making the Business Case for OSI.
Open Systems: the Technical Case for OSI.

(Available from the Open Systems Information Unit, DTI, Kingsgate House, 66–74 Victoria Street, London, UK.)

Chapters 5–6

Peter G. W. Keen, *Computing in time: using Telecommunications for competitive advantage*, Ballinger, 1988.
Michael T. Earl (ed.), *Information Management: The strategic dimension*, Clarendon Press, 1988.
Michael T. Earl, *Management Strategies for Information Technology*, Prentice Hall, 1989.

Chapter 7

For a discussion of the feasibility phase in systems analysis:

H. L. Capron, *Systems Analysis and Design*, Addison-Wesley, 1986.
Alan Daniels and Don Yeats (eds), *Basic Systems Analysis*, 3rd edn, Pitman, 1988.

Chapter 8

For a detailed treatment of application sizing and the use of queuing network models:

E. S. Simon, *Service Levels and their Links with Application Development and Infrastructure Management*, UKCMG Proceedings, 1989, pp. 356–64.
C. U. Smith, *Performance Engineering of Software Systems*, Addison-Wesley, 1990.

Publications from the CCTA in the UK:

SSADM and Capacity Management – An Exploratory Study, Information Systems Engineering Report Number 9, CCTA, November 1987.
SSADM Version 3 and Capacity Planning, Information Systems Study Guide, CCTA, October, 1990.
Capacity Management, IT Infrastructure Library Module, CCTA, 1991.

(Available from the Central Computer and Telecommunications Agency (CCTA), Norwich, UK.)

Ed Downs, Peter Clare and Ian Coe, *SSADM: Application and context*, Prentice Hall. (Note: The first edition (1988) covers SSADM Version 3, the second edition (1992) covers SSADM Version 4.)

The following book has a particularly good section on network security and control:

Jerry Fitzgerald, *Business Data Communications: Basic concepts, security, and design*, 3rd edn, Wiley, 1990.

Chapter 9

The following texts provide a thorough treatment of theoretical and practical issues of performance analysis and modelling:

Raj Jain, *The Art of Computer Systems Performance Analysis: Techniques of experimental design, measurement, simulation and modelling*, Wiley, 1991.

M. Schwartz, *Telecommunications Networks: Protocols, modelling and analysis*, Addison-Wesley, 1987.

R. L. Sharma, *Network Topology Optimization*, Van Nostrand Reinhold, 1990.

Chapter 10

J. P. Meredith and S. J. Mantel Jr, *Project Management: A managerial approach*, Wiley, 1989.

The *IT Infrastructure Libraries* set of guidance books from the CCTA in the UK provide practical guidelines on implementing and managing networks.
(Available from the Central Computer and Telecommunications Agency (CCTA), Norwich, UK.)

References (cited in the text)

Bal, H. (1990), *Programming Distributed Systems*, Prentice Hall, 1990.

Bertsekas, D. and Gallager, R. (1987), *Data Networks*, Prentice Hall, 1987.

Booz Allen & Hamilton (1984), *Productivity in the Office: A survey of European chief executives*, Booz Allen & Hamilton Inc., New York.

Butler Cox (1988), *Network Management*, Butler Cox Foundation Research Report No. 65, August, Butler Cox & Partners Ltd, London.

CCTA (1990), *SSADM Version 3 and Capacity Planning*, IS Subject Guide, Central Computer and Telecommunications Agency, Norwich, UK.

Clemons, E. K., Keen, P. G. W. and Kimbrough, S. O. (1984), *Telecommunications and Business Strategy: Basic variables for design*, AFIPS Conf. Proc., Vol. 53.

Comer, Douglas E. (1991), *Internetworking with TCP/IP*, vol. 1: *Principles, Protocols and Architecture*, 2nd edn, Prentice Hall.

Data General, (1984), *Executive Guide to Estimating Office Automation Benefits*, Data General Corp., Westboro, MA.

Earl, M. (ed) (1988), *Information Management: The strategic dimension*, Clarendon Press, Oxford.

Hartley, R. V. (1928), *Bell Sys. Tech. J.*, **7**.

Hills, M. J. (1979), *Telecommunications Switching Principles*, MIT Press, Cambridge, MA.

Keen, G. W. (1988), *Competing in Time: Using telecommunications for competitive advantage*, Ballinger, p. 143.

King, Peter J. B. (1990), *Computer and Communication Systems Performance Modelling*, Prentice Hall, 1990.

Leung, (1988), *Quantitative Analysis of Computer Systems*, Wiley, 1988.

Martin, J. (1986), *Information Engineering*, vol. 2, Savant Institute, Carnforth, UK.

McFarlan, F. W. and McKenney, J. L. (1983), *Corporate Information Systems Management: The issues facing senior executives*, Dow Jones Irwin.

Nickel, W. E. (1978), Determining network effectiveness, *Mini-Micro Syst.*, **10**, October.

Nyquist, H. (1928a), *Trans. AIEE*, **47**.

Nyquist, H. (1928b), *Phys. Rev.*, **32**, 1928.

Porter, M. E. (1980), *Competitive Strategy*, The Free Press, New York.

Porter, M. E. and Miller, V. E. (1985), How information systems gives you competitive advantage, *Harvard Business Rev.*, July–August.

Reiser, M. (1982), Performance evaluation of data communication systems, *Proc. IEEE*, **70**, no. 2, pp. 171–95.

Rockart, J. F. (1979), Chief executives define their own data needs, *Harvard Business Rev.*, March–April, pp. 81–93.

Rose, Marshall T. (1990), *The Open Book: A practical perspective on OSI*, Prentice Hall, 1990.

Shannon, C. E. (1948), *Bell Sys. Tech. J.*, **27**.

Stallings, W. (1990), *Local Networks*, 3rd edn, Macmillan.

Index

Reference should also be made to Glossary on pages 273–80.